A Portrait of Richard Graves

Richard Graves

Crayon drawing by Thomas Gainsborough

CLARENCE TRACY

A Portrait of Richard Graves

UNIVERSITY OF TORONTO PRESS
Toronto Buffalo

© University of Toronto Press 1987
Toronto Buffalo London
Printed in Canada
ISBN 0-8020-5697-0

Canadian Cataloguing in Publication Data

Tracy, Clarence, 1908–
A portrait of Richard Graves
Includes bibliographical references and index.
ISBN 0-8020-5697-0
1. Graves, Richard, 1715–1804.
2. Authors, English – 18th century – Biography.
3. Church of England – Clergy – Biography.
4. Clergy – England – Biography.
I. Title
PR3499.G77Z86 1987   823'.6   c86-094270-8

This book has been published with the help of
grants from the Canadian Federation for the Humanities,
using funds provided by the
Social Sciences and Humanities Research Council of Canada,
and from the Publications Fund of
University of Toronto Press.

Contents

Illustrations

CHARTS

Preface

I made my discovery of Richard Graves many years ago when as a graduate student I was combing the library shelves for eighteenth-century novels to read in preparation for the qualifying examination. By pure chance I lit upon *The Spiritual Quixote*. Enchanted by its rollicking humour and endless variety of character and incident, I decided to write my dissertation on Graves. But I was frustrated. I was told that somebody else had just done what I proposed doing and so had pre-empted the field. Turning reluctantly elsewhere for an acceptable subject, I nevertheless tucked Graves away in the back of my mind for some indefinite time in the future. That time seemed to have come in the 1960s when I was asked by the general editor of the Oxford English Novels to edit *The Spiritual Quixote* for that series, but the work I did then only convinced me that a lot more needed to be said about Graves than could be squeezed into the introduction and notes to an edition of one of his works. So the present volume is the fulfilment of a promise made to myself almost half a century ago.

Graves, I had found out, had written a great deal more than the novel, in a variety of forms, none of it perhaps quite up to the standard of *The Spiritual Quixote* but all of it lively and readable. Above all, he himself had emerged in my mind as a complex and fascinating person fully deserving to be studied as a man as well as an author. He was an example, moreover, of a class of men characteristic of his time whom one can seldom get close to except in novels, the well-educated parson of good family who kept aloft the flag of eighteenth-century culture in an isolated community. Graves had opened for me a door into an important room in the eighteenth-century establishment.

One of his outstanding characteristics, his articulateness, makes him a good subject for a biography. He not only loved to write but loved to write about himself, drawing much of his material, especially for his novels, from his personal experience. One of the novels he described as an 'embellished narrative of real fact,' and many of the characters and incidents in all of them he labelled 'real facts.' Of course it is difficult to tell how much he 'embellished' any of those facts, and so I have proceeded with what I consider due caution, without denying myself the pleasure of introducing a vivid detail or two that seemed imaginatively right even if factually unsupported, usually under cover of a 'perhaps.' In that way in the pages that follow I have made Graves tell as much as I could of his own story.

Acknowledgments

Of the many friends and colleagues who have taken an interest in this work and have helped me with it, grateful mention must go first to the late Mary Graves Hamilton, the last of the Graves clan and until recently owner of Mickleton Manor. She discussed knotty points in Richard Graves's story with me and read drafts of a couple of chapters. Although she made suggestions and supplied information, she left me free to form my own judgments, so that in no sense of the word is this an official biography. For its faults and whatever merits it may have, I am solely responsible.

To the Reverend Dennis Harvey, present rector of Claverton, I am indebted for many kindnesses, not the least of them being unrestricted access to the records of his church. Similarly, Dr D.J. Fleeman, fellow of Pembroke College in Oxford, allowed me to examine the archives of his college. And my late brother, Dr Herman Tracy, gave me the benefit of his extensive knowledge of the classical languages.

Other friends who gave me unstinting help were Mr Francis Burns of Kingswinford, West Midlands; Dr James Downey, president of the University of New Brunswick, Fredericton; Dr Charles Graves of Geneva, Switzerland; Dr James Gray of Dalhousie University, Halifax, Nova Scotia; Dr Donald Greene of Los Angeles, California; Mr Gavin Murdock of Scarborough, Ontario; the late Peter J.T. O'Hearne, judge of the Halifax County Court, Nova Scotia; Mr John Simmons, fellow of All Souls, Oxford; and Mrs I.U. Todd of Redgrave in Norfolk.

Without the cheerful co-operation of the staffs of the many libraries and record offices at which I either worked or made inquiries, my task would have been much more difficult, and I owe them all my hearty thanks. I am also most grateful to the Canada Council and its successor, the Social Sciences and Humanities Research Council of Canada, for generous grants in support of my research.

Chronology

A chronological list of Graves's publications will be found in Appendix A.

1708 Nov 19 Birth of Morgan Graves, Richard's older brother
1715 May 4 Birth of Richard Graves
1723 June 30 Death of Graves's mother
1727 or earlier Graves starts school in Mickleton under Mr Smith
1728 Graves becomes a pupil in Roysse's Grammar School in Abingdon
1729 Sept 18 Death of Graves's father
1730 Oct Birth of Lucy Bartholomew in Aldworth, Berkshire
1732 Nov Graves becomes a student in Pembroke College, Oxford
1736 June 25 Graves proceeds BA.
1736 Nov 15 Graves elected a fellow of All Souls
1740 or earlier Graves has a love affair with Utrecia Smith
c 1740 Graves studies anatomy in London
1740 Graves seriously ill and afterwards returns to study of divinity at Oxford
1740 Oct Graves proceeds MA.
1741 May 24 Graves ordained deacon
1741 May 29 Graves becomes curate of Tissington
1743 Mar 5 Utrecia Smith dies
1743 May 28 Graves ordained priest
1744 Graves tours the Peak District
1744 Graves returns to Oxford to live and become curate of Aldworth,
     Berkshire. Has love affair with Lucy Bartholomew
1746 Graves now living in Whitchurch with Anthony Whistler
1747 Aug 2 Graves and Lucy Bartholomew marry in London
1747 Oct 22 Baptism of Richard Graves, first child of Graves and his wife
     Lucy

1748 The Graveses move to Whitchurch, where Richard becomes curate

1749 Jan 15 Graves resigns his fellowship at All Souls

1749 Jan 25 Birth of Morgan, second son of Richard and Lucy Graves

1749 June 11 Graves inducted as rector of Claverton

1750 May 22 Birth of Danvers, third son of Richard and Lucy Graves

1754 May 10 Death of Anthony Whistler

1756 Graves meets Robert Dodsley

1763 Death of William Shenstone

1763 Graves becomes vicar of Kilmarsden in addition to Claverton

1765 Feb 26 Birth of Lucy, only daughter of Richard and Lucy Graves

1770 Apr 8 Birth of Charles, fourth son of Richard and Lucy Graves

1770 Dec 26 Death of Morgan Graves, Richard's older brother

1777 May 1 Death of Lucy, Graves's wife

1780 May 20 Death of Richard, eldest son of Richard and Lucy Graves

1794 Graves resigns living of Kilmarsden

1802 Graves presented to living of Croscombe

1802 June 14 Death of Morgan, second son of Richard and Lucy Graves

1804 Nov 23 Richard Graves dies in Claverton

1822 Mar 10 Death of Lucy, daughter of Richard and Lucy Graves

NB The dates of death of Graves's two other children are unknown.

A Portrait of Richard Graves

CHAPTER ONE

Family

For three generations the successive heads of the Graves family had been lords of the manor of Mickleton, their manor house dominating the little Gloucestershire village in which it stood, when Richard Graves, the novelist, poet, and essayist, was born there in 1715.[1] Their position in society as gentry was important to them, as it would be to their writer offspring, and at various times they made efforts to trace their pedigree backwards as far as it would go, and sometimes farther. The first member of the family of whom they could find a reliable record was a dour-looking old man who had his portrait painted at the age of 102 (see plate 1) and shortly thereafter died of the smallpox whilst on a visit to his son in London. He was buried in the church of St Martin, Ludgate, in 1616. So far the searchers were on solid ground. But where had the old man come from, and, indeed, what was his Christian name? The clerk who had recorded his burial in the parish register had left a blank, which had never been filled in, but in the family tradition he was called John. He was also said to have come from Beamsley in Yorkshire and to have descended from a John Grave (note the different spelling) who had lived in Heyton or Cleck-heaton in the West Riding in the reign of Edward IV. But there is no authority for either the name John or the alleged Yorkshire origin. The Graves of Yorkshire had undoubtedly been gentlemen, for in 1591 they had been granted a coat of arms by the College of Heralds. That coat the Graveses of Mickleton took over as their own. Eventually they made slight modifications in it to placate the college, which gave a blessing to it so modified, not because their right to use it was admitted but because nobody had objected, the Graves of Yorkshire having died out. By these means the Graveses, whose own provable pedigree was short, acquired a genteel ancestry of respectable antiquity and a coat of arms, both essential

CHART 1

The Graves Pedigree

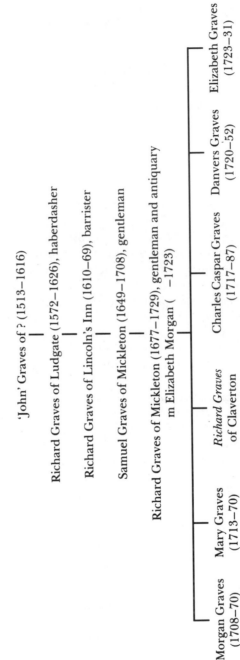

'John' Graves of ? (1513–1616)

Richard Graves of Ludgate (1572–1626), haberdasher

Richard Graves of Lincoln's Inn (1610–69), barrister

Samuel Graves of Mickleton (1649–1708), gentleman

Richard Graves of Mickleton (1677–1729), gentleman and antiquary
m Elizabeth Morgan (–1723)

Morgan Graves
(1708–70)
m Ann Walwyn

Mary Graves
(1713–70)
m John Taylor

Richard Graves
of Claverton
(1715–1804)
m Lucy Bartholomew

Charles Caspar Graves
(1717–87)

Danvers Graves
(1720–52)

Elizabeth Graves
(1723–31)

adjuncts to the status of gentleman. Richard Graves the novelist, who is the subject of this book, accepted the Yorkshire ancestry and included a brief account of the centenarian called John in one of his last books, *The Invalid*, describing him as of 'Kirk-heaton [sic], near Pomfret, in Yorkshire.'[2] Also, in two or three of his books he used as his pseudonym the name Peter Pomfret. He never mentioned the coat of arms, unless the complaints made by some of the characters in his novel *Columella* about the irresponsible way the College of Heralds permitted tradespeople and even innkeepers to put up coats of arms is an allusion to its odd action with regard to the Graves arms.[3] If it was, the comment is typical of the author's quizzical attitude towards life and his ability to laugh at himself and his friends.

It is far from clear that old John was a gentleman at all in the eighteenth-century sense of that word. A writer who published a book on the Graves family some years ago suggested that he was a yeoman and that he had come not from Yorkshire but from Cumberland or Westmorland, where the name was common among the farmers.[4] (John Woodcock Graves, who wrote the well-known song 'Do ye ken John Peel,' was descended from one of those Graveses.[5]) Moreover, the son whom the old man was visiting in London when he died was not a gentleman either but a citizen, or 'cit,' as he would have been called in the upper-class slang of the eighteenth century, belonging to a class frequently satirized by sophisticated writers of the time as uncouth and socially unacceptable. He was a haberdasher and was successful enough in his business not only to be able to acquire some valuable urban property but also to give his son a legal education. Both father and son were called Richard. (That name now became so common in the family that I am constrained to add a descriptive phrase to it each time I use it in this section of my book: for example, Richard of Ludgate [the haberdasher], Richard of Lincoln's Inn [his lawyer son], Richard the novelist or Richard of Claverton [the subject of this book], and so on. Chart 1 shows where each of these fits in.)

Richard of Lincoln's Inn practised law in London and filled a number of important and doubtless highly remunerative public posts in the troubled middle years of the century: in 1644 he was member of a committee for raising volunteers for the defence of Middlesex; in 1645 clerk of the parliamentary commission for raising money; in 1646 High Collector of tax assessments in parts of Middlesex; in 1647 member of a committee for the militia of Westminster; in 1650 counsel to the trustees for the sale of forfeited estates; in 1655 counsel-at-law practising before the Committee for Compounding, and afterwards receiver-general for Middlesex.[6] In addition to carrying these responsibilities, he was financially interested in companies of 'adventurers' operating in the fen district and in Ireland. Definitely he was a man on the make. He far outdid his father in acquiring real estate, buying along with many other properties the manor of Mickleton in 1657. It was he who also high-handedly adopted the Grave coat of arms, which he stuck in a window of the chapel of Lincoln's Inn, of which he became a bencher in 1660, and it was he who discovered or invented the Yorkshire connection. In all this he was making a determined effort to transform his family into gentry. He knew what was necessary. According to the Vinerian Lectures on the English Law (1766–8), written by Robert Chambers with the help of Samuel Johnson, 'A Gentleman in the legal Sense is a Man possessed of Coat Armour and in the popular Sense, a Man that inherits it. Thence the common Axiom that the King can make a Lord but not a Gentleman. But whatever be the Power of the King, it is the Opinion of Sir Thomas Smith that every Man (who has Money) may make a Gentleman of himself, nothing more being requisite in his Opinion than that a Man be able to live without Work and that he bear the Port and Charge of a Gentleman.'[7] Richard Graves of Lincoln's Inn could certainly afford 'to live without Work' and 'bear the Port and Charge of a Gentleman,' and though he apparently continued the practice of law in London during the twelve years of life remaining to him after the purchase of Mickleton Manor, probably he intended to retire there ultimately and become a country gentleman. In the popular imagination the possession of a country estate was inseparable from the idea of a gentleman. His great-grandson, Richard Graves the writer, devoted a large part of his second novel, *Columella*, to exploring this aspect of the structure of English society, sketching various examples of men who had 'retired' from active participation in business, politics, or a profession in order to lead lives of leisure in the country, believing that to be a sure way to recognition as gentlemen. It is not known when the Graves family actually took up permanent residence in Mickleton, but it was the seat of Samuel, son and successor to Richard Graves of Lincoln's Inn, and it remained in the family until recently.

Little is known about Samuel Graves except that he lived in Mickleton, married into a family of sea captains, and begot another Richard, whom I shall call Richard of Mickleton (see plate 2), the father of Richard the subject of this book. Richard of Mickleton comes alive for us more than any of his predecessors do, thanks to his friendship with the Oxford antiquary and librarian Thomas Hearne, who saved many of his letters and often mentioned him in his diary, all of which is still preserved in the Bodleian Library in Oxford.[8] Lacking his grandfather's obsession with

money and power, Richard of Mickleton was content to live quietly in his
manor house the life of a gentleman. After his death Hearne wrote of
him: 'He was one of the most worthy and virtuous gentlemen I was
acquainted with. He was ... a man of great modesty and of a most sweet
Temper, and a great Friend to his Tenants and to the Poor, so that all
People are very sorry for his Death ... '9 His son Richard, who always
admired the country gentleman when he was the genuine article and
prepared to accept the responsibilities that went along with the status,
wrote an enthusiastic description in one of his earliest poems of the life led
at Mickleton Manor during his father's lifetime:

> *... here those ancestors – a virtuous train!*
> *In health contented dwelt, thro' many a reign. –*
> *Each country-seat was then a well-stor'd farm,*
> *Which knew no beauties but in snug and warm.*
> *Pleas'd, round their barns they heard their oxen lowe,*
> *And the same steeds then drew the coach and plough.*
> *Strangers to form, their neighbour was their guest,*
> *Where mirth and rural plenty made the feast:*
> *Nor hyson yet, nor Gallic wines were known,*
> *Nor deem'd polite the annual jaunt to town.*
> *While summers thus, and chearful winters pass'd,*
> *They liv'd thrice happy ...* [10]

This theme recurs often in his writings, most particularly in the character
of Mr Aldworth in *The Spiritual Quixote* (note the significant name), a man
in whose house it snows meat and drink and who acts towards the suspects
brought before him as justice of the peace with exemplary fairness.
Richard of Mickleton may also have been the model for the character of
Mr Townsend in the same novel, some trace of whose sternness as well as
gullible enthusiasm may have been present in the old squire's character. If
so, perhaps some of the chapter on country squires was also based on him.
Rusticity and naïveté are seen there as central characteristics in a man of
this class.[11] As all these things, however, are the traditional stuff of
caricature, it would be rash to read the passages in which they occur as
genuine biography. Nevertheless, there may well have been laughable
sides to the character of Richard of Mickleton, which his son could quietly
enjoy without damage to the affection and esteem in which he held his
father's memory.

Richard Graves of Mickleton married a Welsh woman, Elizabeth,
daughter of Thomas Morgan, Esquire. In his *Reveries of Solitude,*

published several years after her death, her son Richard, the novelist, wrote whimsically: 'As I am myself a Welchman by my mother's side, and am possessed of a pedigree of the *Morgans'* family five yards long; and can prove my descent from a knight of King Arthur's round table; no one I trust, will suspect me of any disrespectful intention, towards that ancient race of Britons.'[12] Wales must have played a significant part in his life, for there are Welsh scenes in all four of his novels, mostly penned with lyrical fervour. In *The Spiritual Quixote*, for example, the two pilgrims who are its chief characters visit 'a romantic valley, on the banks of the Uske, the coolness of which, as the sun was near its meridian, was extremely refreshing. After winding along the river's side for about half a mile, they came in sight of a pleasant village, at the foot of another hill, covered with hanging woods, which formed a beautiful amphitheatre; in the centre of which the Parish-church, with its little spire, rose amongst some old pine-trees; and the ruins of a Monastery, near which the river formed a natural cascade, shewed that the place had formerly been dedicated to devotion and solitude.'[13] It sounds as if the writer had visited the spot he described, like most of the other Welsh scenes in his writings. Unfortunately the five-yard-long Welsh pedigree cannot now be traced, and consequently nothing is known about the family of the mother of the novelist. In a book published in 1788, however, he mentioned that his older brother, named Morgan after his mother's family, had been adopted after his parents' deaths by 'a distant relation, a Mr M—rg—n, of W—rl——s, in Essex.'[14] In a footnote he wrote that W—rl——s was 'near Waltham Abby,' and a typescript history of Warlies in the parish of Waltham Holy Cross, deposited in the Essex Record Office in Chelmsford, informs one that a Richard Morgan, who was described as 'Esq. of London,' was admitted tenant of the copyhold estate of Warlies in 1720. He died in 1740, and in 1742, according to a document now in the Harrowby MSS Trust, Morgan Graves claimed ownership of properties in Middlesex that had been bequeathed to him by Richard Morgan of Warlies, in the parish of Waltham Holy Cross, Essex.[15] All that fits together reasonably well, but it does not tell us who Richard Morgan was. But since he was a 'distant relation,' he must surely have belonged in some way to Elizabeth Morgan's family.

Richard the novelist's contact with his Welsh relations must have been kept up on his own, for his mother died in 1723 when he was a mere child. Her death was a tremendous blow to her husband, who wrote two weeks later to his friend Hearne: 'it hath pleased God to visit me with one of the Greatest Afflictions that could have befallen me in this world, the Loss of the nearest and dearest Relation, who has left me the Father of 6 poor motherless Children.'[16] Almost the only surviving reference her son made to her was to imply in his essay 'On Health' that she had cared for him tenderly and that after her death his health declined in the hands of servants.[17] The glow with which he always wrote about Wales must reflect the tenderness of his memories of his mother and his Welsh relations.

Richard Graves of Mickleton had intellectual interests. Most of the letters that he wrote to Thomas Hearne as well as the conversations recorded in Hearne's diary have to do with antiquarian subjects, for, as Hearne remarked, Graves was 'a most excellent Scholar and Antiquary.' They talked and corresponded about Domesday Book, about the inscriptions in Pershore Abbey, about a copy of Schedel's *Chronicle* that Graves had found in a bookstore in Stratford-on-Avon, about Grave's 'fine MS Polychronicon' that he would not part with even for fifteen guineas, about the distinction between *moor* and *meer*, about 'a Copper coin of Theodora, the second Wife of Constantius Chlorus,' found near Chipping Campden, and about a hundred other similarly fascinating subjects. Graves, who had the money and leisure that Hearne lacked, helped the latter in his researches by lending him books, copying inscriptions for him, and collecting subscriptions to make possible the publication of his edition of the *Chartulary of Worcester*. When it came out, Graves was dismayed to find himself thanked in the preface in what he considered too complimentary a style, but, reflecting that Hearne meant the epithets he had used 'out of kindness and Respect,' he was prepared to 'take 'em as such, and accordingly return you Thanks.' He himself was almost as avid a collector of valuable books, manuscripts, and coins. He never completed his own contribution to scholarship, a work on the antiquities of Evesham and various other abbeys. Nevertheless, a protégé of Hearne's, George Ballard, wrote of Graves: 'He was a compleat master of the Greek, Latin, and Saxon tongues; was admirably well read and skilled in the Roman and British antiquities, and was a most curious historian, antiquary, and medalist ... He had made vast collections towards the history and antiquities of those places, where the several parts of his estate lay; which he had collected, with very great pains and expence, from Domesday book, from MSS. and records in the Tower, and divers other places; which he designed by way of annals, ... and just before his death had designed to have methodized and compiled in 3 vols. fol.'[18] He was clearly a better antiquary than the Mr Townsend of *The Spiritual Quixote*, who mistakes a modern folly for a genuine Roman ruin. It was Richard of Mickleton who became sceptical about his family's right to use the Grave arms and who, after doing a lot of unavailing research on his own, appealed to the College of Heralds.

His interests, however, were not purely intellectual. Writing to Hearne in 1725, he remarked: 'I have been very much taken up of late with Building and Planting, that my Thoughts have been but little upon Books.'[19] Building and gardening were favourite obsessions of many eighteenth-century gentlemen, as every reader of Pope's satires knows. The improvements he made at Mickleton were described by his writer son in the earlier part of the poem from which a few lines have already been quoted:

> *Is this the place where late, in tonsile yew,*
> *Crowns, dragons, pyramids, and peacocks grew?*
> *Where quaint parterres presented to the eye*
> *The various angles of a Christmas pye?*
> *Or alleys met, with correspondent glades,*
> *And trees in rows cast equi-distant shades?*
> *Where terraces you scal'd by many a step,*
> *From which at once poor frogs in panics leapt?*
> *And walls surrounding, thirty cubits high,*
> *Left to the view scarce thirty ells of sky?*
> *Around, the mansion, barns, and stables lay,*
> *And spread night's mantle o'er the face of day.*
> *These spacious lawns an hundred hedges shar'd,*
> *Like tenements of cards, by children rear'd.*

His father's 'want of taste' is held up to ridicule:

> *What taste perverse our ancestors inspir'd,*
> *Who banish'd oaks, and mournful yews admir'd!*
> *Who rais'd huge walls to guard a few jonquils,*
> *Pent up from flow'ry meads and verdant hills!*
> *Disdaining nature, in her richest dress,*
> *Till tortur'd into Gothic littleness!*[20]

But the satire is double edged. In spite of their bad taste our ancestors, he says, like Richard of Mickleton, lived happier and better lives than their new-fangled successors do. The poem on the whole expresses genuine admiration for the author's father, in spite of his stiff, old-fashioned tastes.

Richard Graves of Mickleton died suddenly in 1729 at the early age of fifty-two and was succeeded by his eldest son, Morgan, aged twenty, then a student at Oxford. The father had died intestate, but Morgan, now lord of the manor, told Thomas Hearne, whom he met accidentally on the

High Street, that he was assuming responsibility for his brothers and sisters, who were of course all minors, and had made 'a prudent settlement and provision' for them.[21] He did not explain what that provision was, but his statement is corroborated in a document, now in the Harrowby Trust, in which the financial history of the Graves estates since 1729 was recapitulated. From this it appears that in December 1729 Morgan had raised three thousand one hundred pounds on mortgage for the purpose of 'paying certain portions to his Brothers and Sisters.'[22] No particulars were mentioned, but apparently some capital was transferred to each of them, an action that explains what Richard meant later when he said that he had 'only a younger brother's fortune,' and perhaps also Morgan paid Richard's school expenses and helped him out later while he was at Oxford, for his scholarship would not have met all his needs. Morgan probably did as much for the others as well. But the bulk of the estate, said to be worth eight hundred pounds per annum, must have gone to him. His first action was to transform himself from a commoner of University College into a gentleman commoner, a much more socially prestigious personage. Nevertheless, though not in all respects an ideal elder brother, he undertook his new responsibilities as head of the family with commendable seriousness, seeing all his siblings well launched on the world.

But Morgan was not interested in his father's intellectual pursuits. Naturally Thomas Hearne was concerned over the fate of his late friend's collections of books, manuscripts, coins, and other antiquarian curiosities, which turned out to be even more fabulous than he had thought, and was not reassured by Morgan's announcement that he meant to sell the lot, 'Antiquities, he said, being a dry, unprofitable Study.' Hearne tried to persuade him to keep them in the family but, having little success, growled into his diary: 'I suppose he had been talking with & byassed by some illiterate fine sparks.'[23] In the end the collections were dispersed; the coins, valued by Ballard at 150 guineas, went for 21, and the printed books 'in a most scandalous manner' for forty or forty-five pounds. The papers, including historical mss, went to a Mr West, who at least would understand their value.[24] It was a heartbreak for Hearne, especially as he knew that young Richard, even at the age of sixteen, was showing an aptitude for antiquarian studies. Hearne, however, did Morgan an injustice in implying that his Oxford friends were all 'illiterate fine sparks,' for one of them was Charles Wesley, one of the two brothers later famous as founders of the Methodist movement, and Morgan may have become a fringe member of the Holy Club, founded by Charles Wesley at Christ Church. He remained on friendly terms with Wesley for some years, Charles visiting him in Mickleton. Morgan probably never committed himself to Methodism or experienced the New Birth, but he was at least for a while favourably disposed.[25]

At Oxford Morgan decided to follow in the footsteps not of his father but of his great-grandfather, declaring it his intention to study law and eventually look for a job in the Court of Chancery.[26] In that direction lay riches and sophistication. He was accordingly admitted as a student of the inner Temple on 12 February 1731 and in 1732 acquired a chamber in the inn (8 Kings Bench Walk), where presumably he lived and worked when he was in London. The manor house in Mickleton was apparently either closed up or let, and when not in London he seems to have lived at Warlies, probably with his two sisters. In 1766 he joined the bench of his inn on invitation and attended meetings of the Bench Table regularly thereafter until within a few weeks of his death in 1770. There is evidence that he practised law, and he held on to his chambers until 1748,[27] though how he divided his time between London and Mickleton is not clear. In 1735 he was called to the bar and opened up the manor house certainly by 1736, when it was hospitably ready to welcome guests. In 1756 he was in Mickleton taking a stand on turnpike roads.[28] How rich he grew is not clear. He added a little to the size of the family estate but, as will presently appear, was once rejected as a suitor by a woman who preferred a wealthier man. But he made many 'improvements' at the manor house, completely doing over the garden. He was a pioneer in the new natural taste and an enemy to his father's garden walls, hedges, parterres, and symmetrical flower beds. The ha-ha with which he replaced the garden wall still survives, as well as a fragment of one of the statues with which he ornamented the grounds. As Jerry Tugwell says: 'Why, ... there is our Squire has got a naked *thing-em-bob* stands up in the middle of the grove.'[29] William Shenstone, who later became famous as an exponent of the new taste, seems to have got his first impetus in that direction from the work Morgan did here.

Whatever sophistication Morgan may have also acquired evidently did not include the knack of writing graceful verses to a lady. Edmund Hector remembered that on one occasion in 1731, when his friend Morgan Graves waited upon a lady in the neighbourhood and was presented by her with a sprig of myrtle, he 'wished much to return the compliment in verse.' But the rhymes would not come, and so on his behalf Hector applied to his friend Samuel Johnson, who composed the desired poem in about half an hour and turned it over for the use of the inarticulate young man.[30]

If a 'key' to *The Spiritual Quixote*, published years later, is correct in identifying Morgan Graves as the model for Mr Clayton, a minor character in that novel, he was later involved in another, even more unsatisfactory affair. He had wooed and, as he thought, won a young lady whom the key identified as Anna Maria Brace but who, according to the novel, ditched him on her mother's advice in favour of a man rich enough to offer her two hundred pounds a year pin-money. Mr Nicholas Lyons, who has done some valuable research on the biographical background of this novel, has learned that the real Miss Brace married a Mr Copley but that they soon quarrelled and were legally separated. When Richard Graves moved to Claverton in 1750, Mrs Copley was living by herself in Bath, no doubt on her pin-money, and, as Mr Lyons believes, met her former suitor's brother Richard, who proceeded to tell her story in the novel that he had then begun. In it he presented her as a demanding, short-tempered woman and a great advocate of women's rights, who would have made his brother a bad wife. In 1742 however, Morgan had married Ann Walwyn of Longworth in Herefordshire, who, if the parallel with the fortunes of Mr Clayton is still valid, was 'a very agreeable heiress' worth thirty thousand pounds. It was a happy marriage, and Morgan must long before have forgot the sting of his rejection by the avaricious Miss Brace.[31]

Besides Morgan and Richard, there were four other children, of whom Mary was the eldest. At one time she was engaged to marry William Shenstone, but that alliance was broken off and instead she married a clergyman named John Taylor.[32] Charles Caspar, the third of the sons, became a Methodist while a student at Oxford and will cross our path again in a later chapter. Danvers, the youngest son, struck out in a different direction, not going to the university but entering the service of the East India Company. He was the prototype for Young Barty, a character in Richard Grave's novel *Columella*, who goes out to India, amasses a large fortune for himself in private trade, making a profit of 100 per cent on his trading stock, successfully conducts some delicate diplomatic negotiations for the company, and comes home to marry the sweetheart who has been waiting for him all the while. Danver's career was much the same up to a point but lacked the happy ending, for after becoming the company's chief agent in Persia, he fell a victim to an epidemic fever and died at Bandar Abbas (Gambroon) on 19 May 1752. He was remembered at Mickleton by a pompous Latin epitaph and a simple stone urn that looks like the work of his brother Richard, who had a taste for urns and had set up a very similar one ten years before in memory of a childhood sweetheart.[33] The youngest of the children was a girl, Elizabeth, whom George Ballard described as 'the most beautiful creature' he ever saw. She died of smallpox at the age of about nine in 1731.[34]

There is no need to trace the family fortunes any further or to comment except briefly on its alleged ramifications. Claims were made that the centenarian called John had a brother or other near relation who became lord mayor of York in the sixteenth century and that he had a younger son, also called John, who sired two famous sons, one of whom was Savilian Professor of Astronomy at Oxford and the other Physician in Ordinary to Charles II[35]. But though these men certainly existed, their connection with the Graveses of Mickleton cannot be proved. Even without them, however, it is clear that the Mickleton Graveses were a vigorous and interesting family, full of variety of character and talent. They were all positive personalities, and they brought in fresh blood by seeking their wives outside their immediate communities. And, if they survived infancy, they tended to live to a great age. Richard of Mickleton told Hearne one night that he had an aunt living who was 101 and who 'is still a Woman that is vigorous, & hath her senses perfect. She is a tall, upright Woman, and still comely, she having been formerly very handsome.'[36] According to the family tree, he had no less than nine aunts on his father's side alone, and so I have no idea who the one referred to was. But she was typical of the clan.

CHAPTER TWO

Childhood

Mickleton, the little north Gloucestershire village in which Richard Graves grew up, is reflected in the 'sequestered village' that is the ancestral home of Geoffry Wildgoose, hero of *The Spiritual Quixote*. In the novel Graves produces the necessary impression by mentioning the spire of a Gothic church standing in a grove of pine trees and making a picturesque appearance against the backdrop of a wood hanging on the edge of the Cotswold Hills. One may still see that picture at Mickleton today. The author also informs us that the garden belonging to the Wildgoose house, like the one at the manor house in Mickleton in his childhood, is laid out in the old-fashioned style, 'with high walls and thickset-hedges.' Even the surrounding country is like that about Mickleton, which lies close to the boundary between the grazing lands of the Cotswolds and the rich arable and orchards of the Vale of Evesham, for when Wildgoose, accompanied by Jerry Tugwell, his squire, steals away from his home one morning to begin his travels, mounting the Cotswold Hills and pausing to look back over the way they have come, he sees spread out before him 'the rich vale of Evesham' and, in the far distance, the Malvern Hills.[1] That is the panorama one sees today from Mickleton Wood three-quarters of a mile east of the village. These scant details are supplemented in a pen and ink sketch made by Graves himself (see plate 3) to guide the hand of the artist who was to prepare illustrations for the second edition. Complaining in a covering letter to his publisher that the village shown in a vignette on the title-page of the first edition was too regular, too much like a village in the London area, he explained that what he wanted was one with irregular houses and mountains in the background.[2] He may not have seen Mickleton for some years, and the village in his sketch is shaggier and more up and down than Mickleton was or is. His memory of it had exaggerated those romantic elements in the conception that accorded with the taste for wild scenery that became one of the passions of his mature years, influenced, no doubt, by his three years' residence in Derbyshire and his travels in Wales. Nevertheless the sketch is valuable evidence of how he remembered his childhood home. All the essentials are there. It is irregular; it is rustic; it is tied in with the beautiful countryside; and above all it is feudal. The great manor house, whose gable ends and iron gates are seen at the left, dominates the scene, almost obscuring the parish church whose spire rises among the trees behind it. Here are the elements that made up the environment in which he passed his boyhood.

The countryside about Mickleton had its quota of great houses inhabited by the gentry, but young Richard's father probably did not mix much in society, devoting himself instead to his books, his coins, and his historical researches. He found the gentry uncongenial. They had 'little or no taste for Books,' he complained to his friend Thomas Hearne, 'being altogether taken up in the Diversions of the Field and Good Fellowship.'[3] A few of these hearty gentlemen appear in his son's novels, but it is uncertain whether they were drawn from the life or from the novels of Fielding. One incident, however, certainly came from real life, the story told in *The Spiritual Quixote* about Sir William Keyte, who committed suicide by setting his house on fire and burning himself up in its flaming ruins.[4] Norton Hall, his house, stood almost exactly a mile west of Mickleton Manor and within the boundaries of the parish. A brief report of the disaster appeared in the *London Magazine* for September 1741,[5] but Graves, who was in Derbyshire at the time, probably got the details for his much fuller account from his friend George Ballard, who was an eyewitness, having run thither when a man came riding furiously through the village crying out that Norton House was on fire, and who sent a gruesome description of the scene to his mother two days afterwards.[6] Kyte, according to Graves, had built Norton Hall some years before in order to accommodate his mistress, who had been his wife's maid, and for years he had lived there a life of increasing extravagance and debauchery, finally alienating not only his son but even his mistress. He was drinking heavily, and either drink or (as the magazine suggested) insanity or a deep fit of remorse led him to end his life in this terrible way. It is unlikely that the neighbourhood provided many stories as lurid as that one, but Graves was keeping his eyes and ears open and was in a good position to know what was going on.

Despite the weight that he later attached to gentility, Graves was free from what he once called 'tapino-phoby, or dread of every thing that is low.'[7] By 'low' he meant ungenteel in either writing or behaviour. Obviously he felt that more positive character and more lively comedy was to be found among rustics than among the gentry, and his novels are blessedly free from the curse of gentility that lay heavily on some of the other literature of the time. Much of the raw material out of which he fashioned the many low-life scenes in his novels, especially *The Spiritual Quixote*, must have been his memories of his Gloucestershire home. His masterpiece in the genre of the low is Jerry Tugwell in *The Spiritual Quixote*, one of the most delightful yokels in all eighteenth-century literature. Unlike Joseph Andrews, Tugwell is pure rustic and not a gentleman incognito. A cobbler who has lost much of his business through his addiction to cheap novels of adventure and who has just enough learning to possess some hard words whose proper meanings and pronunciations elude him, he nevertheless is totally down to earth and has a common sense that his romantic young master lacks. Though he is the typical fall-guy of comedy, to whom most of the more uproarious mishaps in the novel occur, he is constantly jerking his master back to reality, sensibly reminding him of the need for food and drink and puncturing his more inflated oratorical bubbles. Makers of keys to this novel, in which Graves's fictional characters are identified with real people, have produced at least two originals for Tugwell: one, a William Taylor, Mickleton shoemaker, who is said to have died in 1783; the other, 'Old Bacon, a noted cobbler of Aldworth.'[8] Neither identification is helpful, since nothing is known about either Taylor or Bacon and neither can be confirmed. But even if Graves had no one model for his character sketch, all the strokes that went into it must have come from his own observations, most of them made in Mickleton. Even Tugwell's language, larded as it is with colloquialisms, was genuine peasant talk.[9]

In the country surrounding Mickleton, as all over England at that time, fairs, race meetings, wakes, festivals, and revels of various kinds were traditionally held, like the Warwick Fair at which Wildgoose comes to grief towards the end of the novel. One of the most picturesque of them, Dover's Games, was held every Whitsuntide close to Mickleton, well within reach of the legs of a sturdy boy. Sometimes known as the Cotswold Olympics, they were first held in the time of James I under the direction of Robert Dover, whose name is still given to the hillside, now the property of the National Trust, where they were held, and with some interruptions they have been held there annually down to the present time. A number of Jacobean poets, including Drayton, Jonson, and Randolph, wrote verses celebrating them, which were published in 1636 in a now scarce volume entitled *Annalia Dubrensia*, whose chief interest lies in a frontispiece (see plate 4) in which the various sports and revels are quaintly depicted. Women are dancing, men jumping, wrestling, sliding, standing on their hands, throwing hammers, and handling pikes, while others on horseback are hunting. Feasting and other revels are underway, the whole presided over by Robert Dover himself on a horse. As the two pilgrims in the novel approach Dover's Hill, as Graves himself must often have done, they hear 'a confused noise of drums, trumpets, and whistle-pipes,' and on coming closer they see 'a great number of swains in their holiday-cloaths, with their belts and silk handkerchiefs; and nymphs in straw hats and tawdry ribbands, flaunting, ogling, and coquetting (in their rustic way) with as much alacrity, as any of the gay flutterers in the Mall.'[10] The crowd of spectators is made up mostly of farmers and farm labourers with their women, though a few of the local gentry, who have turned up in their coaches, hang about feeling out of place and pretending to be bored. Stepping briefly at Jerry's insistence into one of the booths to refresh themselves with pints of ale, the pilgrims hear the smock race announced. It must have stuck particularly in Graves's memory. The prize, a smock, a piece of feminine underwear, is hung up on a pole for everybody to behold in all its flagrant immodesty, creating 'unchaste conceptions' in puritanical minds like young Geoffry's, especially when the contestants, six young women, 'began to exhibit themselves before the whole assembly, in a dress hardly reconcilable to the rules of decency.'

A similar scene is depicted in an engraving in the 1773 edition of William Somerville's *Hobbinol* (see plate 5), and the race itself is vividly described in the poem. In the engraving one may also see the conclusion of a bout of cudgel playing, the victor strutting before the admiring eyes of a group of female spectators while his opponent lies bleeding and unconscious on the ground, his wife or sweetheart swooning away beside him. Eighteenth-century England liked its sports to be rough and bloody. Though there is no reason to think that Richard Graves ever participated as a contestant in such games, he was not one of the supercilious gentry who observed them from a distance, but soaked everything up in his memory and stored it away for later use.[11]

Elsewhere on the Cotswolds, according to Samuel Rudder, who published *A New History of Gloucestershire* in 1779, Whitsuntide was celebrated with a mumming held in a barn with dancing to the music of pipe and tabor, fancy costumes, and favours for the girls.[12] How Thomas Hardy must have enjoyed the account if it ever came his way!

Even closer to Mickleton than Dover's Hill but in the opposite direction lay Meon Hill, Michael Drayton's 'fruitful *Meene*,' a favourite grazing place for sheep, where, according to the poet, the shepherd whose ewes produced the first lambs traditionally gave an al fresco feast –

> In his gay Bauldrick sits at his lowe grassie Bord,
> With Flawns, Curds, Clowted-creame, and Country dainties stor'd:
> And, whilst the bag-pipe playes, each lustie jocund Swaine
> Quaffes Sillibubs in Kans, to all upon the Plaine,
> And to their Country-Girles, whose Nosegayes they doe weare,
> Some Roundelayes doe sing, the rest, the burthen beare.[13]

– a folk custom that, if it persisted into his time, Graves might have seen in a less romantic light!

The centre of his childhood world, of course, was the manor house (see plate 6). Nowhere in his letters or writings has he recalled what it looked like inside, but knowing what we do of his father, we may safely guess that it too was old-fashioned and heavily Jacobean in feeling, lacking the lightness characteristic of more fashionable eighteenth-century interiors, and that the rooms were crowded with cases for books, manuscripts, medals, and curios of every kind. It was also full of people. Richard's family provided companionship, though how congenial they all were is questionable. In later years all the boys developed markedly different tastes and interests, and so it is possible that as children each went his own way. So long as she lived, their mother no doubt held them together, but she died in 1723, when Richard was not yet eight years old. His education must have been supervised by his father, and since Richard alone of his children shared his intellectual interests, it is likely that he was closer to his father than were any of the others. The father more than once boasted to Thomas Hearne about Richard's aptitude for antiquarian studies and his precocity in them.

Who taught Richard to read and write is unknown, but according to the article on him in *Public Characters of 1799–1800*, he 'received the first part of his classical education under a Mr Smith, the curate of the parish, who ... made him read Hesiod and Homer at twelve years of age.'[14] Graves described his schoolmaster, William Smith, as 'a worthy and learned clergyman' who raised four children 'in a genteel manner' on a meagre income.[15] Where he came from, where he was educated, and where ordained, are unknown, though Smith was a common name in nearby Chipping Campden and in 1730 a Smith was a schoolmaster there.[16] But in 1718 or 1719 William Smith had become curate of Mickleton.[17] In addition to his duties as curate, he kept a school, to which young Richard in due time must have been sent, one of his fellow pupils being Howard

Hastings, whom Graves mistakenly identified as the father of Warren, the famous governor-general of India.[18] (He was actually uncle and foster father.) Smith is said also to have conducted a charity school in Mickleton, but it is inconceivable that the son of the lord of the manor should have attended such a school or that it would have admitted a boy, like Hastings, from outside the parish. Mr Smith must have been a good teacher to have put young Richard through Hesiod and Homer at the age of twelve, laying the foundation for the reputation his pupil later took with him to Oxford of being a 'tolerably good Grecian.'

When he reached the age of thirteen, Richard was taken out of the hands of Mr Smith and sent away to a boarding school in Abingdon in Berkshire, not far from Oxford. Why his father chose that school, so far from home, out of all the schools available to him, is unknown, but it evidently was a good one. Founded at least as early as the fourteenth century, it had been reorganized in the sixteenth by a John Roysse, a local mercer, to help fill the gap created in the English educational system by the dissolution of the monasteries, and ever since has been unofficially known as Roysse's School.[19] In the seventeenth century it got a further boost from a generous endowment left for the purpose of enabling it to send several of its best pupils each year on to Oxford, a purpose that resulted in the founding of Pembroke College, the youngest of Oxford's colleges in Graves's time, which came into being primarily as a home for Abingdon scholars. The town council, which administered the endowment, had a respect for learning that town councils seldom have today and that must have been above average even in the eighteenth century. What Richard Graves did during the four years he spent there is also unknown, no family letters or diaries having survived, not even his term bills. A class list dated 1732, however, of which a copy is preserved among the Preston papers in the Shire Hall in Reading, gives us an idea of the kind of boys who populated the school in his time.[20] There are ninety names, including those of three peers or peers' sons, a baronet, and a large assortment of sons of country gentlemen. One name stands out, that of Thomas Head, later Sir Thomas, scion of an old Berkshire family, who became a close friend of Graves's and remained through life his friend and benefactor. Possibly a family friendship had already existed, which would account for the choice of Abingdon in the first place.

That Richard was happy in school is unlikely; sensitive and precocious boys like him seldom are. Atticus, one of the characters in his novel *Columella*, very likely spoke for him when he remarked: 'I remember ... for some years after I had left school, I could not bear the sight of the place where we had been so long confined under a rigid discipline; and yet

I now think it one of the most agreeable country towns in that part of England; being situated ... on the banks of the Thames, amidst flowery meadows and fruitful fields, and abounding in pleasant walks, and a tolerable neighbourhood.'[21] Abingdon answers the description. The 'rigid discipline' would have been that of the headmaster in Graves's time, Thomas Woods, who reigned there for thirty-seven years and who was known to generations of his pupils as 'Flogging Tom.'[22] But Graves was a good pupil. On the Monday after the first Sunday in August following the end of his final term there, a board consisting of the master of Pembroke College in Oxford, two of the senior fellows of that college, the master and two of the senior governors of Christ's Hospital in Abingdon, and the master of his own school, sitting in solemn conclave, chose him and two others to go to Oxford in the fall on scholarships.[23] So it had all been worthwhile, even at the cost of sore buttocks.

CHAPTER THREE

Pembroke

Graves went to Oxford in the fall of 1732, moving into his room in
Pembroke College, according to the buttery books, some time during the
week of 27 October; he was classified as a 'scholar,' that is, as a student
partly supported on the proceeds of a scholarship – in his case, one of the
Abingdon ones. On 1 November he paid his caution money to the bursar
and on the following day his entrance fee to the master. Then on the
seventh, according to the university archives, he matriculated into the
university and further complied with its statutes by subscribing the
Thirty-nine Articles of the Church of England. These formalities
completed, he was an undergraduate member of the university in good
standing.

The move to Oxford must have been relatively easy for him. It was not
his first absence from home, and since his father's death the manor house
had been shut up. Moreover, he was the sort of young man who gravitates
naturally to a university. At first, however, being seventeen, like all young
students at the outset of their university careers he floundered, moving
from one set of friends to another, sometimes drinking too much and at
others not drinking at all. But soon he settled down to a steady and
sensible routine. He must have found the easy discipline of even
eighteenth-century Oxford, in spite of its proctors and tutorial supervision, a welcome change from the iron rule of Flogging Tom. The buttery
books, which record not only the charges made against each member of
the college for his room, board, tuition, and extras but also mulcts, that is
fines, for various kinds of misbehaviour, on the whole give a good account
of him. He seems to have been seldom if ever fined. Misbehaviour in
students, when it is not due to mere high spirits, is usually a sign of
deep-seated unhappiness that can find no other means of expression.

Graves was not unhappy. More and more he was to make Oxford his home, sometimes staying there during the holidays. At the university he found friendship and intellectual stimulus, and best of all he could be his own man.

If he wrote any letters during his years in Oxford, neither they nor the ones he received in reply have come to light, and there are no diaries or other personal papers to inform us about his daily life. But he has given us a glimpse or two of it in the memoir he wrote many years later of his college friend and contemporary William Shenstone.[1] Upon his arrival in Oxford, Graves tells us, he found the college divided into cliques, as colleges always are, and the first group he fell in with was 'a very sober little party, who amused themselves in the evening with reading Greek and drinking water.' There is irony in his use of the word 'amused,' which, as Johnson explained in his *Dictionary*, is 'frequently taken in a sense bordering on contempt,' an irony underlined a few sentences farther on when he described the group as a 'mortified symposium.' But that was a later feeling. At the time he enjoyed the Greek, sticking with the group for six months while they read Theophrastus, Epictetus, Phalaris, and other authors outside the usual fare provided in the schools of his time. Eventually, getting loose from them, he bounced in the opposite direction, taking up with 'a set of jolly, sprightly young fellows, most of them west-country lads; who drank ale, smoked tobacco, punned, and sung bacchanalian catches the whole evening.' Usually they opened their proceedings with this song:

> *Let's be jovial, fill our glasses,*
> *Madness 'tis for us to think,*
> *How the world is rul'd by asses,*
> *And the wisest sway'd by chink.*

From that rowdy group he soon graduated to a tonier one presided over by two former Abingdon boys, John Thynne Howe and his younger brother, Henry Frederick, who later became successively the second and third barons Chedworth.[2] They treated him to port wine and arrack-punch, often finishing up with a bottle or two of claret. They drank their favourite toasts on their knees and considered themselves, in the slang of the time, 'bucks of the first head.' Graves was attracted to them because alongside his intellectual propensities he had a great love of genteel society and saw in these two young men persons able 'to bear the port and charge' of gentlemen. He had sense enough to realize that he could not afford the kind of life the young Howes were leading him into and that his health was being injured by their late hours and hard drinking. Yet he much preferred them to another group that he called the 'flying squadron of plain, sensible, matter-of-fact men ... They had come to the university in their way to the Temple, or to get a slight smattering of the sciences before they settled in the country.' Years later, when he wrote about them, he realized that they were 'a good sort of young people, and perhaps the most rational of the college,' but at the time they must have seemed hopelessly lacking in style and liveliness.

Fortunately two genteel young men of a different stamp from all the others had come up to Pembroke at the same time that Graves had, the one from Solihull and the other from Eton. He met both of them casually at various gatherings, though never among the water-drinkers. One of them was William Shenstone and the other Anthony Whistler. Both were commoners of the college, that is, students who were not on scholarship but were supported either by themselves or by their families. Both were better off than Graves was and lived rather more extravagantly, as the buttery books show, though neither was a son of Comus and both were interested in literature and matters of taste. Both became intimate friends of Richard Graves, forming with him a triumvirate that ended only with their lives. They were very close to each other during their undergraduate years, so close, as Graves afterwards admitted, that the other members of the college felt resentful and even a little threatened by them.[3]

Their close friendship dates from a breakfast party given in his rooms by Shenstone several months after their first arrival in Oxford, at which the three got on so well together that they did not break up until late in the day. They talked about literature. Shenstone produced a copy of Cotton's *Virgil Travestie*, which detained them for some time while they sampled it, Graves finding it to be 'a most laughable performance' though 'full of indelicacies and low humour' – faults not likely to put off a trio of young men let loose on the world for the first time. Whistler said that he preferred Pope's *Rape of the Lock* for its 'higher species of humour,' and Graves slyly suggested that Echard's *Causes of the Contempt of the Clergy* was to his mind a work of *'equal humour.'* Whether or not either of his new friends realized that his leg was being gently pulled is not clear, but Echard's book is a Puritanical attack on the work of the Restoration dramatists that betrays not even the slightest trace of humour. Graves must have laughed at it partly because of its pompous solemnity and partly because it contained an extensive florilegium of the naughty passages that Echard took exception to in those plays. Graves no doubt took secret pleasure in citing a work that neither of his friends had read or known about. This little shaft was typical of him. Years later he added an equally sly footnote to *The Spiritual Quixote* in which he described Bishop Warburton's solemn treatise *The Doctrine of Grace* as a work of 'exquisite humour'[4] because of its numerous quotations of absurdities found in the published journals of Wesley and Whitefield.

The breakfast party was such a success that it was repeated again and again. At length the three friends were meeting almost every evening in the rooms of one of them. They talked, they sipped Florence wine, and they read aloud plays, poetry, and essays from the *Tatler* and the *Spectator*. In *Columella*, written by Graves many years later, he described the similar way in which several of his characters spent their leisure time as students: 'Their vacant hours each day were spent in conversing and walking together; as their evenings were, either in conferring about their studies, or in reading some modern poem, a play, or a paper in the Spectator or the Rambler; or in very sober and philosophical compotations.'[5] Much has been written about the decay of Oxford and Cambridge in the eighteenth century, and no doubt neither university was then enjoying one of its most distinguished periods, but no university is wholly bad in which at least some of its students talk together freely about books and ideas and read widely outside the prescribed course of studies. The urge for self-education was stronger in the eighteenth century than it seems to be now, and Samuel Johnson, who had been at Pembroke College a few years earlier, was by no means the only student who found the atmosphere congenial for serious study.[6]

One morning during their third year together at Oxford Shenstone came into Graves's room and, finding him preoccupied with his studies, sat down and wrote an extemporary sketch of his character. Graves remembered its having been written on a piece of paper and left on his table, but Shenstone its having been written with a black lead pencil on a wall of the room. Though when eventually published in volume two of Shenstone's *Works* it lacked Graves's name, the subject was obviously Graves himself.[7] It is a remarkably perceptive piece of writing, even if at times it leans to the side of panegyric. Shenstone saw Graves as the embodiment of the eighteenth-century ideal of the scholar-gentleman: 'He had indeed all the learning and erudition that can be derived from universities, without the pedantry and ill manners which are too often their attendants. What few or none acquire by the most intense assiduity, he possessed by nature; I mean that elegance of taste, which disposed him to admire beauty under its great variety of appearances. It passed not unobserved by him either in the cut of a sleeve, or the integrity of a moral action.'

'Taste' was a great word with Shenstone and his friends, who derived many of their principles from the writings of Lord Shaftesbury. For them a gentleman was one who got or seemed to get not only his principles of judgment, ethical as well as aesthetic, but also his knowledge effortlessly from within himself. Shenstone must have overlooked the fact that even while he was writing those words, Graves was slogging away at one of his assignments! After developing that point further, Shenstone went on to remark that the only impediment standing in the way of Graves's rise to fame was his modesty: 'He had nothing in his character that could obscure so great accomplishments, beside the want, the total want, of a desire to exhibit them. Through this it came to pass, that what would have raised another to the heights of reputation, was oftentimes in him passed unregarded.'

The subject of Graves's diffidence came up repeatedly in the letters Shenstone wrote to him in later years, and in an essay on envy, also published in the *Works* and dedicated to R.G.,[8] he urged his friend to shed his diffidence so as to allow his talents to shine forth in the world and be the cause of emulation in other men. The only other fault that Graves had, in Shenstone's eyes, was that 'his knowledge of books had in some degree diminished his knowledge of the world; or, rather, the external forms and manners of it.' The pebble, in other words, was not yet perfectly polished. His ordinary conversation, Shenstone explained, 'was, perhaps, rather too pregnant with sentiment.' By that he meant that Graves expressed his opinions too freely and with too little deference an 'awkwardness,' as Shenstone described it, that was felt mainly among his little circle of friends. To counterbalance it Graves had a gift that all his friends admired: 'He gave delight by an happy boldness in the extirpation of common prejudices; which he could as readily penetrate, as he could humourously ridicule: And he had such entire possession of the hearts, as well as understandings of his friends, that he could soon make the most surprizing paradoxes believed and well-accepted.' In those two sentences Shenstone conjured up the image of the archetypal bright under-graduate, eager to show off his wit and his knowledge and clever at defending novel opinions, even apparently absurd ones. That was Richard Graves: an articulate young man of high intelligence and great personal charm who could fascinate his friends by his witty and informed talk. One must be grateful to Shenstone for having left on record such a vivid picture of him at the age of twenty.

Like many students at the time who had means and intended to lead a quiet life afterwards, neither Shenstone nor Whistler took a degree. That does not necessarily mean that they idled away their time. Graves took umbrage at Johnson's writing in his life of Shenstone that at Oxford

Shenstone 'employed himself upon English poetry.'[9] English literature did not become a respectable academic discipline in that home of lost causes for another hundred years, and so to say of anyone that he *employed* himself at it amounted to a sneer. Instead, Graves insisted, Shenstone '*employed* himself in the study of the mathematics, logic, natural and moral philosophy, and the other sciences usually taught in the university.'[10] Later Shenstone turned briefly to the study of law, and his letters written to Graves after he left Oxford reveal also a considerable interest in public affairs. Though eventually he settled down quietly in the country and devoted much of his time to landscaping his paternal estate, The Leasowes, he was a man of many intellectual interests. While he was at Oxford, however, even if he had not 'employed himself' in the study of English poetry, he was certainly reading and writing it. Just before he left the university in 1737 he published anonymously a little volume of occasional poems written characteristically, as the title page explains, 'for' the Entertainment of the Author, And Printed for the Amusement of a Few Friends, Prejudic'd in his Favour.'[11] That did not mean that he took his writing lightly. In fact, he was a perfectionist who fussed endlessly over the revision of his work. But it was the dilettantish attitude he thought proper for a gentleman to affect and present to the world.

Less is known about how Anthony Whistler spent his time at Oxford. His family was of much longer standing as landed gentry than Shenstone's, who were relatively speaking upstarts, and he had come into possession of the family estates on the death of his father a dozen years before his matriculation. He was a true dilettante. At Eton, Graves informs us, Whistler had failed to learn either Latin or Greek,[12] and since those languages were about all that was taught in schools at that time, one wonders what Whistler did learn. But Graves assures us that, in spite of his inability to read classical works in the original, he was a 'young man of great delicacy of sentiment' and that 'no one formed a better judgment in them.' But he was not content to be merely a critic. He began writing a tragedy on the story of Dido and actually published a drearily mythological mock-heroic poem called *The Shuttlecock* (1736), written in imitation of *The Rape of the Lock*. The tragedy remained incomplete, like a number of other works in manuscript that Graves assures us 'would do no discredit to his memory.' A few of Whistler's letters to Shenstone have survived.[13] They reveal a lively mind and a ready wit as well as boyish charm, and are full of expressions of affection for both Graves and Shenstone. Graves later recollected him as a person who combined 'manly sense, and a fine genius,' with 'a delicacy of taste, and softness of manners, bordering on effeminacy.'[14] But he lacked drive, and one suspects that he picked up most of what he knew the easiest way, that is, at second hand. Shenstone wound up the sketch of Graves's character from which large quotations have already been made with a comparison between Graves and Whistler that confirms one's suspicions. Graves 'differed from W[histle]r,' Shenstone wrote, '[in] that he had the talents of rendering the greatest virtues un-envied: Whereas the latter shone more remarkably in making his very faults agreeable.' Eight years later Shenstone still held the same opinion and repeated it in much the same words in a letter written to Whistler himself.[15]

Once, in August or September 1735, Graves paid a visit to Shenstone, who was then living at Harborough Hall, a fine old half-timbered house a share in which had come to him from his mother's family.[16] Graves stayed for a month, enjoying one of those leisurely visits that the relaxed pace of eighteenth-century life made possible. They saw little company either at home or elsewhere, for Shenstone, having spent most of his youth in boarding schools, was awkward and embarrassed in society and had few friends. But they read and talked together. Inevitably they sometimes got on each other's nerves, and once they had a falling out. But it lasted only twenty-four hours. In the following year Graves invited Shenstone to Mickleton, where Morgan Graves had recently returned and taken up residence along with his sister Mary. it was a very different kind of holiday. Morgan, an elegant and reasonably well-to-do young bachelor, had made his house the rendezvous of most of the young people of both sexes in the neighbourhood, and life there was a continual round of balls and card-parties. This was probably the first time in his life that Shenstone had ever mixed freely in a lively group of people of his own age, and though he refused to dance, declaring such leaping about allowable only in savages, he paid attention to a number of young ladies. Several of the poems published in his collection of the following year were addressed to these girls concealed under such fancy names as Selinda, Delia, Silvia, Chloe, and Ophelia. According to Graves one of those young ladies, who was not named, flirted outrageously with all the men: 'She sung, she danc'd, and laugh'd, and romp'd; and, as one of [the men] observed, came hop-stride-and-jump into one's affections.'[17] But she failed to make any impression on Shenstone's heart. He was much more attracted to Utrecia Smith, bluestocking daughter of Graves's old teacher, of whom more will be said later. His most lasting affair of the heart, however, was caused by Graves's sister Mary, whose good looks and pleasant personality capti-vated him.[18] Meanwhile, his friend Richard, who had few if any of his inhibitions and who was always highly susceptible to female charms, was undoubtedly also paying attention to the young ladies. The Chloe to whom he addressed his first published poem several years later, expressing his disappointment in his love for her, may have been the same Chloe whom Shenstone met at Mickleton. It was a happy holiday for both young men and a welcome change from the semi-monastic atmosphere of an Oxford college. Several years later and after further visits to Mickleton Shenstone wrote to Graves: 'there is ... no place at which I have spent more agreeable hours than Mickleton.'[19]

Whether or not young Geoffry Wildgoose was following the example of his creator, Richard Graves, in also making occasional excursions to London during term in order to visit the theatres is an unanswerable question, but Graves acquired a great interest in the drama and in later years made holiday trips to London as often as he could. So it is far from impossible that he had done so also during his student years. Wildgoose's time at Oxford was later than Graves's undergraduate years, and so he was able to see Quin acting in his meridian splendour and Garrick at the dawn of his even brighter day.[20] Graves too may have seen Quin; later on he certainly saw Garrick many times, and there was an earlier generation of actors who may also have entertained him. Perhaps Wildgoose was also imitating Graves on these more or less furtive expeditions to London when he visited taverns and 'eat a jelly' – whatever that may imply – with Betty Careless at Covent Garden. Betty was a desirable young prostitute well known to the rakes of London, who appeared in Fielding's *Amelia* and when grown old is said to have been the model for the procuress in the third plate of Hogarth's *Marriage à la Mode*. Her charms were evidently well known also in Oxford, for a 'Gentleman of Trinity College' celebrated them in a Latin ode published in a volume of occasional verses written by various Oxonians that came out in 1738. Graves slipped a quotation from it into *The Spiritual Quixote* in a footnote, adding in the decent obscurity of a dead language: 'Carlesis! ah! nostris & fleta & flenda camœnis.'[21] How lucky it is that Puritans so often do not understand Latin! The quotation is not attributed to Wildgoose in the novel but stands as Graves's own sentiment. Betty did not die until 22 April 1752, when the *Gentleman's Magazine* published an obituary of her: 'was buried from the poors' house of St. Paul's Covent Garden, the famous *Betty Careless*: who had helped the gay gentlemen of this nation to squander above 50,000 £.'[22]

But Wildgoose is also imitating Graves in applying himself 'to the sciences with great assiduity' and in going through 'the business of the college with diligence and regularity.' Graves's mornings were kept sacred for study, as we have seen; friends might come into his room if they would while he was at work, look at his books and papers, and even write essays on his walls, but he ignored them. Oxford did not neglect its instructional obligations and kept serious students occupied. A nephew of Sir Joshua Reynolds, for example, who was a student at Pembroke in the seventies, once took the opportunity afforded him by a cancelled lecture to write a letter to his sister to explain that he was usually kept too busy by his studies to write to her as often as she evidently expected.[23] Letters home, of course, do not always tell the whole truth, but there is no doubt that then as now the life of a conscientious student was a busy one.

Graves himself described the routine at Pembroke in a poem entitled 'A College Life,' published in the second edition of his miscellany called *Euphrosyne*. His lines may be more than a little tinted by reminiscences of 'Il Penseroso' and may also have been romanticized in other respects, but they give as reliable a first-hand description of the daily life of a student as one is likely to find anywhere. His day began at dawn with the ringing of the bell calling all members of the college to prayers in the chapel, where (though Graves did not say so) the dean called the roll. After chapel everybody trooped off to 'the public hall' for the 'moral lecture' – that is, a lecture on moral philosophy, a little hard to take, one would think, on an empty stomach. That was followed by breakfast, which was also a time of pleasant relaxation and conversation. The rest of the day, according to Graves, was spent by each student on various studies under the direction of his tutor – logic, ethics, physics, metaphysics, and classical literature. Surprisingly, Graves included among them readings in such English writers as Milton, Locke, and Newton. The day was interrupted at noon by a 'frugal meal' but otherwise went on until sunset, after which, in summer, there were pleasant walks in the fields or in the public gardens, where the sight of pretty girls cheered one up:

> *Their radiant smiles, their charms divine,*
> *The soul revive, the thoughts refine.*

In winter there was good conversation over a temperate glass with one's fellow students in 'some warm chearful room.'

> *Thus calmly glide the hours away,*
> *Thus chearfully they pass the day,*
> *In quest of truth and useful knowledge,*
> *Within the precincts of a college.*

The routine followed in the college in the time of Samuel Johnson, only four years earlier than Graves's freshman year, has been investigated by the present librarian and archivist of the college, Dr J.D. Fleeman.[24] Thanks to his researches some of the gaps in Graves's account may be filled in, though even Dr Fleeman is not sure that the teaching program that he has reconstructed was invariable or ever wholly followed. The daily timetable, according to him, however, was much as Graves remembered it: prayers in chapel at six, breakfast at eight, lunch at noon, and dinner about five. Dr Fleeman does not mention the daily moral lecture, but he does schedule other lectures on every day of the week including Sunday, with the exception of Thursday, which was a relatively free day, as well as declamations (that is, formal speeches in Latin by students on set subjects) and disputations (that is, debates). In addition to those requirements each student was expected to report regularly to his tutor and to hand in written work once a week, usually on Saturday morning just after prayers. These were themes written in Latin, sometimes in a mixture of prose and verse but oftener in prose only, on such well-worn subjects as 'Dulces ante omnia musæ,' or 'ut ameris amabilis esto.' Special occasions, such as Guy Fawkes Day, were celebrated in verses written by all the undergraduates, copies of which were stuck up in hall for all to admire.

The undergraduates received virtually all their instruction within their own colleges, of which the university was little more than a loose federation. Though professors were appointed by the university, neither Graves nor Johnson made any mention of them, their instructors being all fellows of Pembroke College. The university at that time had largely ceased to function as a teaching institution, having become mainly an examining and degree-granting one. Even its examinations seem to have become perfunctory. Graves made no reference to any except for a casual reference to a 'wall-lecture.'[25] The candidate for an MA was required to deliver a lecture of a prescribed length but was thoughtfully shut up for the purpose in an empty room, where he lectured to the walls until the beadle came with the joyful news that his time was expired. What other hoops he was expected to jump through before he took his degree is not clear, but it is certain that in relatively non-competitive eighteenth-century Oxford more emphasis was placed on the daily routine of studies and on collegiate life than on a solo performance in the examination hall at the conclusion of it all. The daily routine, however, was obligatory. Fines were levied on students who skipped lectures, missed prayers, or failed to turn in written assignments on time. Samuel Johnson rebelled against the system in his final term, more because he was unhappy and threatened with poverty than because he disliked Oxford, but there is reason to believe that Richard Graves threw himself into his work in the college with a whole heart.

The only evidence as to the quality of the work Graves did at Oxford is contained in three Latin proses, dated 1735 (his penultimate year at Pembroke), that survive in the college archives. Extending to about two dozen lines of rather cramped handwriting apiece, unlike the free-flowing cursive in which he later wrote his letters, each is an elaboration of a theme suggested by a quotation from Horace or Juvenal that had no doubt been set by his tutor. They show a good knowledge of Latin vocabulary and sentence structure but are rather lacking in style. An experienced professor of Latin in a Canadian university to whom they were shown said that if they had been turned in by one of his students he would have given them B+ with the comment: 'The word order is prim and lacks the tang of Latin.' But they were evidently sufficient to satisfy the unexacting requirements of eighteenth-century Oxford. On 25 June 1736 Graves took the bachelor's degree in the university, and on the following day in the college buttery books the title 'Dˢ' (Dominus) was consequently prefixed to his name. He let his name stand in the books for at least a year longer and did not ask for his caution money back until July 1739. The reason is not clear, unless in both cases he was expressing his reluctance to sever his ties. Shenstone was still at the college, where he remained for another year, and Whistler even longer. Meanwhile, in November of 1736 Graves was elected to a fellowship in the College of All Souls, an elite and richly endowed society devoted to postgraduate scholarship. This, Graves thought, gave him the entrée into what he once called a 'bright career in learning,' and he moved at once into rooms in his new college. In spite of the excessive modesty noted by Shenstone, he seemed about to rise 'to the heights of reputation.'

1 / 'John' Graves
Engraving by George Vertue
From T.R. Nash *Collections for the History of Worcestershire* 1781–2

RICHARDUS GRAVES
de Michleton in Com Gloucestriæ Armiger
Obiit   1731. A: Ætat: 51.

2 / Richard Graves of Mickleton
(NB The correct date of death is 1729.)
From T.R. Nash *Collections for the History of Worcestershire* 1781–2

3 / Richard Graves's Mickleton
From a letter from Graves to James Dodsley, dated 30 October 1773,
showing the sequestered village that was the ancestral home of
Geoffry Wildgoose, hero of *The Spiritual Quixote*, and that resembles Mickleton.
Graves analysed the scene as follows:
'An handsome old Elm in the fore-ground,
under which Wildgoose with his hat on, harangues his first little audience:
the principal of which is Tugwell, with his apron on – a peasant or two;
one leaning on a pitchfork, another with a rake upon his shoulder[.]
On the right hand Tugwell's Cottage, his wife Dorothy leaning over the gate[.]
On the left hand, the Squire's great gates just appear –
The steeple of the Church on a Bank on the right [sic] hand. in the
background a remarkable hill with a few trees about half a mile distant &c.'

4 / Dover's Games
From *Annalia Dubrensia* 1636

5 / At Dover's Games
From sixth edition (1773) of
William Somervell
The Chase and Hobbinol

6 / Mickleton Manor

7 / Mickleton parish church

8 / William Shenstone at twenty-four
By Thomas Ross, 1738
Once in the possession of Richard Graves, the original of this portrait now hangs
in Pembroke College, Oxford.

9 / Roman coins from Graves's collection

Coins of the Emperor Carausius
From William Stukeley's *Medallic History* I (1757) plates 10, 31

Coin of Marcus Aurelius
From Graves's translation of the *Meditations* 1792

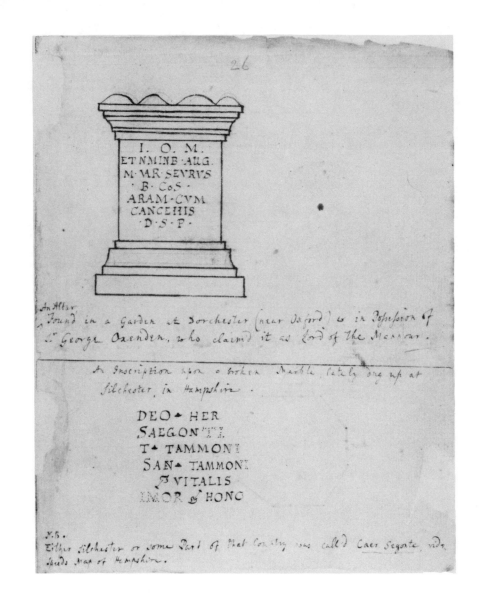

26

I. O. M.
ET NMINB AUG.
M·VR·SEVRVS
·B·CoS·
ARAM·CVM
CANCELIS
·D·S·P·

An Altar.
Found in a Garden at Dorchester (near Oxford) & in Possession of
Sr George Oxenden, who claim'd it as Lord of the Mannor.

An Inscription upon a broken Marble, lately dug up at
Silchester, in Hampshire.

DEO⬧HER
SAEGONTI
T⬧TAMMONI
SAN⬧TAMMONI
℘VITALIS
IMOR & HONO

N.B.
Either Silchester or some Part of that Country was call'd Caer Segate, vide
Speeds Map of Hampshire.

10 / Archaeological notes by Graves
ms Ballard 37, folio 36ʳ

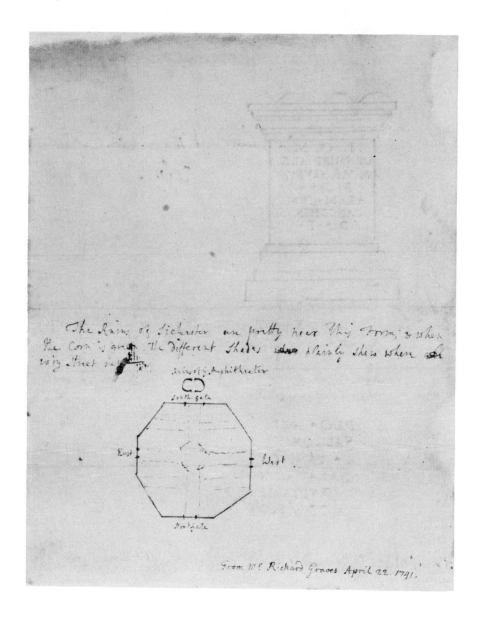

The Ruins of Silchester are pretty near this Form; & when
the Corn is green the different Shades ~~are~~ plainly shew when ~~the~~
very street ~~...~~

Ruins of y Amphitheater

South gate

East

West.

North gate

From Mr Richard Graves April 22. 1791.

11 / Archaeological notes by Graves
ms Ballard 37, folio 36ᵛ

12 / Tissington Hall

13 / Picnic in Dovedale

Graves's sketch in a letter to James Dodsley, dated 30 October 1773, of a proposed frontispiece for volume 3 of *The Spiritual Quixote*: 'A view amongst the rocks in Dovedale ... Wildgoose & Tugwell appear at a distance on the top of a rock; a gentile party seen at the Mouth of a Cave, one playing on German flute, another on a fiddle; one with bottles & glasses, &c. &c.'

14 / Utrecia's urn

CHAPTER FOUR

All Souls

All Souls, the college in which Graves had just been elected to a fellowship, occupies a special place in the loose structure of federated colleges that constitutes the university. Unlike the others, it had no undergraduate members, only fellows with at least three years' standing in the university before election. Founded in the fifteenth century as a chantry in which 'twenty poor and indigent Scholars' were to be supported in order to pray for the souls of the late king and his relations as well as of 'others faithfully deceased in the French wars,' it had developed since the Reformation into a society of scholars devoted to study, the worship of God, and the practice of a profession.[1] Some of the fellows remained in the college all their lives, studying, writing, and – as their critics charged – drinking, eking out the income from their fellowships by serving as curates in churches in Oxford or rural parishes within easy reach. Others, taking advantage of the privilege of non-residence, might be found all over England in parishes, cathedral closes, and law courts making use of their academic knowledge in their professions. They might retain their fellowships so long as they remained unmarried or unless they inherited a fortune or accepted a valuable benefice. Though the fellows were often criticized over the years for being preoccupied with their own comfort, many of them eventually rose to the highest places in church and state and made valuable contributions to the public good.

When Graves was elected, he had already been in the university for four years and, having just taken the degree of bachelor of arts, was largely free from any set curriculum of studies. His immediate task was to qualify himself for ordination, since all fellows of his new college, except those going in for medicine or the civil law, were expected to enter holy orders. This he could do in his own time. His further outlook, however, is less clear. He did not enjoy being idle. He was not one of those 'decent easy men,' described by Gibbon, 'who supinely enjoyed the gifts of the founder' of the college and who had 'absolved their consciences' from 'the toil of reading, or thinking, or writing.'[2] Even the relaxed way of life chosen by his friends Whistler and Shenstone was not for him. Moreover, being a younger son and having most likely already exhausted the financial support that his older brother had given him, he needed a profession. One day-dream may have been recalled in an academic success story told long afterwards in his novel *Columella*:

Atticus, according to the excellent plan long established in our Universities, had ... applied assiduously for the four first years to logic, geometry, natural and moral philosophy; and after that confining himself particularly to the study of divinity, he became a celebrated preacher in the University; an ingenious and diligent tutor in his own college; and being of a considerable family, and some independent fortune, as well as a man of great discretion, and an amiable temper, he was unanimously chosen by the time he was thirty, the Head of a very respectable and learned society [that is, a college]: in which station his behaviour being equally free from a pedantic haughtiness, and too easy and submissive a condescension, he gained both the love and esteem of his college, and the harmony that subsisted between them constituted their mutual felicity.[3]

But that was only a day-dream. Graves had no independent fortune and must have already suspected that he would never be a great preacher. Moreover, he was far more of an intellectual than the genial and extroverted Atticus.

His own statements about his future career, though tantalizingly brief, indicate beyond reasonable doubt that his primary interest was not in a cure of souls. In his poem entitled 'A College Life' he wrote that he had gone to All Souls 'on literary fame intent,' and in another poem, entitled 'A Cottage Garden,' of his hopes for a 'bright Career' in learning. 'Literature' and 'learning' were words of wider scope then than they are now, but both of them point to humane interests rather than to clerical ones. As a schoolboy he had earned a reputation on account of his knowledge of Greek, and during his undergraduate years in Oxford he had read widely in Latin and Greek literatures, acquiring enough proficiency in both languages to enable him later to produce and publish competent and lively translations of several classical works. His aptitude for antiquarian studies, also noted in him at an early age, tied in with his classical interests, for he was particularly fascinated by Roman Britain, about which relatively little was known at that time. So it is more than likely that over and above his necessary reading in divinity he was giving much of his time to ancient history and that the career he looked forward to was in humane scholarship. As a fellow of All Souls or as the vicar or rector of a parish he would provoke neither surprise nor censure by devoting much of his time to such pursuits. Many beneficed clergymen in the eighteenth century found sufficient leisure for interests unrelated to their clerical callings. Gilbert White, for example, though a curate, made numerous contributions to the study of natural history that are still held in high esteem, and John Skinner, a protégé of Graves and later a Somerset rector, had time to fill nearly a hundred volumes of a diary, now in the British Library, with the notes he had made on archaeological expeditions. A volume of extracts is in print and popular. The eighteenth-century Church of England did not number among its faults a distaste for learned parsons.

Positive evidence that Graves's interest was turning towards the archaeology of Roman Britain is provided by a sheet of paper with notes and diagrams in his handwriting preserved among the Ballard manuscripts in the Bodleian Library in Oxford (see plates 10 and 11).[4] Ballard was a countryman of Graves's, having been born in Chipping Campden. Brought up in what John Nichols, who wrote a brief sketch of his career, called 'low life,'[5] he became a stay-maker or mantua-maker, but, possessing brains and a good share of that eighteenth-century drive for self-education, he took time off from his sleep to teach himself 'the Saxon language' and became an archaeologist and antiquarian scholar. At a relatively early age he made the acquaintance of Graves's father, whose intellectual interests he shared, Hearne recording in his diary frequent references to him made in the letters and conversations of Richard Graves of Mickleton. After the latter's death Ballard transferred his friendship to the son, his junior by nine years, and the piece of paper just now referred to shows that by 1741 they were exchanging archaeological information. It was subscribed in Ballard's hand: 'From Mr Richard Graves April 22 1741,' and contains a plan of the important Romano-British town of Silchester, then largely unexcavated, and notes on two archaeological finds made in the Oxford area, one of which was not reported to the Royal Society until three years later.[6] Graves must have been keeping well abreast of what was happening in the world of archaeology. In 1750, after Graves had left Oxford for Claverton, Ballard moved to Oxford, where he was appointed a clerk at Magdalen College.[7] In the same year Graves sent him a manuscript copy of his poem entitled 'The Cabinet,' in which he celebrated the collection of antique medals and coins of archaeological interest made by the Reverend George Walker of Whitechurch, stepfather of his friend Anthony Whistler. Ballard was also interested in Graves's other poems, but archaeology formed the basis of their friendship. He died in 1755, leaving Graves in his will almost the whole of his collection of Roman coins, both silver and brass, 'containing about an hundred different Emperors and Empresses,' as well as his collection of old English ones, 'Being a Series from William the Conqueror down to Charles II' (see plate 9).[8] Graves treasured it all his life, though he made fun of himself and his hobby in the character of Mr Townsend in *The Spiritual Quixote*.

Eighteenth-century Oxford has had a bad press. The dreary pictures painted by Parson Woodforde and Edward Gibbon of life in the colleges are well known to all students of the period. Though, as we have seen, the college tutors performed their duties conscientiously, they were tied hand and foot to an obsolete curriculum, a relic left over from the Middle Ages, which they made little attempt to revitalize by the infusion of new knowledge and ideas. The empirical sciences were left almost entirely to the virtuosi of the Royal Society, and even in the humanities only a few university scholars were doing original work. Gibbon could recall only three names of scholars from his time worth mentioning: Richard Lowth, who wrote a seminal work on Hebrew poetry, William Blackstone, author of the celebrated *Commentaries upon the Laws of England*, and William Jones, the pioneer orientalist.[9] Dame Lucy Sutherland, in her lecture on *The University of Oxford in the Eighteenth Century, a Reconsideration*, adds two others to the list: Benjamin Kennicott, a Hebrew scholar of international reputation, and Thomas Warton, who inaugurated the study of medieval literary history. But even so enlarged, the list is lamentably short. In fact the university was out of touch with the main tendencies of modern thought, especially those of the European Enlightenment, and so tutors and students alike found little challenge in what they were expected to teach and learn.

Whether the name of Richard Graves might have been eligible for inclusion in that short list is a hard question to answer, for he was frustrated in the realization of his academic ambitions and was never given a chance to show what he was capable of. Most of his writings were the rapid productions of leisure hours snatched from his preoccupations as parson and schoolmaster. In addition to novels, poems, and essays, he made translations, one of which achieved some measure of earthly immortality in the Loeb Library. And all his life he continued his active interest in archaeology. John Skinner, who spent a short time in Claverton as a young man reading for orders under the supervision of the aging Richard Graves, recalled the long walks he took with his mentor through the countryside and the wealth of archaeological information that poured out from the old man as he strode along beside him over the hills. But Graves published no contributions to archaeology, significant or other- wise, and it would be idle to speculate further on what he might have done. It is sufficient praise of him to note that his bent turned actively towards original scholarship at a time when most of the social pressures bore in the opposite direction, towards intellectual apathy and the mechanical performance of light duties.

At first Graves's social life at All Souls must have been a continuation of what it had been at Pembroke, for Shenstone and Whistler were still in Oxford, and All Souls is only a short walk from his old haunts. Graves's new associations and interests, however, may have led to a slight slackening of the bonds that held the triumvirate together. Shenstone, for example, remarked to Graves that he was a little reluctant to visit All Souls on account of the 'enemies in the gate' there.[10] But they remained on good terms. Shenstone was granted graduate status in 1736, though he had taken no degree, probably because he had begun preparing himself for the study of law, having, as Graves wrote, put on the 'civilian's gown.' The following summer, after entertaining Graves at The Leasowes, he left Oxford for nearly two years, spending most of that time in London. In Recollection Graves had much to say about Shenstone's doings in the metropolis that could only have come from Shenstone himself, though only a few of the letters that must have passed between the two friends have survived. It was Shenstone's first time in London, and though he may have gone there to study law, he seems, according to Graves, to have spent much of his time in the theatres, the coffee-houses, the Mall, and the public gardens, 'scenes,' as Graves expressed it, 'of uncommon amuse- ment to a man of reflection and an active imagination.'[11] Graves felt that he could not spare the time from his studies to visit him there. Shenstone was back briefly in Oxford in 1739 and then removed his name from the books of Pembroke College.

Whistler stayed in Oxford more or less continuously until 1740, and a few undated letters written by him from Oxford to Shenstone that are now in the Osborn Collection at Yale were probably mostly written before 1740 during the periods of Shenstone's absence.[12] They are breezy and gossipy and full of protestations of his warm friendship for both Shenstone and Graves. But in one of them Whistler made this astonishing remark: 'Mr Graves is still a prude.' What meaning he attached to 'prude' is unclear. Normally one thinks of a prude as a woman, but it is unlikely that Whistler was hinting at a streak of effeminacy, for nobody else ever discovered a trace of it in Graves. Bailey's dictionary, however, defined *prudery* as 'an affected or conceited womanish Reserve, a shyness,' and so Whistler was probably complaining of a slight aloofness in Graves's manner that perhaps had developed since his move to the more rarefied atmosphere of All Souls. 'I see Him sometimes,' Whistler continued, 'but shou'd be glad to see Him oft'ner.'[13] Some incident may have occurred that caused just a little coolness between them, a suspicion that is strengthened by a typically adolescent effusion on the subject of friendship that followed in Whistler's letter, which seems to be concealing a slight sense of grievance. In another one of his letters, also undated, he made a longer reference to some incident, perhaps the same one, that might have caused hard feelings among all three members of the triumvirate had Whistler not been at pains to smooth things out. He wrote of Graves: 'All that I hinted at was some little shyness he lately shew'd to me, on the account you and I have often mention'd.'[14] Again his choice of a word is odd. By 'shyness' he must have meant not timidity or the modesty Shenstone had noted in his Pembroke College character sketch, which could not have hurt anybody's feelings, but probably again reserve or aloofness. The trouble may have been that Graves, having entered into a new university circle, was making new friends and seeing less of his old ones than they expected. Also he was becoming even more fully committed to his academic work than either of his old friends ever were. Fortunately the coolness did not persist, and though in later years Shenstone and Whistler drew apart, Graves's friendship with both of them remained in good repair during the rest of their lives.

Of his other friends, Ballard, of course, was one, but since Ballard did not arrive in Oxford until after Graves had left it, this friendship must have been maintained chiefly through letters. Another Oxford friend was mentioned in *The Triflers*, where Graves recalled spending 'three or four evenings in the week with a gentleman whose chambers were so near the tower, in which the bell called Great Tom hung, that the sound shook the room, and made the windows jar, yet we often read or conversed till twelve o'clock, really ignorant that the bell had tolled, as it always did at nine.'[15] The gentleman was unnamed and the anecdote undated; he may have been a Pembroke man, for Pembroke College is just across the road from Christ Church, where the big bell hangs; but he also may have been a Christ Church man whose acquaintance Graves was cultivating after the triumvirate dispersed.

But the new friend of these years who meant the most to him was William Blackstone, who had entered Pembroke College a precocious youngster of fifteen in 1738, the year after Shenstone left for London, and who to some extent took Shenstone's place in Graves's affections.[16]

He was elected fellow of All Souls in 1743, though not actually admitted until November of the following year, and so he was in residence during Graves's later period in the college. He made many contributions to its life and work, the most enduring of them being the completion and organization of the splendid Codrington Library. Graves in his 'Trifling Anecdotes' of him told of another contribution of a different sort. Noticing that many of the resident fellows were in the habit of going to a tavern across the way from the college every day after dinner to drink wine and loiter a good part of the afternoon, Blackstone, who was then bursar, had the happy thought of laying in wine by the pipe so that the fellows might enjoy a pint, 'or even half a pint,' in their own common-room before returning to their studies. In that way, he hoped, less time would be wasted,[17] Graves evidently thought that this stratagem had worked, for he called it a 'no less important' contribution to the college than the completion of the library. At this time Blackstone was also writing poetry, though presently, to Graves's regret, he was to abandon the gentler muses in order to embrace that sterner maiden, Justice. In volume 4 of Dodsley's *Collection* are his lines 'The Lawyer's Farewell to his Muse,' written when he was about to leave Oxford for London and the Inns of Court. Addressing himself to his muse in accents imitative of Milton's minor poems, he spoke to her of his happy undergraduate years:

> *How blest my days, my thoughts how free,*
> *In sweet society with thee!*
> *Then all was joyous, all was young,*
> *And years unheeded roll'd along.*[18]

Graves was about to leave Oxford too, and though Graves made some attempt to keep in touch, their ways did not cross again.

CHAPTER FIVE

The Gentleman and
the Christian

The one thing that disturbed the otherwise unruffled calm of Oxford life
in the eighteenth century was the Methodist movement, which had begun
there in a small way while Richard Graves was still a schoolboy in
Abingdon.[1] Unlike more modern student-protest movements, which set
out to change the 'system' by violence, the Oxford Methodists kept their
profile low, being concerned mainly with the salvation of their own souls.
In so far as it was a protest movement at all, it was directed against the
prevailing scepticism of the age through a reassertion of the doctrine of
supernatural grace coupled with a determination to make religion more
personal and more meaningful. It began when Charles Wesley, then a
student at Christ Church, gathered together a small group of like-minded
friends who agreed to meet regularly in the evenings for serious reading
of both classical and religious books, promising to obey all the statutes of
the university faithfully and to take communion once a week. The latter
practice gradually made them known to the generality of the university
population and brought down ridicule on their heads, for in an age when
most people communicated no more than three times a year, their
practice seemed almost scandalously high church. But the little group
quietly persisted. Its membership, like that of all student clubs, was fluid,
and there was always a fringe of persons of varying and doubtful degrees
of commitment. The charter members, in addition to Charles Wesley,
were the genial Bob Kirkham from Stanton Harcourt, an emotional
Irishman named William Morgan, and probably a young man named
Boyce from Berkswell near Coventry. John, Charles Wesley's older
brother, who had already taken his degrees, was away helping his father
as curate in his country parish when the movement began. But in 1729 he
returned to residence as a fellow at Lincoln College and immediately took

dynamic charge of the little club, leading its members out to minister to the sick and to visit the Oxford prisons, where they gave spiritual guidance to the inmates and taught some of them to read and write. The Wesleys never accepted the Calvinist doctrine of justification by faith alone, and from the start expressed in both words and deeds their belief that, though salvation cannot be bought by good works, good works are the sign a man gives when his feet are on the road to salvation. Dubbed the 'Holy Club' by a Merton undergraduate and presently to be widely and pejoratively known as 'Methodists,' the little group encountered a good deal of scorn and even hostility.

How and when Richard Graves became involved in the movement and to what extent he ever was involved are mysteries. His contact with the Methodists may have begun during his undergraduate years at Pembroke College; brother Morgan, who is said to have been a fringe member[2] of the Holy Club and who knew Charles Wesley, may have put him in touch with some of the other members or fringe members, and in any case the Kirkhams must have long been known to the Graveses. The little club of water-drinkers, moreover, with whom Richard associated on his first arrival in Oxford, may have been a spin-off from the Holy Club.[3] He stuck to it for several months, mainly because of his interest in Greek literature, and the contempt with which he afterwards described it as a 'mortified Symposium' reflects a later mood. At the time he may have to some extent shared their serious outlook on life. He was a complex personality, full of conflicting impulses, and a tender conscience was notable in him all his life. A year or so later he admitted in conversation that formerly religion had been his chief pleasure in life.[4] He may have had his undergraduate years in mind. But it is difficult to draw any precise conclusions from this evidence.

By 1737, however, Graves was intimate with Charles Wesley. In the latter's diary under date of 10 October of that year there is the following entry: 'Being determined not to leave England till I had come to a full explanation with Dicky Graves, this morning I went to his rooms; talked the whole matter over, and were both entirely satisfied.'[5] The matter was evidently important since Wesley was unwilling to return to Georgia, as he then intended, until he had settled it, but what it was is unknown, there being no other reference to it in the journals of either of the Wesleys. Since it was of deep concern to him, it must surely have had to do in some way with religion. Whatever it may have been, it was amicably settled without involving Richard Graves, so far as can be learned, in any public actions that would have been labelled either 'Holy' or 'Methodist.' Nevertheless, the words imply an acquaintance of some standing, and the fact that Charles Wesley referred to him as 'Dicky' indicates a considerable degree of familiarity and good will, for at that time the use of nicknames was not common except among intimates.

At the same time as he met Charles Wesley, Graves may also have met some of the other Methodists, even if he had not done so earlier. It seems likely that he met John Wesley at some time, through either Charles or brother Morgan, but there is no evidence in either Graves's writings or John Wesley's journal of any friendship between them, the one personal appearance made by John Wesley in *The Spiritual Quixote*, though vivid, having been worked up from an entry in Wesley's published *Journal*.[6] Two of the minor characters in that novel, however, have been identified by J.L.N. Lyons with other possible Methodist friends of Graves: Hammond with Bernard Kirkham, older brother ot Robert Kirkham, one of the charter members of the Holy Club; and Gregory Griskin with Richard Boyce. Since the latter, according to Lyons, was rector of Berkswell, Warwickshire, from 1713 to 1759 he cannot have been the same man who was a member of the Holy Club, but he may have been his father. Though not much is known about them, Lyons tells us that the Boyce family 'was associated with the same circle of Cotswold society as were the Graveses of Mickleton, and the Wesley brothers,' and that Susan Boyce 'may have been the "Serena" of John Wesley's early correspondence.'[7] Both Kirkham and Boyce were of assistance to Graves during a crisis in his personal life in the late forties, if this identification is correct and the interpolated story of Mr Rivers in *The Spiritual Quixote* may be accepted as autobiographical,[8] but Graves's characterization of them in the novel does not associate either of them particularly with Methodism. Even Griskin's emphasis on good works, though anti-Calvinist, is not necessarily Wesleyan, being quite consistent with the most orthodox Anglican theology. By the time of writing the novel Graves may have been playing down a Methodist past, but the evidence produced by Lyons proves only a very marginal commitment.

By the mid-forties Graves was also associating with another friend who served as a listening-post for his reconnaissance of the Methodist movement. This was Thomas Seward, father of Anna Seward, the 'Swan of Lichfield' and friend of Samuel Johnson. He was a cleric and literary man who contributed to Dodsley's *Collection* and edited the works of Beaumont and Fletcher. Writing to Mrs Piozzi in 1799, Graves said: 'in the earlier part of my life, I had been extremely intimate' with him,[9] and according to *Public Characters of 1799–1800* he and Graves went on a holiday excursion together in the picturesque northern counties.[10] Boswell described him as 'a genteel well-bred dignified clergyman' who 'lived much in the great world,'[11] and if he was the model for the character of the Canon in Graves's novel *Columella*, as has been suggested, he was a worldly and ambitious prelate, the very antithesis of a Methodist preacher. The narrator of the novel, addressing the Canon, says: 'I fancy by this round belly you have not lived the austere life of an hermit, upon roots and acorns, and the crystal brook.'[12] Indeed, he had not. His only known connection with Methodism is through his brother William, who was deeply involved in it and who perished in an anti-Methodist riot in Wales.

From this review of Graves's possible Methodist friendships it is clear that though he must have been acquainted at some time with a number of the early Methodists, through both family contacts and personal encounters, on the whole he preferred to associate with the members of those Methodist families who were not themselves enrolled under the banner, however sympathetic they may have been – except, of course, for Charles Wesley, and even he, founder of the movement though he was, played second fiddle to his forceful older brother.

But more was said by Charles Wesley and Richard Graves in that interview on 10 October than has so far been considered. 'Then,' Wesley continued, 'I spoke of my making his brother Charles mad.'[13] Charles Caspar Graves, one of Richard's younger brothers, had entered Magdalen College the year before and in May 1737 had met Charles Wesley at breakfast. The latter had just returned to Oxford after spending more than a month at Mickleton with Morgan Graves and his sister. Morgan had perhaps suggested that on his return to Oxford he look his brothers up. Charles Caspar proved a ready convert, owning 'with tears, he had never felt any true joy but in religion.' Wesley recommended that he read William Law's *Serious Call to a Devout and Holy Life,* a powerful work of practical piety much admired and studied by both Wesleys. In July, returning once more to Oxford, Wesley found Charles Graves 'in an excellent temper' and encouraged him 'to go on in the narrow way.' Three days later Charles Caspar reported to him that on that day 'he first felt the beginning of the change.' 'He appeared full of joy and love,' Wesley added. Consequently, two and a half weeks later he was thunderstruck to learn that 'Charles Graves had been carried away by his friends, as stark mad.'[14] The friends who had carried him away must have included Richard, for in the eighteenth century the word often referred primarily to members of one's own family. But who else was involved is not clear, though Morgan may very likely have been summoned, for Charles was eventually taken to Mickleton to recover his sanity among the green Cotswold Hills in a less tense atmosphere than that of Oxford.

The 'madness' that afflicted Charles Caspar Graves was undoubtedly the hysteric symptoms that often accompanied religious conversion, or 'the change,' as he called it. Although conversion is a part of all Christian experience and as much a part of Catholic and Anglican theology as of nonconformist, eighteenth-century Methodists laid special emphasis on it, viewing it as a wholly non-rational and involuntary experience, the mysterious operation of supernatural grace within the soul. Though it would ultimately result in unspeakable joy and confidence, in its early stages it was likely to be accompanied by intense pain. People in the throes of conversion groaned, uttered loud and bitter cries, threw themselves on the ground, and frothed at their mouths as their Saviour harrowed the hells that were within them. Such behaviour was a staple subject of ridicule in the copious literature of anti-Methodist satire; the satiric parts of Graves's *Spiritual Quixote* are full of such episodes. Many level-headed and unemotional people thought it madness. In fact, in some cases it was. All the Methodist leaders were embarrassed from time to time by followers who caught religious mania, many of whom were committed to Bedlam as 'Methodically Mad,' like Joseph Periam, who sold everything he had, including the clothes he was wearing, in order to give to the poor. Even William Morgan, one of the charter members of the Holy Club, went mad and died, owing, as his father believed, to his religious austerities. So it is no wonder that the friends of Charles Caspar Graves were concerned, blaming his plight on Charles Wesley. Law's book alone, recommended by him, was enough to upset any highly strung and serious-minded young man; reading it produced a severe depression in Samuel Johnson.

The character and career of Charles Caspar Graves are of interest because they were a quarry from which his brother got some of the materials out of which he constructed *The Spiritual Quixote*. Charles Caspar recovered his sanity and his Methodism before the end of September, and when he met Charles Wesley again, he fell on his neck and burst into tears. 'It is hard to say,' Wesley reflected, 'whether his friends' hatred, or his love, of me exceeds.'[15] In the following year the change that had been interrupted by his friends was completed, and presently he became an itinerant preacher, joining forces for a time with John Wesley, who considered his new recruit 'rooted and grounded in the faith.'[16] In 1740 Charles Caspar seems to have been in London trying out the Christian virtue of humility by working as a bricklayer, where he led Silas Told, a reformed slave-trader, into the Methodist fold.[17] But his roots were shallower than John Wesley had thought, for in December of that year Charles Caspar formally recanted his Methodism in a letter to the fellows of Magdalen College. Two years later, however, he renounced his renunciation, asserting that he had made it under compulsion.[18] Shortly thereafter he set out on a preaching mission into the north with Charles Wesley, but very soon he began to diverge in theology from the Wesleys, disagreeing with them on the doctrine of perfection and on good works. In 1746 John Wesley found 'poor C[harles] G[raves]' in Bristol, 'proclaiming open war,' but felt that his former supporter had done 'neither good nor harm,' and dismissed him from his thoughts with: 'Oh poor head and honest heart!'[19]

One night in midsummer of that year, Charles Caspar, then on a missionary tour in Cornwall, was seized in his bed at the instigation of Satan, as Charles Wesley believed, and shanghaied on board a man of war[20] – one of a number of incidents from his life effectively used by his brother in his novel. He was soon released. The next decade in his life is obscure, but by 1755 he was in Tissington, where, as we shall see in the next chapter, his brother Richard had lived in the early 1740s. Charles Caspar found the little village involved in a struggle. A group of villagers had organized a Methodist society and was holding a prayer meeting in the church every Wednesday and a lecture every Friday – all in the absence of Mr Fitzherbert, lord of the manor and upholder of the establishment. Charles Caspar could not avoid involvement and was caught in a squeeze. On his return Mr Fitzherbert might be counted on to disapprove, probably in the strongest terms, of the initiative taken by the Methodists, but in the meantime they were to be reckoned with, led by Miss Hill Boothby, a pious and aristocratic lady who had undertaken the care of Mr Fitzherbert's children on the death of her dear friend their mother and who was formidable enough to engage Samuel Johnson in theological arguments. 'Poor Mr. Graves,' wrote Miss Boothby, who had had great hopes for him; 'while he is encouraged and spoke plainly to he seems to forget the fear of man; but, alas! it returns upon any opposition.'[21] At some time the poor bewildered man must have recanted again, for in 1759 he became incumbent of Tissington, a position he held until his death in 1787. The Reverend Francis Kilvert, who read a paper on Richard Graves to the Bath Literary Club in 1857, reported that Charles Caspar was still spoken of in Tissington as 'a good man of kindly disposition and quiet habits.'[22] John Wesley had summed him up shrewdly when he spoke of his good heart and weak head. A good deal of his well-meaning idealism went into the character of young Geoffry Wildgoose.

Charles Wesley's long talk with Richard Graves in October 1737 took place against the immediate background of his emotional meeting with Charles Caspar, who had revealed the hatred of his friends. Nevertheless Wesley aimed to win Richard over. '[I] hoped,' he continued in his journal, 'he himself would be one of those whose life fools count madness; explained the nature of true religion; "no other than what you once laboured after, till the gentleman swallowed up the Christian."' Obviously Richard had formerly been considered an ally but had since fallen away, the prison visitations of the Methodists, their austerities in dress and diet, and their continual soul-searching and agonized praying seeming to him ungenteel. Wesley had put his finger on the central dichotomy in his friend's character: the gentleman and the Christian. But he still had hopes. Graves, he wrote, was 'greatly moved' by what had been said and complained that 'he could not pray,' though confessing that he had 'formerly felt more solid pleasure in religion than in all the caresses of the world.' It was a large admission, revealing in one flash the depth of the cleavage in his personality. Wesley again recommended Law and daily periods of quiet meditation and prayer. 'My heart's desire to God for you,' he went on to say, 'is that you may be saved. In a little time, all I can do will be to pray for you; and I hope you will now pray for me, as for a friend, not an enemy.' That Graves promised to do, and the two newly reconciled friends bade each other farewell, in Methodist fashion, with a kiss.

There is no need to doubt the sincerity of Graves's promise while recognizing the power of the conflicting impulses at war within him – not unusual in a man of twenty-two undergoing a religious crisis. But according to all that is known about him, this incident marks the end rather than the beginning of his involvement with Methodism. His inability to pray perhaps remained with him, aborting the fulfilment of his promise, and when he searched his soul, most likely he failed to find there any evidence of a vocation for an intensely religious life or capacity for the perfectionism of William Law. In an open letter to his son Charles, written in 1787, in which he may have been referring to this period of his life, he confessed that when he was a young man he was inclined to think very freely about religious doctrines and 'was a little staggered, particularly at the doctrine of the Trinity.'[23] In 1787 he recommended an acquiescence in what the church had always taught, but in 1737 his feelings may have been different. Almost at once his life changed direction. He abandoned his studies in divinity and turned his thoughts towards medicine, a profession that from Chaucer's time down has been hospitable to free-thinkers in religion. As a medical man he might retain his fellowship in All Souls, subject to the usual restrictions, without becoming a priest. It was a major about-face.

From that time onwards all his causal references to Methodism and Methodists are hostile if not satiric. In a poem called 'The Invisible,' composed in 1747, he wrote:

E'vn Wesley's saints, whose cant has fill'd the nation,
Toil more for fame, I trow, than reformation.[24]

In later printings of the poem the name Whitefield replaced that of
Wesley, as Whitefield came more and more to seem to Graves to be the
major reason for his antipathy to Methodism. From Shenstone's letters it
is apparent that Methodism had become the subject of jokes shared
between them. In 1759, for example, Shenstone reported to Graves his
disappointment in the new edition of Whitefield's journals, of which a
copy had just reached him, because they had been cleaned up, having
been purged, as he put it, of 'that *gross* absurdity which I saw in your
brother's at Mickleton.'[25] The two friends had apparently come to think of
those spiritual autobiographies as funny books. And in 1762, in a letter to
an unidentified correspondent, Graves himself expressed his approval of
Warburton's flogging the Methodists in his *Doctrine of Grace*, accusing
John Wesley in particular of enthusiasm and spiritual arrogance.[26] In *The
Spiritual Quixote*, however, he adopted a more ambivalent attitude towards
Methodism.[27] The putative author of that novel, Christopher Collop, is
represented as favouring them in his heart even though he satirizes them
extensively, and from numerous passages in the work it is clear that
Graves himself admired many of the Methodists for their sincerity and
their devotion to duty, seeing them as examples that many of the regular
clergy might follow with advantage to the established church. But he
could not stomach their theology whenever it deviated from the traditional teachings of the Church of England, and much of their behaviour
he thought ludicrous if not dangerous. Nevertheless, even his own
marginal contacts with the movement had a lasting influence on his mind.

CHAPTER SIX

Tissington

In order to practise medicine in the eighteenth century, at least in the London area, one had to be licensed by the College of Physicians, which would grant a license only to a person holding a medical degree from either Oxford or Cambridge. Neither the college nor the universities provided much in the way of instruction. The college, in fact, provided none at all, except for an occasional commemorative lecture delivered in elegant Ciceronian Latin. The universities did a little better, but only a little, the medical staff at Oxford consisting of only one professor and two or three lecturers. The most serious faults in the university's teaching of medicine, however, were the absence of laboratories and teaching hospitals and the fact that it treated medicine as book-learning, concentrating attention on the ancient works of Galen and Hippocrates. A good knowledge of Latin was consequently considered the prime need of a medical student and doctor. The universities did, however, publish curricula of the further requirements for medical degrees. Having done that, they left the student to his own devices. Fortunately for him, private medical schools that followed the university curricula and did provide instruction had grown up in London and to a lesser extent in the university cities. One of the best of these was run by Dr Frank Nicholls, a brilliant anatomist, who introduced some new medical procedures and published several medical books of importance in their time. He, like Dr Hunter and others concerned in these private schools, brought into medical education what was badly lacking in the universities, laboratory demonstration and practical experience. In their schools students themselves did no dissecting, but they were at least able to watch while the lecturers dissected cadavers, pointing out the significance of what they were finding. The rooms in which this procedure took place, however, which were generally in private houses, were so crowded that students often could not see clearly what was being done, and the time so short that material parts of the subject had to be left out. Dr Nicholls advertised courses in the London newspapers from 1727 to 1741, making claims like this: 'A Course of Human and Comparative Anatomy, in which the Animal Œconomy, the pathology of most diseases, and the action of most medicines will be explained from the structure of the parts.' He charged each student four guineas for a course, which in 1739 consisted of thirty-nine lectures, most likely extending over thirteen weeks. In that year his course was given in a house 'at the corner of Lincoln's Inn Fields, near Clare Market,' where he was a near neighbour to Orator Henley. The atmosphere in such a school must have been very different indeed from that of Oxford.[1]

The first step in Graves's medical education was most likely the lectures, such as they were, given in the university, though there is no reference to them in any of his letters or other writings. But the second was study in London. The biography in *Public Characters of 1799–1800* states positively that, 'soon after Mr. Graves was chosen at All-Souls, instead of pursuing his theological studies, as he had intended, he conceived the idea of studying physic, which he thought a more *genteel* profession; and ... went through two courses of anatomy in London, with that celebrated anatomist Dr. Nicholls.'[2] Those two courses were most likely in 1738 and 1739, Graves moving down to London for the few weeks they required. How well he liked his medical studies is recorded nowhere, but his choice of medicine as a profession on the ground that it was more genteel was characteristic. At the end of his second course, however, he fell seriously ill. *Public Characters of 1799–1800* speaks of a 'nervous fever which had been some time coming upon him,' and in *The Invalid*[3] Graves himself gives a fuller account of this illness and of its cure in terms that suggest not only a physical collapse but a psychological one as well, of which persistent headaches, a tendency to catch colds, and too much drinking on an empty stomach were tell-tale symptoms. He blamed his slow recovery on the bad advice given him by his physician and took credit to himself for acting on the more sensible advice found in such medical books as Luigi Cornaro's *Discourses on a Sober and Temperate Life*, George Cheyne's *English Malady*, and the same author's *Essay of Health and Long Life*. On 12 May 1740 Mary Graves, his sister, wrote from Mickleton to William Shenstone to announce a stage in Richard's recovery: 'His Physicians have thought him out of Danger these three Weeks, as to his Fever, but are apprehensive of a Consumption.'[4] Happily the consumption was avoided, and in the following week his brother Morgan, who had been with him in London, brought him home to the country by easy stages in a hired chaise, making three or four days of the trip. The experience left Richard with a lifelong interest in medicine, which led him to become what many people might call a health faddist, though his prescription for good health – a moderate diet, fresh air, and exercise – seems sensible when compared with the horrendous remedies often prescribed by physicians in his time. But it also cured him of any desire to practise medicine professionally. In her letter to Shenstone his sister went on to say that Dick 'is quite determined to leave the Study of Physick, and turn Friar, which I am delighted at, as I believe it will be conducive to his Health.'

When Graves returned to full residence in the college, he went on with his former academic studies. In October he took the degree of MA, and on 24 May the following year (1741) he was ordained deacon by the bishop of Oxford.[5] Nowhere has he told us what examinations he had to undergo, but some twenty years later, when James Woodforde presented himself before the bishop of Oxford's chaplain for the same purpose, he was merely asked to construe a chapter in St Paul's Epistle to the Romans.[6] If Graves was set a similar task, he must have done well. He had 'turned Friar' after all. But it would be wrong to infer that he had experienced a renewal of his religious faith. The acquiescence in what the church had always taught that he long afterwards recommended to his youngest son would describe his state of mind in 1741 more accurately. The scruples that in 1737 and 1738 had led him to abandon divinity in favour of medicine had been hushed. Though in many ways an intellectual, he was never much interested in theological speculation, the few sermons he published having to do mainly with conventional morality and piety. The tenor of his thinking on theological matters is much like that of Dryden's 'Religio Laici':

> 'Tis some Relief, that points not clearly known,
> Without much hazard may be let alone:
> And, after hearing what our Church can say,
> If still our Reason runs another way,
> That private Reason 'tis more Just to curb,
> Than by Disputes the publick Peace disturb.
> For points obscure are of small use to learn:
> But Common quiet is Mankind's concern.

Graves had come to think of the church as a career, the only one now open to him, a career that could be, and must be, pursued conscientiously but without allowing oneself to be upset by difficult questions of doctrine. He came to see the parish priest as an essential part of the traditional structure of English society rather than as an inspired interpreter of the ultimate mysteries.

Apparently he did have scruples about taking orders, but characteristically they had to do with the ungenteel external appearance made by the clergy. What he wrote to his friend Shenstone in announcing his ordination is unknown because the letter has been lost, but it is likely that Rouvell in *The Spiritual Quixote* speaks for him when on the eve of his own ordination he says: 'I have been so long accustomed to the gaiety of the world, and to dress like a Gentleman, that I do not at all relish the peculiarity of the Clerical habit. Indeed, I can see no reason why a Clergyman should be distinguished from the rest of the world by such a funereal appearance, nor what connexion there is between Religion and a black coat; as if Christianity were such a gloomy affair, and so fatal an enemy to all kind of enjoyment.'[7] Shenstone's reply to Graves's letter has survived. Writing on 1 June 'as a man of the world,' he considered the question whether or not clerical apparel and 'the *avowed profession*' of religion would spoil his friend's 'genteel character' and ended by expressing the belief that Graves was 'very capable of *shining* in a dark-coloured coat.'[8] One hopes that Graves was reassured, for evidently he had feared that it would be ungenteel to let his religion show. The gentleman and the Christian in him were still at odds.

Almost immediately after his ordination Graves accepted an appointment as curate in the Derbyshire village of Tissington, four miles north of Ashbourne.[9] The position he was to hold was an unusual one. According to the will made in 1695–6 by William Fitzherbert, then lord of the manor of Tissington, the curate of the parish was not only to look after the spiritual welfare of the inhabitants of the village but also to act as chaplain in residence to the manorial family, reading prayers daily according to custom. The Fitzherberts were an old family that had held the lordship of the manor at least since the thirteenth century; they had remained Catholic during the reign of Elizabeth 1 and royalist during the Civil Wars. Old William, by whom the curacy-chaplainship was endowed, was a man of old-fashioned views and staunch Anglican principles. Graves may have come by his appointment through a long-standing family relationship, though there is no evidence of one, or through his brother Morgan, who became friendly with William Fitzherbert, grandson of the founder of the endowment, when they were both students at the Inner Temple. Fitzherbert returned to live in Tissington Hall, a fine Jacobean building directly across from the Norman parish church, at about the same time,

1736, as Morgan returned to Mickleton, and their friendship must have been kept up, for when the curacy fell vacant five years later, Richard Graves was the man chosen to fill it. As domestic chaplain he was to live at the great house when it was open and to associate with the family and its guests. He was to receive twenty pounds a year as salary, so long as he lived in, but double that amount if he had to live elsewhere. He would lose his position if he married, but in no way was it a menial one, and it is easy to understand why it appealed to the genteel Richard Graves. It meant, of course, leaving All Souls, though without relinquishing his fellowship, but it meant also moving into good county society and having the opportunity of meeting a number of unquestionably genteel people through whom he might make his fortune. It looked like a promising position for him.

Graves's letters to Shenstone written during the three years he lived in Tissington have not survived, and Shenstone's replies to them, which have, provide little information except that both Graves and he were writing poetry, copies of which they sent to each other for critical comment, correction, and admiration, and that Graves travelled a good deal. In the fall of 1741 he was expected in Birmingham; in the spring of 1742 he was in Oxford; in June in Herefordshire, probably to attend the wedding of his brother Morgan; in November back in Tissington, after what Shenstone described as his 'travels,' a trip that included a visit to Mickleton; in May of the following year in Oxford again, this time to be ordained priest by the bishop of Oxford;[10] in July perhaps again in Mickleton; and in November in London. Evidently he enjoyed a good deal of freedom, though on many of these trips he was most likely accompanying his employer, who, taking his spiritual needs with him, required a chaplain in constant attendance.

At home in Tissington Graves's life was probably lively. In a letter written in 1799 to his friend Samuel Jackson Pratt there is an allusion, tantalizing in its brevity, to 'our Tory Club at Ashbourne.'[11] He recalled that Mr Fitzherbert had once privately suggested to his neighbour the duke of Devonshire that his son, then marquis of Hartington, might join it, whatever it was. Graves wished this fact to be hushed up and not published in *Public Characters of 1799–1800*, for which Pratt was arranging an account of Graves. One can understand why. The Fitzherberts and their friends were Whigs, and Hartington, after succeeding to the dukedom, was briefly prime minister in a Whig government. So being known to have a Tory club in their past might be an embarrassment to the family. The anecdote was accordingly cut. But what was the 'Tory Club?' Eighteenth-century Tories are thought to have lacked organization, certainly nationally and most likely also locally, and so if the club at

Ashbourne was the nucleus of Tory political power in the area, it is something that political historians would like to know more about. Until more information becomes available, if it ever does, one is free to speculate that it was not a serious political club at all but a comic one, a kind of charade, a political hell-fire club, in which the members drank copiously and mimicked the Tories for their own amusement. What Graves's politics were at the time is unknown, although later he was certainly a Pittite Whig and domestic chaplain to Lady Chatham. But he would have thrown himself whole-heartedly into a burlesque, especially among the socially exalted people involved in it. It would have been exactly his idea of fun.

A closer look at life in the Fitzherbert household, though in the following decade, is provided in the letters of Miss Hill Boothby. 'Mr. Fitzherbert loves company,' she wrote, 'and has a good deal.' In August 1755, for example, she reported that 'he and his company arrived here on Thursday last, all at a loss what to do with themselves in *still life*. They set out yesterday to Derby race, and return on Friday, with some forty more people, to eat a turtle; weight, an hundred and thirty. This feast, I ... am preparing for them.' And, she went on to say, 'next week Mr Fitzherbert and his guests go to dance at Buxton, and see the Peak ... I shall have resting time, before they return again to stay a few days; and then they all go to Lichfield race.' Evidently she did not like being 'whirled about by a succession of company' and insisted on sending her employer's six-year-old son to boarding school, away from too much exposure to fox-hunters and turtle soup.[12] She herself took refuge in religion. Graves, however, evidently liked his life in the Fitzherbert household.

The adventures of Geoffry Wildgoose and Jerry Tugwell at Tissington, which occupy one of the longest and liveliest episodes in *The Spiritual Quixote*, must also to some extent reflect Graves's own experiences there.[13] In an appendix to his edition of Boswell's *Life of Johnson* Croker printed a key to the characters cast in that episode, a key that had come into his hands from Lord St Helens, one of William Fitzherbert's sons, who assured him that Graves had described 'the several members of that family, and their visitors, with great accuracy.'[14] Since Lord St Helens had not yet been born when Graves was in Tissington, his assurance must be accepted with some scepticism, and in any case it would be naïve to assume that this or any other episode in a novel, even one of Graves's, was a literal transcript of actuality. However, the pictures Graves painted of the principal characters are vivid and (so far as one can tell) true. Fitzherbert appears as Sir William Forester, and the pious Hill Boothby, who (according to his lordship) 'was attached to Mrs. Fitzherbert by an enthusiastic and spiritualized friendship,' as Miss Saint Hill. The other characters are too minor to be of any concern now, save that they illustrate the catholicity of Fitzherbert's social tolerance.[15] Sir William is introduced by Graves as 'a Gentleman of fine sense; and ... of fine taste, not only in the polite arts, Music, Painting, Architecture, and the like; but in life and manners. He had the art of making every company happy; and the greater art of making himself happy in every company.'[16] Graves does not include in his characterization of Sir William the intellectual interests that led Fitzherbert later to become a fellow of the Royal Society of London and vice-president of the Society of Antiquaries – interests that could hardly have been carelessly overlooked. Actually there is little evidence in the novel even of interest in the fine arts; instead, Sir William is presented as an amiable and tactful host, a man skilful at making a miscellaneous assortment of people associate together without quarrelling – qualities in Fitzherbert that Graves must have come to admire greatly.

Graves kept in touch with Fitzherbert after he left Tissington at least until 1769, as references in his correspondence show. But he cannot have been aware of the canker gnawing at Fitzherbert's soul that led him to kill himself in January 1772. The first draft of the novel had been written long before then, but final revision was still in progress, for the book did not get into print until December of that year. Nobody knows whether the anecdote, referred to earlier, about the suicide of Sir William Keyte and the ensuing discussion of the ethics of self-destruction had been in the first draft or not, but whenever it was written, its retention in the final draft by Graves, who must have known of his old friend's death, seems callous. For Sir William is made to say decidedly that 'it is a very serious affair ... for a man to destroy himself; and rush into the presence of his offended Judge, with all his sins and follies unrepented of about him.'[17] Perhaps, however, Graves left this passage in the text deliberately, or put it there for the first time during his final revision, not to point a moral but to show his friend's better self, impersonated by Sir William Forester, condemning the rash and wicked action of his worse self. The episode, then, serves to preserve the memory of his friend, so recently tarnished, by perpetuating the image of him as a charming and level-headed man of good Christian principles.

In 1744, Graves's last year at Tissington, Fitzherbert married Mary, oldest daughter of Littleton Poyntz Meynell, a woman 'distinguished,' as the *Gentleman's Magazine* said, 'for her piety and fine accomplishments.'[18] Lady Forester differs from her in having been married for some years before the novel opens and in having several children, but like her prototype she is a 'woman of uncommon merit.' Her religious beliefs incline 'to the mystic, or rather the seraphic, Theology' of Fénelon and Norris of Bemerton.[19] What Graves meant by *mystic* may be hard to define, though a tinge of disapproval may be detected in his words. But he may not have meant anything very different from what Lord St Helens, Mrs Fitzherbert's son, meant when he described his mother's friendship with the pious Hill Boothby as 'enthusiastic.' In that respect both ladies must have reminded Graves of the Methodists he had known. Yet he presents Lady Forester as admirable in her character and her actions. She is his ideal of both the Christian woman and the gentlewoman who cheerfully accepts her responsibilities as wife of the lord of the manor. She is kindly and hospitable, capable of intellectual conversation, and a shining example to all Christians in the charitable work she did among the village poor. If she reflects his memory of Mrs Fitzherbert faithfully, Graves must indeed have been fortunate in his position in the family at Tissington.

There is no further evidence to show how Graves spent his own time in Tissington, unless the various incidents narrated in the novel paint a true picture: walks in the country, charitable missions in the village, elegant food in the dining-room, sophisticated conversation *à la mode* in the parlour, and picnics in romantic glens with flute and horn music echoing among the rocks. But if so, how did he reconcile the conflicting claims made on him by the Fitzherbert household and his parish? In particular, who looked after the latter while he was travelling? The parish, of course, was small, but the needs of parishioners will have been no less urgent because his flock was small. Probably they had to wait. But when he was in residence he faithfully posted the parish register, and he was present on each Visitation Day to sign the transcripts.[20] Sometimes he treated the register as a diary, adding comments of his own to the official record that reflect his awareness of the village life around him. When he recorded the marriage of William Smith of another parish and Anna Milward of his own, for example, he added a footnote recording the fact that a few months earlier the same man had fornicated with Mary Bagshaw of the parish of Fenny Bentley, a couple of miles away, for which crime she had done public penance in Tissington church, though her partner in sin had bought his way out of public penance by commuting with the spiritual court in Lichfield. And a year or two later the register recorded that Graves baptized 'John ye 2^d base born Son of John Taylor & Mary Tunnicliff his *Concubine*.' His '2^d' was added above the line with a caret, and '*Concubine*' was heavily underlined. Mary must have been the village whore, for the baptisms of one or two other of her children by different fathers are also recorded in their places. Undoubtedly the curate had his problems, of which these entries give a glimpse or two, but how he coped with them remains unknown.

The Methodist faction of the parish, headed by Hill Boothby, found Graves unsatisfactory and gave a poor report of him to a certain John Bassett, one of their persuasion, who chanced to be in Tissington early in September 1744, just before Graves gave up his duties there and returned south. The people in Tissington told him, Bassett wrote in his diary, that Graves 'was a Gentleman it was below him to preach.'[21] Graves, it is true, was never happy in the pulpit and probably preached fewer sermons than the Methodists in his congregation wished to hear. They attached what the orthodox clergy like Graves considered inordinate importance to sermonizing among the various duties of a parish priest. Yet Graves, who was riding high at Tissington Hall, may have found it hard to reconcile the Christian and the gentleman. According to Lord St Helens, Graves called himself a 'sporting parson' – laughing at himself, no doubt. Though there may have been a little truth in this, his lordship also assured Croker that Graves was in fact 'a worthy and conscientious parish priest.' Consequently it would be wrong to take *The Spiritual Quixote's* scenes of elegance and leisure as a true picture, for there is neither curate nor domestic chaplain among the characters in the novel, Sir William reading daily prayers in the household himself. In real life Graves shared the pleasures enjoyed by the company at the hall and also did the work expected of him.

In Derbyshire Graves also became familiar with a type of scenery wilder and more entrancing than the relatively tame landscape of the Cotswold Hills and Oxfordshire. Tissington itself lies in a rich and lovely vale leading north to Buxton and the Peak District, the roof of England, and it is flanked on the west by Dovedale, famous as a haunt of nature-lovers in both the eighteenth and nineteenth centuries. The pilgrims in *The Spiritual Quixote* travel through Dovedale on their way to Tissington, and its scenery is described at some length (see plate 13). In the summer of 1744, before leaving the district, Graves and his friend Thomas Seward, who was curate of Ilam a mile or two west of Tissington, made a holiday excursion in the north, no doubt visiting as many as they could of the natural marvels often recommended to tourists in the guidebooks of the time.[22] Graves kept no diary, so far as is known, but several of the places they must have visited are described in *The Spiritual Quixote*. At Ilam itself, where the tour started, 'the river Manifold, after running three or four miles under ground, bursts forth from a hollow rock in the garden [of Ilam House], which is laid out with grottoes and cascades, suitable to so grotesque a scene.'[23] Graves and Seward probably also visited various of the Wonders of the Peak missed by Wildgoose and Tugwell, though described in the novel with gusto and embellishments by an old gardener. First, Mam tor, the Shivering Mountain, 'that was continually moulder- ing and shivering down earth and parts of the rock; and yet neither was the hill visibly diminished, nor the valley beneath raised up, in the memory of man.' Next worth a visit was a bottomless pit called Elden-hole, and after that 'Peak's hole,' named by Tugwell less elegantly 'the Devil's A[r]se o' Peak,' a large cavern in the side of a mountain that could be entered only through a narrow aperture by means of a boat and that is the site of a magical kingdom either in local folklore or in the gardener's own fertile imagination. They probably also visited Chatsworth, the magnificent seat of the duke of Devonshire, and, as will appear, Scar- borough, the much frequented seaside resort where Matthew Bramble in *Humphrey Clinker* has his unhappy experience of sea bathing. These scenes Graves afterwards recalled with real pleasure, for as all his four novels show, natural beauty was to him one of God's greatest gifts to mankind.

That expedition was his final fling before leaving Tissington, as he did after 21 September, when he made his last entries in the parish register. Word had arrived from All Souls informing him that his turn had come to serve in one of the various elective offices that the fellows customarily shared among themselves in turn. In 1744, accordingly, he became Custos Jocalium, that is, custodian of the silver plate belonging to the college; in 1745, dean of Arts; in 1746 and 1747 successively, Rector Theologiæ and Naturalis Philosophiæ Prælector, offices involving his attendance at theological and philosophical disputations; and in 1748, bursar of Arts.[24] None of these was onerous, though they meant a welcome increase in stipend, but they did require residence closer to Oxford than Tissington. So he looked about for a curacy nearer the university. Luckily, when he and Seward were in Scarborough, 'he was accosted by an old clergyman, with an immense beaver and a long cravat,' who, after staring at him, asked him if his name was not Graves.[25] The clergyman turned out to be Dr Samuel Knight, archdeacon of Berkshire, a distant relation, who had had Graves to dinner in London a few years earlier and who was himself a literary man as well, being author of lives of Colet and Erasmus. Knight was a good friend to Graves. Morgan Graves had told him that brother Richard needed a curacy near Oxford, and one being vacant in Knight's own archdeaconry, at Aldworth, he had secured it for him. Richard had only to present himself in Newberry, within a few miles of Aldworth, in order to notify his acceptance and meet his new employer. He must have done so, for the official transcript of the parish register for 1744–5 now in the diocesan record office in Salisbury carries his signature: 'Ric Graves Curate.'

CHAPTER SEVEN

Utrecia

Graves was always gregarious. Although the semi-monastic state of English schools and colleges in his time must have made social contacts with women difficult during term, there were always the vacations. During one of them he may have met Molly Aston, if indeed that is the identity of the lady who was called Molly A——n in one of his poems. Samuel Johnson described her as 'a beauty and a scholar, and a wit and whig,' and was much impressed when she explained to him a difficult point in political economy. If it was she whom Graves met, he was inspired to write a poem in her praise, the typical work of a precocious schoolboy deep in classical mythology:

> When for the prize the heav'nly rivals strove,
> Before the Phrygian prince, in Ida's grove,
> Venus in vain had brib'd her judge with Helen,
> Had Pallas nam'd her *fav'rite Molly A——n.*[1]

He published the poem twice, each time with the lady's name garbled as above. On its first appearance it was entitled 'On the Accomplish'd Miss ——' and on its second, 'On some flowers drawn by Miss ——,' but patently the poem has nothing to do with flowers; it is a celebration, if a pedantic one, of the lady's beauty, which had moved his adolescent soul to express itself in verse. On his part it may have been true love, but as she was nine years older and he at the most seventeen, likely it was just speechless admiration. Molly Aston was worth it. When Johnson was once asked what had been the happiest period in his life, he said, 'it was that year in which he spent one whole evening' with her. 'That indeed ... was not happiness, it was rapture.'[2] No wonder that young Richard was smitten! But there is no record of further acquaintance between them.

Molly may have been the first of his loves, but she was certainly not the last. The next of whom record has survived was Utrecia Smith, daughter of his Mickleton schoolmaster. The date of her birth is unknown, but it is reasonable to assume that she and Richard were much of an age, and the Smiths probably moved to Mickleton when Richard was only three or four years old. In a Latin inscription composed after her death, he wrote of their having spent their childhood together.[3] When at the age of ten or twelve he began attending school in her father's house, opportunities for meeting must have occurred frequently. Though he was sent away to boarding school when the age of puberty drew near, the holidays still gave them occasions for meeting. Utrecia was often one of the young people who filled the manor house with music and laughter. Insensibly during these years their relationship deepened and they came to mean much to each other. In the inscription just referred to he described her as 'unaffected, kindly, and gracious.'[4] Apparently she also possessed some of the same qualities that had appealed to him in Molly Aston, for he found her intelligent, well educated, and not afraid, like many other young women of her time, to voice her opinions in mixed company. In *Recollection* he went out of his way to introduce a paragraph about her. He remembered her still as 'an extraordinary young woman' whose father had given her a genteel education and kept her supplied with books, so that she 'had formed to herself so good a taste of polite literature, and wrote so well in prose (and sometimes in verse), that a very ingenious clergyman, bred at a public school, and a Master of Arts in the university, often said, he was afraid to declare his opinion of any author till he previously knew hers.'[5] That clergyman was probably not Graves, who would not have described himself as 'ingenious,' but his respect for her taste and judgment is obvious.[6] There is, however, significantly little in his words about her concerning her physical appearance. Evidently she was not a raving beauty like Molly Aston.

This amiable bluestocking attracted not only Graves but also other young men belonging to his circle of friends. Shenstone made the first of several visits to Mickleton in the summer of 1736, meeting Utrecia there and several other attractive young women, including Richard's sister Mary. He flirted with them and wrote poems about them, calling them by various fancy pseudonyms, Utrecia being Ophelia.[7] He liked her for her refusal to dance and her preference for sitting in a corner discussing poetry. He dashed off an impromptu poem in her praise:

> *Whilst round, in wild rotations hurl'd,*
> *These glittering forms I view,*

Methinks the busy, restless world
Is pictur'd in a few.

So may the busy world advance,
Since thus the fates decree:
It still may have its busy dance,
Whilst I retire with thee.[8]

Another of her admirers was Montague Cholmondley or Chalmley (at least four different spellings of his name have been noted), a member of Magdalen College in Oxford, who may also have visited Mickleton at Graves's invitation in 1736 or on some later occasion. His passion for Utrecia evidently had made him conspicuous, for in writing to Graves in June 1742 about his own recently acquired love of Spenser's poetry, Shenstone wrote: 'I am now (as Ch[al]mley with [Utrecia Smith]), from trifling and laughing at him, really in love with him.'[9] In editing that letter for inclusion in Shenstone's *Works*, Graves deleted or obscured the proper names, but he fortunately inked in the missing letters in his own copy of the book.[10] Cholmondley may have been the original of the young fellow of an Oxford college already referred to as overawed by Utrecia's judgment of literature, who after a long engagement jilted her 'for prudential reasons.'[11] The poet William Somerville was still another of her admirers.[12]

On 5 March 1743 Utrecia died.[13] It has been said that she died of smallpox,[14] and her death was certainly premature, for most likely she was not yet thirty. At the time of her death Graves was in Tissington, and how soon the bad news reached him is unknown, but the following year, when he was back in Oxford, he had a handsome stone urn carved with an inscription in her memory and set it up beside the altar in the north aisle of the parish church in Mickleton (see plate 14). Parts of this inscription have already been quoted, but the whole of it ought to be printed here:

UTRECIÆ SMITH
PUELLÆ SIMPLICI, INNOCUÆ, ELEGANTI;
R. G.
UNA ÀCTÆ MEMOR PUERITIÆ
LUGENS POSUIT.
M.D.C.XLIV.

(Richard Graves has dedicated this urn in sorrow to Utrecia Smith, an unaffected, kindly, and gracious young woman, in memory of a childhood spent together, 1744.) Those Latin words express only sorrow, yet his action itself suggests something more. Young men do not ordinarily put up elaborate memorials in honour of their childhood playmates or even their youthful sweethearts unless there is some special reason for their doing so, and Graves's urn conveys a suggestion of a sense of guilt. A glimpse of what may have been in his mind is given in a poem that Shenstone addressed to him entitled 'Ophelia's Urn. To Mr. G——.'[15] Written in the sombre metre of Gray's churchyard elegy and imitative in style of both Gray and Collins, Shenstone's poem seems intended to assure Graves that he need fear no ghosts when he visits Ophelia's tomb, for it will be guarded by a host of phantoms of a 'celestial kind' – fame, young simplicity, candour, elegance, beauty, and fancy. Had Graves, in one of the letters that he was then writing to Shenstone, hinted at fears that haunted him? There is no means of knowing, his letters having disappeared. Shenstone, however, returned to the subject of ghosts in an undated prose essay entitled 'An Opinion of Ghosts.'[16] Denying any objective reality to them, he yet allowed them a psychological reality as products of either superstition or a disturbed state of mind caused by such 'passions' as 'grief for a departed friend,' 'horror for a murdered enemy,' 'love for a mistress killed by inconstancy.' Did Graves feel that he had been inconstant, that he had in effect jilted Utrecia after having aroused feelings and hopes in her that he could not or would not satisfy?

That question cannot be answered now except speculatively. But it is likely that his mind continued to be troubled over the fate of poor Utrecia because he sounded the theme again in 'Mr. Graham's Story,' which forms an episode in *The Spiritual Quixote*, begun in the fifties.[17] The episode, of course, being part of a work of fiction, must not be accepted at face value as biographical evidence, though it rests on a foundation of fact at several points. The heroine, whom Graves calls Ophelia (using Shenstone's fancy name), is described as 'tolerably handsome' and 'a young woman of great good sense and delicacy of sentiment.' Unlike other young women of her time she is 'thoroughly versed in all the best writers in the English language' and even acquainted with the classics, though, of course, through translations, a knowledge of Latin and Greek being thought unladylike. Her original was obviously Utrecia Smith. Mr Graham, the raconteur, is both hero and villain of the story. Attempts have been made to identify him with both Montague Cholmondley and Graves himself, but though there are obvious points of resemblance, neither identification is convincing.[18] Whoever he was, Mr Graham falls passionately in love with Ophelia, engages himself to marry her, but jilts her when he receives an anonymous letter full of abuse of her character.

She dies of a broken heart, and he, full of remorse, retires from the world to spend the remainder of his life in self-reproachful seclusion.

Mr Graham's story differs in important particulars from the account given by Graves in the more factual *Recollection* and from the other facts known about Utrecia Smith, and its atmosphere is overcharged with that melodrama common in the popular fiction of the time. But though some of its facts may be only inventions, the sense of guilt that breathes from it seems deeply felt. So Mr Graham is best thought of not as an avatar of either Graves or Cholmondley or any other of the young men who flirted with Utrecia Smith but as the objective correlative of that sense of guilt. The romantic notion that she died of a broken heart rather than of smallpox or any of the other plagues that stood ready to strike down people in the eighteenth century may not have been meant very seriously when Graves put it into *The Spiritual Quixote*, but by the 1780s, when he wrote *Recollection*, it had hardened in his mind into fact.

Utrecia's tragedy seems to have been that though she attracted many young men, especially intellectual ones, good talkers, men full of literature and ideas, she had the misfortune to make them feel threatened in the very bastion where they ordinarily felt most secure, their fancied intellectual superiority. The 'very ingenious clergyman' who was 'afraid to declare his opinion of any author, till he previously knew hers,' would have needed more sympathy and understanding than most men of his time possessed to be happily married to her. Graves himself may also have been a little afraid of her wit and penetration. On the other hand, his interest in her may always have been more intellectual than sexual. He was surprisingly tolerant of the other young men who flirted with her, and though Mr Graham allowed Ophelia to have been 'tolerably handsome' – a somewhat tepid compliment – there is no mention of physical charms in any of the non-fictional descriptions of her. Most likely she lacked what is now called sex appeal. Graves's crime, if that is not too strong a word for it, was most likely not an excess of ruffian passion in his relations with her but rather too little of it. Whatever his feelings about her may have been during her lifetime, her death upset him badly. How seriously he believed her to have died of a broken heart cannot be estimated, but he may have been right in thinking that disappointments had robbed her of the will to live and made her an easier prey for the illness that killed her. That he felt responsible more than any of the others may only mean that he had a more sensitive conscience, and that he had known her longest.

CHAPTER EIGHT

Lucy

Aldworth, where Graves held his second curacy, was a small village of brick cottages scattered along prettily wooded by-roads, with a thirteenth-century church on its western edge that looked out over the rich farmlands of Berkshire. Icknield Street ran through the parish, and Roman coins and tiles were often found along its route, which must have greatly interested the young curate. The exact length of his stay there is unknown, but approximate limits may be set. He must have taken up his duties there as soon as possible after his return to Oxford late in 1744, and in May of the following year he was certainly present on Visitation Day, for he certified the accuracy of the official transcript of the parish register by affixing his signature: 'Ric: Graves Curate.'[1] The transcript for the year after that, which ended in March 1746, is unaccountably missing from the diocesan archives, and by 6 April he was living in Whitchurch.[2] How long before that he had left Aldworth is unknown. That is only one of many unknowns in this part of his life.

Officially he was still a full-time resident in All Souls, taking his turn at various offices and, like many other fellows of colleges, riding out at the weekend to do duty in his parish. Since Aldworth was at least twenty miles from Oxford and not on a direct road, he must often have been obliged to spend a night or two away from his own bed; so, finding the parsonage house in poor shape, he retained a room for himself at a farmhouse called Dumworth just across the road from his church. His landlord, Edward Bartholomew, was a gentleman farmer or yeoman who had been a churchwarden twice in the previous decade. He had five daughters by his first wife and was now married for the second time, but there is no record of any children by this marriage or of any belonging to his new wife from a previous one of her own. Lucy, the youngest of the girls, had been born in

1730 and so was not yet fifteen when Graves came to live in her father's house. Nevertheless, according to him, she was already a dazzling beauty. Before long he fell head over heels in love with her.[3]

This was the great passion of his life. The history of it is better known than that of his affair with Utrecia Smith, thanks to datable references in the letters of his friends, to various public archives, and to what he himself has told us. The latter, however, mainly took the form of fiction. He gave up the whole of book 6 of *The Spiritual Quixote* to 'Mr. Rivers's Story,' a version of the history of his courtship and marriage,[4] but he changed all the names, calling Lucy Bartholomew Charlotte Woodville and himself Mr Rivers, moved the village from Berkshire into Buckinghamshire, speeded up the action, and most likely made an untold number of other improvements, as the tellers of good tales often do. Consequently, a biographer may accept it as evidence only with caution. How much he told his friends is uncertain because all of his letters to Whistler as well as Whistler's replies have vanished, and so have his letters to Shenstone. Shenstone's replies have survived, but when Graves edited them for publication, he obliterated all references to his courtship and marriage. Fortunately the original of one of the them has survived and is now in the Osborn Collection at Yale,[5] and it is possible to guess fairly accurately at the drift of the deleted passages in others. Moreover, in 1799 Graves permitted a brief and most discreet account to appear in *Public Characters of 1799–1800*, which adds a point or two to what has been recorded elsewhere. So, by various means, much is known. But much is also still unknown or known only indistinctly. The reconstruction of this history that follows may be a little confusing, but it is pinned down to hard fact wherever possible, and the gaps have been filled in cautiously from the less reliable but more imaginative material contained in the novel. 'Mr. Rivers's Story' led one of the first reviewers of the novel to remark that it was 'by far the best part of this novel' and, after reprinting the opening paragraphs of it, to write: 'We have seldom read so natural and pleasing an account of the commencement of an amour; and we give the Author credit for the truth of it.'[6] Certainly the vividness and sensitivity of Graves's narrative still make it sound convincing.

Mr Rivers's word picture of Charlotte is probably a faithful likeness of Lucy as she was when Graves first saw her:

She was rather tall than of a middling stature, but every way finely proportioned, and of a natural, easy shape. Her features were neither too large, nor too small; the extremes in either respect being, I think, less agreeable. Her eyes had always such a brilliant lustre, that I never knew their real colour. But her hair (which she had in great abundance) was of a bright brown, and gave an inimitably fine shade to her complexion. Her complection had, at that time, rather the glossy bloom of high health, than the transparent delicacy which is generally the concomitant of too tender a constitution.[7]

Her mind, he goes on to say, had even greater beauties, for she combined good nature and good sense in her disposition with sprightliness and artless freedom. This beautiful creature was given the task of waiting on the young man who boarded in her father's house, and one day, when the rest of the family had gone to a wedding, he made some joking remark to her about the happiness of the married state. 'She made me some very innocent reply,' he wrote, 'which however tempted me to chuck her under the chin ... She blushed, and retired with some precipitation, and with such a sweet confusion, that I longed to repeat the freedom; and begging her to return for a moment, as soon as she came within the door, I caught her around the neck, and snatched a kiss.'[8] That kiss must be historical. Graves was young, susceptible, lonely after the lively time he had had in Tissington, and overripe for an affair of the heart. The temptation was irresistible. Like Mr Rivers, he had now 'passed the rubicon of discretion.' The development of the affair is traced in the novel with insight, and even if some of the incidents are imaginary, such as Charlotte's sending a dish of wild strawberries to Mr Rivers to signify her forgiveness of the freedom he had taken, the general course of the romance must be true to fact. That course does not always run smooth, or there would be no story. There are lovers' quarrels followed by delicious reconciliations, and separations followed by homecomings. Charlotte's stepmother, jealous of her good looks and of her favour with her father, puts obstacles in his way. Nothing is known about Mary Perry, Edward Bartholomew's second wife, and there is no evidence that she created the role of wicked stepmother. But there are no grounds for saying that she did not.

Graves had worse problems than a stepmother. Like Mr Rivers he knew that if he married he would forfeit his fellowship, and since he had no other source of income, he was reluctant to marry until he had established himself in some lucrative position. For Graves that meant an ecclesiastical benefice. Letters of this period show that he and his friends were in active search of one for him and that all of them were urging him not to marry until his circumstances improved. Graves obviously agreed, though he was not at all averse to marriage, as a letter, now lost, written to Shenstone at this time must have shown. For in his reply Shenstone agreed with him that society is necessary to happiness and that a wife and children are the most important elements of one's social life.[9] But for the moment

Graves looked on marriage as an eventuality rather than an immediate possibility.

Moreover, there was a further objection to his marrying Lucy, similar to one that stood in the way of Mr Rivers. Lucy, like Charlotte, was the daughter of a yeoman, a man of some substance but little education. According to Robert Chambers, a yeoman was a man possessed of land to the yearly value of twenty pounds – a successful farmer.[10] Lucy herself had had only the education available to a girl at that time living in a tiny village – in other words, almost none except in needlework – and was deficient in what Mr Rivers called 'the common accomplishments of the sex' – that is, music, dancing, and other refinements of the kind. These shortcomings undoubtedly loomed large in Graves's mind, for he was still at heart a fine gentleman, fond of the good life as he had experienced it at Mickleton and Tissington. His family, too, would certainly wish him to marry well.

There is no description of the Bartholomew household in any of his writings, but a scene in his novel *Eugenius* set in a farmyard may be a recollection of it. Mrs Owen, a farmer's wife, who had lowered herself in her marriage, is surprised seated outdoors with her hair down and her bosom uncovered suckling her baby while her maid milks a cow and her two older children feed some poultry. It is a genre picture in the style of Nicholas Berghem, and the young hero of the novel, who is a lover of nature, is delighted by it, though Mrs Owen, on seeing him, flees in shame and dismay.[11] In another novel, *Columella*, the hero becomes engaged to marry his servant but recoils from the prospect on account of 'her cursed, vulgar, unclassical language.' 'She tortures my ears every hour in the day,' he complained, 'with her solecisms, her rustic dialect, or her uncouth expressions.'[12] There is no evidence that Lucy's speech was equally barbarous, but it is hardly possible that she did not speak broad Berkshire. Dialect was an important class distinction in class-conscious eighteenth-century society. Clearly Lucy was not the wife Graves family and friends would have chosen for him, however acceptable she might be as a mistress. Graves himself, through all his love for her, must have felt the difficulties.

In 'Mr. Rivers's Story' this first act in the drama culminates in Mr Rivers's having a talk with Charlotte's father, in which he explains why he cannot marry her then but, declaring that he is passionately in love, gives his solemn promise that he will do so ultimately. Meanwhile, to solve one of his difficulties he proposes that he take her to London and put her into a boarding school there at his own expense. Astonishingly, the old gentleman agrees to that proposal, though with some reluctance and perhaps in the mistaken belief, encouraged in him by his wife, that the young people have already been married. She would be glad to be rid of her rival. Accordingly, the lovers set off together for London, where he finds lodgings for her, seduces her, marries her, and finally enrols her in a school.

Though Graves's movements during the corresponding phase of his courtship are not clearly known, their pattern must have been similar, though by no means identical. If he had a long talk with Goodman Bartholomew, as is likely, it is hardly credible, as one of the reviewers of *The Spiritual Quixote* pointed out, that any father outside a novel, unless weak minded, would have agreed to a proposal similar to the one put to Mr Woodville. What was said on the actual occasion, however, if anything, is unknown. Certainly Graves left Aldworth before April 1746 and moved in with his friend Anthony Whistler in nearby Whitchurch, Oxfordshire.[13] Though he went on performing his collegiate duties in Oxford, he gave Whitchurch as his mailing address; all three of Shenstone's letters written to him in 1746 and early 1747 were addressed to him there. But did he have Lucy with him? At this point the evidence fails almost altogether. All that there is to go on is negative; there is nothing whatever to show that in 1746 she was with him either in Whitchurch or in London; it was not until January 1747 that she became pregnant. Most likely in 1746 she was still at home, seeing her lover, surreptitiously or otherwise, whenever he was able to ride to her across the fields.

Eventually he did carry her off, with or without her father's permission, and took her to London. The date of this adventure is unrecorded, though most likely it occurred towards the end of 1746. The history of their journey and of her experiences in the metropolis probably runs reasonably parallel to that of Charlotte Woodville, though the incidents are stuff out of which English novels had been created ever since *Moll Flanders* and may be imitations of other novels rather than imitations of nature. The story of Julia Townsend, told in book 3 of *The Spiritual Quixote*, may also reflect some of Lucy's experiences. In 'Mr. Rivers's Story' there is no suggestion that he kept his promise of sending her at once to school. Instead Charlotte spends her time in various lodging houses, exposed to the evil devices of prostitutes, bawds, young rakes, and elderly mashers and being visited from time to time by her lover, whose occasions seem to require his presence elsewhere much of the time. Apparently Lucy's lot was much the same. There is no reference in any of the extant correspondence to her being in school in either 1746 or 1747. Instead she was the kept mistress of a young man who, however ardent in his feelings about her, was in no hurry to marry her and had much to do elsewhere.

Keeping her in London was a means of preserving a certain amount of secrecy, not that in the lax state of morals prevailing at that time anybody would have been much shocked over a young man's, even a young clergyman's, keeping a mistress. Graves's friend Whistler must have known about the love affair, for they were in close touch at this time, Graves probably using Whistler's house as a base. Shenstone, who had recently made The Leasowes his permanent home, was apparently not taken fully into Graves's confidence until quite a late stage. He makes no reference to the affair in his letters before one dated '1746, ineunte anno' (which must mean the beginning of 1747, new style), in which he wrote: 'Let me hear something in your next of your *domestic affairs*. I beg you would not make any grand decision, without giving me some previous information. I esteem this as due to the friendship I have so long professed for you, and from the friendship you have so long professed for me.'[14] The italic type used for '*domestic affairs*' probably indicates an editorial substitution, made by Graves himself when he edited the letter for publication, replacing a more specific question. In his copy of the *Letters* Thomas Percy wrote in the margin: 'Perhaps about his Marriage.' He would not have said 'perhaps' if the information had come from Graves, yet the 'grand decision' must refer to some important step contemplated by Graves in his relations with Lucy, and if that was marriage, it is our first evidence that he had it in mind. Whatever the request was, Graves evidently resented it, for in another letter, dated 21 September 1747, Shenstone wrote: 'I dare now no longer expatiate upon the affair you have in hand; it is enough for me, if you will excuse the freedom I *have* taken.' Nevertheless, he added: 'I have often known *delay* produce good effects.'[15] Graves responded by a long silence. In a letter that Professor Williams thinks ought to have been dated at the end of June 1748, Shenstone wrote: 'When I wrote last, I discovered a more than ordinary solicitude for *one* immediate answer. It puzzles me to account for your unusual silence, otherwise than upon supposition of some offence you have taken.'[16] The coolness did not last long, but Graves did not at this time keep Shenstone posted about his personal affairs. Since in the eighteenth century it was not unusual for young men to discuss their amours with close friends of their own sex, Graves's reticence with one of his most trusted friends must indicate a certain unease in his conscience. In June 1748 Dick Jago, Shenstone's old college friend, who had evidently heard rumours and like Shenstone was curious, inquired at a pub in Mickleton and was told that Graves's marriage was 'doubtful.'[17] But Jago was not in Graves's inner circle of friends. How much may have been known at the manor house is a mystery.

In his story Mr Rivers, on arriving in London with Charlotte and finding himself alone with her in her lodgings, loses no time in completing his happiness, as he puts it. That happiness, however, is ruffled by an uneasy conscience, especially after she becomes pregnant. In his perplexity he meets two old friends, a Mr Hammond and a Mr Wylmot, who talk seriously to him and urge him to marry Charlotte at once, the latter offering to lend him a house. A third friend offers him a farm at a low rental that will make him financially independent so long as he is content to live a simple life in the country. He does as he is advised and is rewarded accordingly. The Stephens key to *The Spiritual Quixote* identifies Mr Hammond with Bernard Kirkham, an old friend and Gloucestershire neighbour of Graves whose family was Methodistically inclined. There is no corroboration of this identification, but neither is there any reason for rejecting it. The key also identifies Mr Wylmot with the Reverend George Walker.[18] If these identifications are correct, Mr Rivers is telling Graves's own story. Both friends, no doubt, advised Graves to marry Lucy, and Mr Walker also offered to take him on as curate and give him a house to live in. *Public Characters of 1799–1800* corroborates this view of Mr Walker's role though without mentioning his name: 'a curacy of fifty pounds a year ... with a very neat, but small house, was offered him by an acquaintance, a most worthy and respectable man, of a good private fortune, near Reading, but in Oxfordshire.'[19] That fits the Reverend George Walker of Whitchurch like a glove.

On the strength of that promise Richard Graves and Lucy Bartholomew were married on 2 August 1747. Mr Rivers and Charlotte Woodville are married 'by a curate in a remote part of the city,' who performs the ceremony with the utmost secrecy. But that is tame beside the circumstances of the marriage of Richard and Lucy, which occurred in the Fleet, one of the most unsavory districts in central London. Dominated by a great gaunt prison for insolvent debtors, the district was crowded with cheap and noisy taverns, brothels, tumbledown lodging-houses, disreputable coffee-houses, and dens of thieves. It was London's sin-strip. Weddings there were big business. Before 1754, when Lord Hardwicke's act for the prevention of clandestine marriages came into effect, people's minds were greatly confused over what constituted a valid marriage, and the civil courts, which controlled property, were even in conflict with the church courts, which regulated the conditions of marriage. The canons of 1604 stipulated where and when marriages might take place, required the previous reading of banns, and forbade the marriage of persons under twenty-one without their parents' permission. But paradoxically, in some areas like the Fleet, which was Crown property

and where ecclesiastical and municipal control was consequently ineffec-
tual, the trade in clandestine marriages was lively, and such marriages,
however illegal, once solemnized and consummated were considered by
the courts valid and indissoluble. In country districts and the more
respectable London parishes the situation was kept more or less under
control by custom, but London was full of drunken sailors, runaway
children, and adventurers of every sort, who often wished to get married
secretly and in a hurry. For such people the Fleet provided every
convenience. Thomas Pennant, author of the well-known *Account of
London*, wrote that in his youth all through the Fleet district signs could be
seen hanging in front of buildings consisting of 'a male and female hand
conjoined, with, *Marriages performed within*, written beneath.' A dirty
fellow, called a plyer, walked about drumming up trade, accosting
passers-by with the question: 'Sir, will you be pleased to walk in and be
married,' and sometimes the parson, or pseudo-parson, might also be
seen, described by Pennant as 'a squalid profligate figure, clad in a
tattered plaid night-gown, with a fiery face, and ready to couple you for a
dram of gin, or roll of tobacco.'[20] Naturally the district was unsafe for
unattended women. In 1735 a woman wrote a letter to a newspaper
complaining that not long before a relation of hers had only narrowly
escaped being kidnapped on her way home from a theatre by an unknown
adventurer who forced his way into her coach and tried to marry her
against her will in one of the establishments set up for that purpose in the
Fleet.[21] A typical scene in the Fleet is vividly represented in an engraving
(see plate 15) done in the style of Hogarth and published in the same year
as that in which Richard and Lucy were married.[22]

The Graves-Bartholomew marriage was recorded in a small notebook,
one of a series now in the Public Record Office in Chancery Lane,
London, described as 'Dare's Notebooks.'[23] W.W. Dare, whose property it
once was, was one of the most energetic entrepreneurs engaged in the
marriage business in the Fleet, performing, it is said, between 150 and 200
ceremonies a month. His little notebook appears to have been kept handy
in his pocket so that he could jot down all the necessary details of each
transaction as it occurred before he forgot them in the press of business.
Afterwards he always made a more formal entry in a neat hand in a
permanent record book. Dare's marriages, however sordid their circumstances may have been, were legal, and so information about them was a
valuable property. The Graves marriage was formally recorded in one of
them, also in the Public Record Office.[24] But the earlier entry is the more
interesting:

Aug.ˢᵗ 2.ᵈ 1747
Richard Graves of Tissington in Darby Clerk & Lucy Bartholomew of
Alder in Berks Spinster Home m / m – com

Crawford

The significance of the code letters at the end of the entry is not entirely
clear. 'm / m – ' conveys nothing at all to the mind of the present writer,
and 'com' is almost equally obscure, although it has been suggested that it
may indicate the presence of company – that is, witnesses. As for 'Home,'
it is reasonable to guess that it indicated the place where the ceremony
took place, in a private house rather than in a church or chapel.
'Crawford' must be the name of the man who performed it. Dare is known
to have employed an assistant, and the name of Crawford appears in at
least one other entry in the same notebook. He may have been the T.C., a
watch-maker by trade, who, according to another letter in the newspaper previously quoted, went about 'in a Minister's dress, personating a
Clergyman, and taking upon him the name of Doctor to the scandal of the
sacred function. He may be seen at any time at the Bull and Garter, or the
Great Hand and Pen and Star.' Bogus priest or not, he was at least more
presentable than Pennant's fat and greasy parson, for he usually
appeared 'exceeding well-dress'd in a flower'd morning gown, a band, hat
and wig.'²⁵ Fine clothes seem always to have been a part of the picture
where Graves was concerned.

The most remarkable feature of this wedding was its secrecy. Holding it
in the Fleet was a guarantee, for respectable people normally kept away,
and holding it in a private house increased the security. If company was
present, it probably consisted of only Mr Kirkham and the Reverend Mr
Walker, who had helped to arrange it and who were not in touch with
either the Graves or the Bartholomew families. Graves also covered his
tracks by giving Tissington as his address, though he had left there three
years before and now properly belonged to either Oxford or Whitchurch.
Lucy's giving Alder as her address was possibly for the same reason,
though Alder may have been a genuine local variant of Aldworth. Several
reasons for this secrecy suggest themselves. The chief of them was that if
news of his marriage became known at All Souls, Graves would be
deprived of his fellowship. Obviously he would not be able to go on living
this double life for ever, but he did not wish to give up his fellowship until
he had secured more substantial preferment, and at the moment none
was in sight. Another reason for secrecy was the probable disapproval of
his family. The Graveses were proud of their status as gentry, and

Morgan, Richard's older brother and present head of the family, was busy doing over the old manor house and its grounds in the latest fashion, to make it suitable for the sort of people whom he would have as his guests. Although class lines were more sharply drawn in the eighteenth century than they are today, English society was then the most fluid in Europe. The yeomanry, to which class the Bartholomews belonged, were on the way up and so were felt as a threat by the gentry. Readers of Jane Austen's novels will recall Emma Woodhouse's aversion to Robert Martin, another successful farmer, and her warning to Harriet Smith that he belongs to a class of people she ought particularly to avoid. There is no knowing how much, if anything, brother Morgan knew about Richard's liaison with Lucy Bartholomew, but Richard must have had good reason to expect strong disapproval of his marrying into such a family. Richard himself, deeply in love though he was, may also have felt apprehensive over how his friends would receive his wife; not all of them would react as his young idealist Eugenius was to do when he surprised Mrs Owen in her farmyard.

After his marriage Graves apparently spent much of 1747 in London with Lucy, for in a letter written to him during that year Shenstone asked him for news about public affairs that he had better access to in the metropolis.[26] Nevertheless, he was still performing his undemanding duties at All Souls as Naturalis Philosophiæ Prælector, and he must have been carrying on a three-cornered existence by attending to his duties in Whitchurch as well. On Easter Sunday 1749 he was present in Whitchurch and signed the visitation book as curate, the only positive evidence that he ever held that office, but it is likely that he had been functioning in that capacity since before his marriage.[27] Lucy probably remained in London after the wedding. On 22 October 1747 she and her recently married husband presented their first child at the church of St Giles, Bloomsbury, for baptism. They named him Richard after his father, his grandfather, and his great-great-grandfather.[28]

Early in 1748 Graves took steps that he hoped would solve the second of his problems by enrolling his wife in a boarding school in London. Mr Rivers, one recalls, does the same thing. It was a sorrowful parting for them after only five or six months of married life and only about half that long since the birth of young Richard, who was probably put out to nurse. Graves wrote a poem on the occasion, called 'The Parting':

> The rising sun thro' all the grove
> Diffus'd a gladsome ray:
> My Lucy smil'd and talk'd of love,
> And every thing look'd gay.

But oh! the fatal hour was come
That forc'd me from my dear:
My Lucy then thro' grief was dumb,
Or spoke but by a tear.

Now far from her and bliss I roam,
All nature wears a change:
The azure sky seems wrapt in gloom,
And every place looks strange.

Those flow'ry fields, this verdant scene,
Yon larks that towering sing,
With sad contrast increase my spleen
And make me loath the spring.

My books that wont to sooth my mind
No longer now can please:
There only those amusement find
That have a mind at ease.

Nay life itself is tasteless grown
From Lucy whilst I stray:
Sick of the world I muse alone
And sigh the live-long day.[29]

It is not great poetry, but it is simple and sincere, one of his best. Shortly after writing it he sent a copy in a letter to Shenstone, who sent it on to his vivacious friend Lady Luxborough in a letter dated 18 April, with the following explanation: 'Poor Dick Graves (of whom you may have chanc'd to hear me speak) has sent his Farmer's Daughter to a Boarding-School in London ... He indited yᵉ Sonnet I enclose upon leaving her there.'[30] A few years later, when Graves published his poem in volume four of Dodsley's *Collection*, he called it 'The Parting' and added the date 1748. He also inserted after the title the words 'Written some years after Marriage,' but when he reprinted it in his own collection *Euphrosyne*, he corrected 'Years' to 'Months.'[31] By that time the truth did not hurt so much. How long this experiment in education lasted is not altogether clear. Thomas Percy, in one of the notes he wrote in his copy of Shenstone's *Letters*, mentioned 'a year or two.'[32] It is likely that one is nearer the truth than two, for in early 1748 Lucy became pregnant again and by January 1749 was living in Whitchurch.

When Shenstone received 'The Parting' from Graves he had not yet been told about the marriage and jumped to the conclusion that the schooling was to be in the nature of a test of Lucy's suitability as a wife. He explained this to Lady Luxborough: 'Graves looks upon London as a fiery Tryal – If he finds her *false*, he is at Liberty to decline; if *true*, as he *sincerely* wishes, She is all Gold thrice purify'd &c &c.'[33] Shenstone must have made all that up out of his own head. 'Poor Dick,' as he had called his friend, was no longer a free man. Nevertheless a legend grew up among Graves's friends, such as Thomas Percy, that the schooling preceded the marriage, and Graves, who never did tell Shenstone the correct date of his marriage, did little to set the record straight.

There is no trace now of what school Lucy attended. Many such schools undoubtedly existed in London and elsewhere, all of them small, short lived, and probably undistinguished. Their concern was with deportment rather than knowledge, as in the finishing schools that used to flourish in America. They aimed to teach young women to act like ladies, and their clientele generally came from the middle classes, from families having social aspirations but not enough money to let them hire the private tutors who took charge of the education of the daughters of the upper classes. Some idea of what such a school was like may be got from an advertisement that appeared in a later decade in the *Bath Chronicle*:

Ladies Boarding School,
Catharine-Place

Mrs. Bird, induced by the kind encouragement of her friends, intends opening a BOARDING-SCHOOL for YOUNG LADIES, whose improvement in every useful and polite branch of education, (and her care in the cultivation of the mind) will, she presumes, fully convince their parents of her assiduity and attention.

TERMS.

Boarding, Reading, English Grammar, Embroidery, elegant Muslin Work, &c. Twenty Guineas a year; French and Writing included, 25 *l*. a year, two guineas entrance. Every other accomplishment taught by the most approved Masters on the usual terms. – All bills paid every half year.[34]

Graves must have hoped to placate his family by making his Lucy socially acceptable. Shenstone explained Graves's intentions to Lady Luxborough: 'we will suppose that, however he prefer his Lucy to yᵉ good Opinion of the wise world, yet he doesn't so *entirely* despise that Opinion as not to wish to *compromise* Matters ... and to render his Conduct something *less* absurd, by rendering her Behaviour something less exceptionable.'[35] But with his family this experiment in education would turn out to be a failure; they never accepted her.

By the beginning of 1748 Graves had moved to Whitchurch,[36] occupying the house promised him by his employer, the Reverend George Walker, with whom he shared an interest in ancient coins and medals. He wrote a poem about it entitled 'The Cabinet,' dedicated it to Walker, and published it in 1751 in *The Student*, a university periodical. At the beginning of 1749, her schooling completed, Lucy joined him there, where in January she was delivered of her second child, another boy, who was christened Morgan in the parish church on the twenty-fifth.[37] She and Richard were devoted to each other. Anthony Whistler complained in a letter to Shenstone written in October that though Graves lived 'next door' to him the two old friends saw little of each other, Graves giving all his time to his wife.[38] Whistler was a bachelor and remained one for the rest of his short life. Like many other bachelors he took the marriage of an old friend rather hard. Three years later Lady Luxborough made a similar report in a letter to Shenstone, that Graves did not leave his wife 'an inch.'[39] Shenstone himself had not been informed about the marriage until the summer of 1748, a year after it took place. He wrote a letter of congratulation on 21 August but did not post it until the twenty-eighth, worrying perhaps over whether or not he had said the right things. His letter was kind and conciliatory, though hardly enthusiastic: 'It will, I *hope*, be esteemed superfluous in *me*,' he wrote, 'to send you my most cordial wishes that you may be happy; but it will, perhaps, be *something* more significant to say, that I believe you *will*: building my opinion on the knowledge I have long had of your own temper, and the account you give me of the person's whom you have made choice of, to whom I desire you to pay my sincere and most affectionate compliments.'[40]

When the Graves family was informed about the marriage is not known. According to *Public Characters of 1799–1800*, 'Mr. Graves had highly displeased his elder brother, by resigning his fellowship, and by so imprudent a match.'[41] Shenstone, in his letter of congratulations, also mentioned that the Graveses thought Richard had 'acted indiscretely.' That was probably a tactful reference to a great family row. Morgan must have been particularly annoyed, because not long before Richard had rejected a proposal, put to him probably by Morgan, that he marry a highly eligible young lady with a good living in her purse.[42] Afterwards communications between Richard and his family evidently ceased. In his later correspondence, even in his letters to the Dodsleys, which often touch on personal matters as well as business ones, there is a notable absence of references to his family or to Mickleton. After Morgan's death in 1770 Richard got on very good terms with Morgan's eldest son and successor, Walwyn, but the history of his relations with his family during Morgan's lifetime after 1747 is a blank.

As for the Bartholomews, there is no record of how they felt. But in later years Lucy and her husband occasionally visited in Berkshire, and a century after their marriage a Bartholomew was able to give Francis Kilvert some information about the Graves family.[43] So good relations may have been kept up.

Finally, in the middle of January 1749 the blow fell; the steward's book at All Souls recorded that Graves ceased to be a fellow of the college 'on his marriage.' No letter of resignation has been preserved in the archives of the college, but Mr Rivers is described in the novel as having resigned, and *Public Characters of 1799–1800* makes a similar statement. No doubt, if Graves did resign, he was actuated by a characteristic attack of conscience, though why he chose that moment to act on it after having lived a double life for a year and a half is a mystery. If he did not resign his fellowship, he must have been stripped of it by a formal act of the assembled fellows. However it came about, it was a bitter blow to him. It not only cut off his only steady income but also dashed his hopes of a career as a scholar and academic by severing his ties with the university and by putting an end to his prospect of a comfortable church living in the gift of the college. He never ceased lamenting it. Some years later he expressed his feelings in one melancholy stanza in a poem:

> For [Beauty], in youth I chose a wife,
> And sacrific'd the pomp of life;
> Stopt short in Learning's bright career;
> Nor ever thought the purchase dear.[44]

But the brave assertion made in the final line referred only to Lucy. The shipwreck of his career he long lamented. In the summer of 1772, looking back on this crisis in his affairs, he wrote: 'The visionary plans of happiness, of learning, of fame, which dazzled my imagination in the morning of life, are vanished, like the baseless fabric of a dream.'[45]

Between a brisk young Sailor & his Landlady's Daughter at Rederiff.

Scarce had the Coach discharg'd its trusty Fare, / Pray step this way—just to the Pen in Hand. / Th' alarmed Parsons quickly hear the Din! / Till slow advancing from the Coach's Side,
But gaping Crowds surround th' amorous Pair, / The Doctor's ready there at your Command: / And haste with soothing words t' invite 'em in. / Th' experienc'd Matron came (an artful Guide)
The busy Plyers make a mighty Stir! / This way (another cries) Sir I declare / In this Confusion jostled to and fro, / She led the way without regarding either,
And whisp'ring cry d'ye want the Parson, Sir? / The true and ancient Register is Here: / Th' inamour'd Couple know not where to go; / And the fleet Parson splic'd 'em both together.

Publish'd according to Act of Parliament October y^e 20th 1747.

Price 6^d
Oct. 1747

15 / A Fleet Wedding 1748

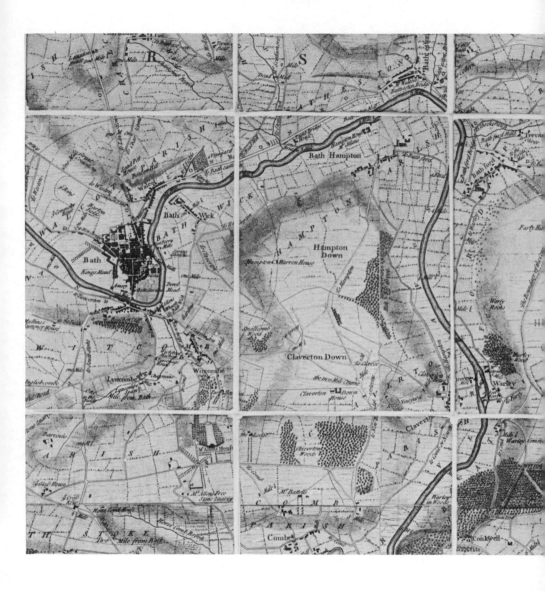

16 / Map of Bath and Claverton, 1742
Part of Thomas Thorpe's *Actual Survey of the City of Bath* 1742

17 / Claverton parish church
Sketch by John Skinner

18 / Claverton House
Sketch by John Skinner

19 / Parsonage-house, Claverton
Sketch by John Skinner

20 / Frontispiece to volume two of the second edition of *The Spiritual Quixote*

21 / Graves's rough sketch

22 / Lucy's urn
From the second edition of Graves's *Euphrosyne* (1783) II, 211

23 / Wildgoose throws down an idol
Frontispiece to volume three of *The Spiritual Quixote*

24 / William Shenstone
From Shenstone's *Works* 1764

Optimus olim
Virgilius, post hunc Varius, dixere quid essem —
Et placui tibi, qui turpi secernis honestum.
Lib. I. Sat. 6.

25 / Frontispiece and title-page of the Baskerville *Horace* 1762

QUINTUS
HORATIUS
FLACCUS.

S. Wale del.   C. Grignion sculp.

MONUMENTUM ÆRE PERENNIUS

BIRMINGHAMIÆ;
Typis *JOANNIS BASKERVILLE.*
M DCC LXII.

26 / *Orange Grove, Bath*
Painted on a lady's fan by George Speren

OPPOSITE

27 / Richard Graves in profile
From *Public Characters of 1799–1800* 1799, facing page 400

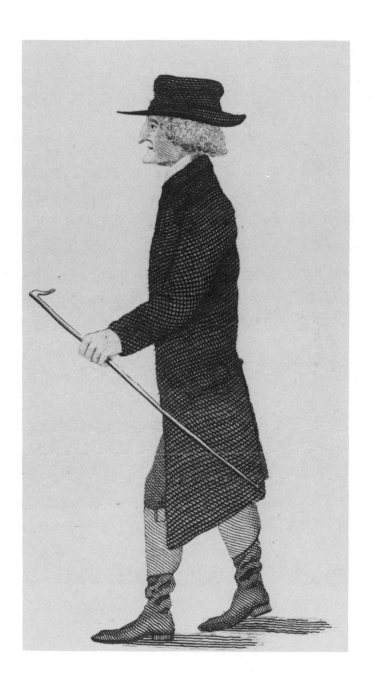

28 / Richard Graves by James Northcote
Mezzotint in the Victoria Art Gallery, Bath

CHAPTER NINE

The Clerical Calling

For some time Graves had been hoping for a benefice of his own in the church. Curacies were very well for a while, but they were badly paid and, unlike rectories, conferred no security of tenure. Shenstone had joined in the search and had given Graves a hint about one that might be available in his own vicinity, but he was perplexed by his friend's failure to follow it up, not knowing that at the time he was busy getting married.[1] Now that he was married and had lost his fellowship, the need was urgent. The only means of getting what he wanted was personal influence, through what today is sometimes called the old-school-tie network, since the right to nominate to livings was normally vested in private individuals, often the lord of the manor or the fellows of a college such as All Souls. At last, early in 1749, word got to Graves through some such channel that a living was vacant in the Whitchurch area and that his friend and former school-fellow Sir Thomas Head of Langley had influence with the patron. Sir Thomas, however, for some reason declined to act. But late in May of the same year, accidentally meeting William Skrine of Claverton near Bath, a common friend, who told him that the rector of his parish, of which he was patron, had just died, leaving him the problem of finding a suitable successor, Sir Thomas mentioned Graves's name.[2] Skrine must have adopted the suggestion at once, for the necessary steps were taken with surprising speed. The Reverend Mr Huson, the former rector, had died on May 27,[3] and only five days later Graves met Skrine in the study of the bishop of Bath and Wells, where he was formally presented to the rectory of Claverton. He had ridden over in such a hurry that he had forgot to bring with him the necessary documents: his ordination papers and a certificate of good character signed by three fellow clergymen. So he had to post a bond for two hundred pounds to guarantee his production of them for his lordship's inspection within three months.[4] But that did not delay his induction into the living, which took place on Sunday, 11 June, in the parish church at Claverton.[5] He was given the keys by one of the wardens and tolled the bell of a church of his own for the first time.

At this juncture in Graves's life chronology ceases to be a matter of primary concern. He remained in Claverton for over half a century, during which time no dramatic changes occurred in the routine that he established for himself. He faithfully performed his duties as parish priest; he taught school; he wrote books; he rode across the down nearly every day to Bath to collect his mail, talk to people, and examine the new books on sale in the shops; he went for long walks and rides visiting spots of aesthetic and antiquarian interest; he cultivated his friendships, and he raised his family. Once or twice a year, during school holidays, he and his wife went to London to see plays and visit friends. But he was never absent from Claverton at any one time for more than a month during all his years there. The 'tenor of his way,' to adopt a phrase from Gray's Elegy, was not only 'noiseless' but unchanging, or changed only slowly as he grew older and his circumstances fell into new patterns.

In worldly terms the rectory of Claverton was no great prize. In 1791 the parish contained only sixteen houses and had about one hundred inhabitants;[6] it was probably much the same size when Graves came into residence in 1750.[7] His income from it seemed inadequate to meet the needs of his growing family, so that for years he felt obliged to supplement it in various ways. It was a clerical backwater, not even the *Bath Journal* seeing any reason for reporting in its issue for 12 June 1749 the induction of the new rector of Claverton, which had taken place on the previous day.

All avenues of further advancement in the church had apparently been closed to him. No doubt the scandal of his secret marriage had offended many potential friends and patrons, including the fellows of All Souls. As late as 1767 he wrote of being 'molested' by '*Scandal*'s darts.'[8] Other friends might have helped had he himself not lost heart. Once, he recalled, when the bishop of Gloucester suggested that he take more upon himself and so rise in the church, he replied: 'Your lordship might as well bid me add, "two cubits to my stature."'[9] Elements in his personality were against him. He had a slight speech defect, and the shyness that Shenstone had noted in him as an undergraduate, which had inhibited him from displaying his abilities except in a circle of friends, still plagued him. In 1759, when planning to dedicate a seat in his shrubberies to Graves, Shenstone suggested inscribing on it these words:

AMICITIÆ MERITISQUE RECONDITORIBUS
RICHARDI GRAVES.

(To the friendship and buried talents of Richard Graves.) Graves apparently objected, for the adjective 'reconditoribus' was dropped, not because it was not true but because Graves shrank from drawing attention to his weakness.[10]

Graves's shyness made him reluctant to preach. Once when asked by his bishop to preach in Bath Abbey, he 'saw all the horrors of mounting ye Abbey pulpit,' as he explained to a correspondent, and refused. He knew that he had acted foolishly, and so when a year or so later his archdeacon insisted, he did preach and, as he reported, 'have gain'd great credit on ye occasion.'[11] That success did not altogether remove his reluctance, but he did sometimes mount the pulpit on special occasions, and in 1799 he published over his own name a handful of those special sermons in a little volume. They are not great sermons, though they measure up well against his own standard of 'plain, intelligible, practical discourses' that avoid boring a congregation with 'metaphysical controversies, and with endeavour to explain, what was not intended to be explained to us in this life.'[12] But they lack the charm, the wit, the vivacity, and the gift for anecdote that mark his best secular prose, qualities that no doubt he felt would be out of place in the pulpit, and they fail to compensate with profound thought or moving eloquence. Perhaps he was less reluctant to preach to his own little flock in the parish church on ordinary Sundays, but none of those sermons has survived. The model he set himself for them may have been what Dr Greville, a character in *The Spiritual Quixote*, calls 'a sett of plain regular discourses, upon the principles of Natural and Revealed Religion: the Being, Attributes and Moral Government of God; and the peculiar doctrines and duties of the Gospel.'[13] Or he may have followed the easier model set for him by some of the 'deep divines' of his own time, which he described in *Love of Order*:

> *In Charles's days the deep Divine*
> *Delighted in divisions nine,*
> *But, in our age, has brought (thank Heaven!)*
> *His numbers something under seven:*
> *Nay, oft those heads reduc'd to one,*
> *A Sermon is an Essay grown.*[14]

If, as is most likely, in drawing the character of Parson Pomfret in *Columella* he was parodying himself, he was probably unfair:

Mr. Pomfret, the little Rector ... is a worthy man, and a man of reading, and had taken his degrees in the University. But he is a poor, hectic, miserable-looking creature; and the want of dignity in his person, the want of spirit in his reproofs of vice, and the want of a good elocution to inculcate his virtuous sentiments, prevent him from doing that good in his parish which he might otherwise have done. He preaches tolerable discourses, but with so little emphasis, that his audience frequently fall asleep in the midst of them. If he has occasion to exhort privately any of his parishioners, he does it in so timorous and undecisive a manner, and with so much hesitation, that it loses its effect.[15]

But there may have been enough truth in it to explain his failure to rise.

Characteristically, Graves took seriously his commitment to a cure of souls. Even if he still felt the spiritual dryness of which he had complained to Charles Wesley in 1737, the gentleman within him was no longer at war with the Christian as he set about his parochial duties with earnestness. When he overcame his objection to the wearing of dark clothes is not known, but later in his life he wrote scornfully in *Reveries of Solitude* about the spruce young clerics of his time. 'Even our Young Divines,' he wrote, 'though doubtless much given to fasting and prayer in private, yet "appear not to men to fast"; but anoint their hair, and exhibit their rosy faces; and, by their dress, are not to be distinguished from prophane sportsmen or country "squires."'[16] Though he must have undergone some searchings of heart before accepting his lot in Claverton, he did not record them in a diary or confide them to friends in letters. The visitatorial sermon 'On the Clerical Character,' however, which comes first in his little collection, probably records the fruits of his thinking during his first year in his own parish.[17] Taking his text from the First Epistle to the Thessalonians – 'Therefore, let *us* not *sleep*, as do others; but let us *watch* and be *sober*' – he addressed himself primarily to the clergy, on the one hand admonishing them to live up to their high calling and on the other defending them against their critics. Though he nowhere used the word Methodist, his sermon was obviously a reply to Methodist criticism of the orthodox clergy. The age, he conceded, was licentious and irreligious, neglectful of church attendance and in need of constant preaching. The clergy, he felt, must consequently stress moral and practical topics in their discourses and avoid theological hair-splitting. 'The truth is,' he declared, 'they [that is, the Methodists] have taken it for granted, that the whole of religion consists in thinking precisely as they do, on a few particular articles of our faith. And therefore, if their curiosity leads them into any religious assembly, where the subject of the discourse happens not to be, at that time, on justification by faith, regeneration, or any of their favourite topics, they immediately condemn the preacher as a mere moral man, and entirely unacquainted with the essential doctrines of Christianity.'[18] The true Christian, Graves felt, was on the contrary one who left such metaphysical puzzles alone and concentrated on living in peace and charity with his neighbours.

At some time during his first decade in Claverton Graves had a brush with the Methodists. One of their itinerant preachers, an unordained journeyman shoemaker, had invaded his parish, preaching and singing psalms in defiance of the rector, and had drawn off part of his congregation.[19] Having dealt with that intruder with firmness, Graves began to write the comic romance to be called *The Spiritual Quixote*, of which one of the themes is a satire on the itinerants who went about preaching the gospel according to Wesley and Whitefield. The principal character is young Geoffry Wildgoose, only son of a widowed mother belonging to a family of minor gentry that, like the Graveses, had lived for generations in a sequestered village in Gloucestershire. Nursing some grievance against the parson of his parish, he turns morose, falls to reading a parcel of old books of piety found in his attic, and eventually sallies forth in the company of an earthy-minded yokel called Jerry Tugwell to preach to the heathen at fairs, in inns, by the roadside, or wherever he can find them. He is the Don Quixote of Methodism and Tugwell his Sancho Panza. Naturally many adventures befall them, mostly hilarious ones, the sources for many of them being the published journals of Whitefield and Wesley as well as the career of Graves's brother Charles Caspar, who had himself taken to the road as a preacher. There is, however, more to the plot than clowning. Wildgoose's theology, which was Whitefield's rather than Wesley's, is given full exposure: the Calvinist doctrines of election and reprobation are emphasized; the more morbid of the phenomena connected with the New Birth are conspicuous in many episodes; the worthlessness of good works is asserted, and such worldly pleasures as the theatre are denounced again and again. In the conclusion Wildgoose is brought back to his senses, ostensibly by means of a blow on his head from a wine decanter flung by one of the heathen. But it causes only a minor concussion, and everything ends happily.

That decanter is just a part of the comedy; the real causes of Wildgoose's reconversion are more profound. Among them is the advice he receives throughout the novel from a number of older and wiser heads. At first he hardens his heart against it, but in the end his defences are penetrated by the good sense and warm humanity of a Dr Greville, the hero of the final fifty pages. Dr Greville is no Methodist, but he feels that the Methodists have done some good by exposing weaknesses in the established church for which reform from within is overdue. 'Dr Greville,' the author explains, 'really was what Mr. Wesley and his associates ought to have been, and what (I sincerely believe) they at first intended to be. He revived the practice of primitive piety in his own person, and in his own parish; and, by his examples and admonitions, excited many of the neighbouring Clergy to be more vigilant in the discharge of their duty.' Graves took for granted that his readers knew what he meant by 'primitive piety.' From other contexts in the novel as well as from his other writings it is clear that it did not mean anything at all like the perfectionism of William Law, whose works were much studied by the early Methodists, but rather something much closer to the teachings of Archbishop Laud. It meant a conformity to the traditional practices and low-keyed faith of the Church of England. In particular it meant that a priest must make himself a real part of the community he serves, avoiding non-residence and the laxity fashionable at the time, and in fact be the shepherd of his flock, exercising discipline when discipline is needed and showing compassion when compassion is called for. Dr Greville, as the author goes on to say, 'had a *Faith*, which worked by *Love*; or, in modern language, his belief of the truths of the Gospel made him consider as an indispensable duty those acts of benevolence which his humanity prompted him to perform.'[20] It is Greville who finally persuades Wildgoose that the itinerant preachers are doing more harm than good by breaking down the parochial structure traditional in English society and introducing a divisive element.

Dr Greville's faith is much like that of Gregory Griskin, another of Graves's fictional heroes:

Griskin was a man of the old-fashioned piety, that shewed his Faith by his Good Works. He gave much in charity, prayed often, and fasted now and then. Having the tithes in his own hands, it enabled him to keep a plentiful table, to which every sober honest man was welcome. He every Sunday invited by turns some of his Parishioners to dine with him, one or two of the most substantial in the parlour, and as many of the oldest and poorest in the kitchen. This made them pay their tithes and dues chearfully; which Griskin exacted of them punctually, but not with *rigour*. If a Farmer had any loss, or remarkably bad year, he made him some little allowance; and, if a Cottager paid him a groat at Easter, which he could ill spare, perhaps he would give his family a six-penny loaf the Sunday following. By this means he kept up his dignity, and secured his right and the love of his parish at the same time.[21]

That must have been the pattern of behaviour that Graves himself tried his best to follow in discharging his own priestly duties.

The Spiritual Quixote must have been nearly completed in at least a rough draft during the fifties, but it was not published until twenty years later. The reasons for such a long delay are obscure, but one of them may well have been reluctance to expose to the public gaze so deeply personal a work, one of which so much had been forged out of his own experience. Though he had taken pains to alter names and particulars in most of the anecdotes he made use of, the publication of 'Mr. Rivers's Story,' for example, so soon after the events occurred on which it was founded, might have revived his own scandal and hurt the feelings of his beloved wife. The central story also might have been interpreted as a slur on his brother, Charles Caspar, reviving episodes in his life that he would have had forgotten. But no such objection could have been raised to Graves's examination of the clerical calling. Steering a middle course between the worldliness and laxity all too prevalent among the orthodox clergy and the sanctimoniousness equally prevalent among the Methodists, he took up his own position on traditional ground, recording in his novel the fruits of his reflections on his new duties as parish priest.

His doctrinal position was simple. In 1787, when his youngest son, Charles, went up to Oxford, Graves was reminded of the doubts that had once troubled him as a young man. The radical Dr Priestley had just published a *Letter* addressed to the divinity students at both universities, urging them to re-examine coolly the accepted doctrines, especially that of the Trinity, before they entered the ministry, lest they preach what their own reason could not support.[22] Graves responded with a *Letter* addressed to his son Charles, published anonymously to avoid embarrassing the young man. He urged his son to steer clear of 'speculative studies' as much as he could, accusing Priestley of ignoring the distinction between 'things *above* and things *contrary* to reason.' Belief in the Trinity, he urged with some justice, was no more difficult than belief in a deity. 'If you live a sober, diligent, and religious life,' he concluded, 'I trust, you will never be called to an account for embracing speculative opinions, which have been held, with little variation, in the same sense, by the greatest and best men for seventeen hundred years, as the doctrines of the gospel.'[23]

Naïve though it was, that view of history and of society lay at the foundation of Graves's religious position, which rested more on political or sociological grounds than on theological ones. Differences of opinion, he believed, were relatively unimportant. In *Plexippus*, a novel that he published three years later, his hero marries a Roman Catholic and lives happily with her, in spite of differences in religious belief and practice, until death does them part. In the incidental discussions of Catholicism that occur in the novel Graves shows a degree of tolerance that must have been unusual in his time. But there were limits. It 'may be *doubtful*,' he writes, 'which system is preferable [that is, the Anglican or the Roman]: but there can be no *doubt* that it is our duty 'to submit to those who have the rule over us,' and to obey the laws of our country.'[24] Children must be brought up as Protestants and public worship conducted according to the canons of the Church of England. That takes us back to a remarkable statement in the *Letter*:

For what confusion must be the consequence, if so many young people of different religious persuasions, *Papists* and *Presbyterians*; *Baptists* and *Independents*; *Methodists* and *Moravians*; if so many different sectaries, who are generally taught to maintain their peculiar opinions with zeal and obstinacy, were jumbled together in one society, and to have separate places of worship; such a discordant multitude, in the heat of youth, would probably not long be confined to cool reasoning, but support their opinions by the strength of their arms, rather than by that of their arguments; and '*smite each other* with the fist of wickedness,' as they would reciprocally term the resistance of their adversaries.[25]

That preview of modern society may seem unduly pessimistic, but though we may not often smite each other with the fist of wickedness over our religious opinions, we have not achieved that harmonious society that Graves believed in, ordered in its social structure and supported by a common faith.

In a verse essay entitled *The Love of Order*, perhaps sketched out at the same time as he was composing the first draft of *The Spiritual Quixote* and published in the same year with it, Graves develops the same theme in a different way.[26] The motto, taken from Shenstone, neatly sums up the thought of the poem: 'An obvious connexion may be traced between Moral and Physical Beauty; the Love of Symmetry, and the Love of Virtue.' Starting from that premise, he elevates the love of tidiness that he felt within himself and had observed in others into a law of nature and a principle of virtue. He pays no attention for the moment to the aesthetic aspects of his subject, which had also been suggested by Shenstone, though these are developed in the novel. The poem is not his best work by any means, but he had expressed in it thoughts that meant much to him. He thought well enough of it to reprint it in the place of honour at the front of his poetical miscellany *Euphrosyne*.

Contemporary rationalism continued to worry Graves, especially during the later part of the century, as several of his other sermons, obviously composed during the revolutionary period though mostly undated, clearly show. About his personal faith he seldom wrote or spoke.

He was entirely without that kind of piety that leads one to wear one's soul on one's sleeve. Once, however, while on a journey, he sat down in a lonely inn to assuage his boredom by writing one of his most intimate essays. Nothing, he declared in it, could remove his disgust of life except revealed religion and the hope it gave him of a future life. At the heart of his faith was the Incarnation. 'When we contemplate the Deity in a cold philosophical light, and address ourselves to him merely as the Creator and Governor of the universe,' he wrote, 'we are lost in the immensity of the divine nature. The imagination ranges through the boundless regions of space and time, like the dove in the universal deluge, and cannot find even an olive-branch to speak *peace* to the soul; we feel nothing to interest the heart and engage the affections.'[27] But, he went on to say, when we think of that deity mingling with men and instructing them through his prophets and particularly through Jesus of Nazareth, 'that gloom that surrounds us is immediately dispersed; we address him as a friend and benefactor; we find our hopes encouraged and our love inflamed.' God, seen in 'this endearing and familiar light,' helped to satisfy Graves's immense need for friendship. Such a faith was much closer to that of Robert Browning than it was to eighteenth-century deism or the Unitarianism of Priestley. That essay was written for himself, however: he kept it in a drawer for fourteen years before publishing it, and he published it then anonymously. Before the world he preferred to appear as a 'mere moral man.'

In the harmonious society he hoped for, the parish priest, Graves believed, occupied an all-important position, and Graves was determined to live up to his own ideal to the best of his ability. The author of the parish history of Claverton reports a tradition that Graves threw himself into his work with energy and devotion.[28] Unfortunately, documentary evidence is slender. The surviving letters that he wrote from Claverton were addressed mainly to his publishers and his literary friends and so naturally made few references to his parochial activities. But the parish registers, which he kept scrupulously posted, give us a few glimpses of the rector at work, presiding, for example, over vestry meetings at which such thorny problems as rights of way and watercourses were settled and auditing the accounts of the churchwardens and overseers of the poor. The rector himself compiled a list of his predecessors since 1581, which he entered on the endpapers inside the front cover of the register. He liked to think of himself as belonging to a great succession. And he made notes of historical interest about changes in the church and parsonage during his incumbency. But of his spiritual functions, other than baptizing, marrying, and burying, and of his good works no trace remains, unless his tongue-in-cheek comments in *Columella* are to be taken seriously. The plaque erected to his memory in the chancel of his own church, after repeating what had been said in *Public Characters* about his never having been absent from his post for more than a month at any one time during his long incumbency, went on to say that he had been 'distinguished ... by the faithful, zealous, and truly christian Administration of his sacred charge.' The evidence of epitaphs is, of course, always suspect. Epitaphs, as Samuel Johnson once remarked, are not written under oath. But in this one we have no reason to suspect more than a little natural bias.

Although Graves failed to rise in the church, he consolidated his position and expanded laterally in it during the fifty-five years he spent in Claverton. In 1763 he undertook the vicarage of Kilmarsden in addition to the rectory of Claverton at the gift of his wealthy friend and parishioner Ralph Allen.[29] Pluralism has often been thought an abuse, but the only way many a small parish could survive was by sharing the services of a priest with another small neighbouring one. Graves did not take charge in Kilmarsden himself but maintained curates there who performed all the duties of a parish priest under his watchful eyes.[30] Two of these curates were his own sons, all of whom entered the priesthood. He remained vicar of Kilmarsden until August 1794.[31] In 1767 he purchased the advowson of Claverton parish and so became its patron. Throughout his life there he spent considerable sums of his own money on repairs and improvements to the fabric of the church.[32] In 1802, at the age of eighty-seven, he accepted still another living, that of Croscombe, in order to oblige a friend who was the patron of that living and who wanted just to keep it warm by appointing an incumbent who would not live long. Graves was amused by the grim humour of the situation and complained only of what the required dispensations cost him.[33] His career in the church did not bring him great wealth. Kilmarsden brought him only forty pounds a year, out of which thirty went to the curate. His reward was mainly the feeling of being a part of a great national institution.

CHAPTER TEN

Home

Claverton must have seemed like an ideal background for a retired life. As plate 16 shows, it perches on the side of the deep valley scooped out by the Somerset Avon, which, passing the village on its left, makes a wide S-curve around the lofty headland known as Hampton Down, in order to embrace the city of Bath on its right before flowing on through Bristol to the sea. Contemporary descriptions are lyrical about the village. Henry Skrine, a son of Graves's patron and one of his own former pupils, wrote in his *Rivers of Note in Great Britain* (1801) of the 'deep and hollow valley between high impending hills' formed by the Avon, 'some of which are rocky, and others profusely cloathed with wood; abundant villages are scattered along these eminences, and some few seats are beautifully dispersed, so as to command the river and its striking accompaniments in perfection.' After devoting two pages to his own seat, Warley (or Warleigh), Skrine came to Claverton. 'About midway in this ascent,' he wrote, 'immediately overlooking Warley and the river, the pleasing village of Claverton seems to hang suspended.'[1] Richard Warner also praised this 'picturesque and sequestered village': 'Every thing around, indeed, in this vale, breathes inspiration, and tends to encourage the dreams of fancy.'[2] Most of the guides to Bath and its surroundings published in the eighteenth century made similarly brief but eulogistic references to it: it was a 'romantic village'; its manor-house was 'goodly looking,' and its parsonage 'one of the prettiest ... in England.' Best of all, the view from the down back over the city of Bath was superb, though, significantly, the tourist had to turn his back on Claverton in order to enjoy it. But the guides urged him, when he had reached the top of the down, at least to peer down the steep slope beyond him and to admire the village as it lay nestled among the trees.[3]

The village has not changed greatly in appearance since Graves's time, and the recent construction of a bypass road has restored some of the quiet it must have enjoyed in the eighteenth century. Sketches of its principal buildings were made in the latter part of that century by Graves's protégé John Skinner and are reproduced here (see plates 17, 18, and 19). The quaint little medieval church with its ivy-mantled tower was extensively rebuilt in the nineteenth century, but the new building is said to be a replica of the old one. The Jacobean manor-house beside it dwarfed the church, which was too close, but by all accounts it was a fine, hospitable building. Now only the terrace steps remain, along with the entrance gates that must have been behind Skinner's back as he sat at his easel. The pretty parsonage-house was enlarged and rebuilt in the nineteenth century by a wealthy incumbent, though parts of the old building were incorporated in the new, and the garden that Graves laid out with what one eighteenth-century topographer called 'that classick elegance of taste which has long distinguished the proprietor as an author'[4] is cherished by the present owners, who use as a shed for their garden tools the little summer-house he built and called his 'Chantry.' The rest of the village consisted of a few houses and the remains of a winery, which down almost to his time was reputed to produce the best wine made in England. Today much of Claverton Down has been covered with urban sprawl. A technical college has been built, and the eighteenth-century race-track has been replaced by a golf course. But thanks to a conservation order the village itself has escaped the developers.

At once Graves set about improving the beauty of his own little property, applying the principles that such contemporary gardeners as his brother Morgan and his friend Shenstone had applied to their own places. Much has been written about those principles both in the eighteenth century and more recently, and since Graves had neither the time nor the money for a major undertaking, not much needs to be said about them here. Shenstone encouraged him, as his letters to Graves show, appealing to his thirst for society by suggesting that if his garden became a show-place, it would bring him welcome visitors. How much Graves did, beyond building the Chantry, is not clear, but there are references in letters to streams, ruinated walls, urns, and illuminations. It must have been on a small scale, yet Graves expected more from it than visitors. He agreed with Shenstone and the other gardeners of his time in the belief expressed a few years later by Thomas Whately that gardening was a fine art. 'Gardening,' Whately wrote, 'in the perfection to which it has been lately brought in England, is entitled to a place of considerable rank among the liberal arts.'[5] The gardener was to use his materials – ground, wood, water, rocks, and buildings – as the poet uses words and the

painter pigments, to produce epic, elegiac, romantic, or whatever
aesthetic effects he has in mind. 'Take thy plastic spade,' cried William
Mason in his poem *The English Garden*:

> *It is thy pencil; take thy seeds, thy plants,*
> *They are thy colours; and by these repay*
> *With interest every charm she [Nature] lent thy art.*[6]

Like all eighteenth-century art, moreover, the garden taught useful
moral lessons, and the motto Graves borrowed from Shenstone for *The
Love of Order* was echoed again and again, especially by Shenstone himself
in his letters to Graves. Graves could not attempt any of the grand genres
in his little rectory grounds; the best he could do was to create little lyrics,
sometimes comical ones, according to his taste. But he loved his garden
and by means of it provided an ambiance for himself and his family that
was at once agreeable and ennobling. Besides, gardening was fashionable
and unquestionably genteel. In later years he appeared to have come to
prefer wild natural scenery, but as his novels demonstrate, he continued
to associate in his mind natural beauty with virtue, whether or not nature
had been assisted by art.[7]

More important than beautiful surroundings was happiness in human
relationships. Such evidence as there is suggests that Lucy and Richard
were still as devoted to each other as they had been at Whitchurch, Graves,
in Lady Luxborough's memorable words, leaving his wife not 'an inch.' At
least twice during the fifties Graves gave expression to his delight in their
life together. In a poem called 'Domestic Happiness,' composed in 1750,
he wrote:

> *Though chill descends the drizzling rain,*
> *And hollow blows the wind:*
> *Of wintry storms I'll not complain,*
> *While thus my Lucy's kind.*[8]

During the same decade he probably wrote the description of Mrs Rivers
in *The Spiritual Quixote* that is an idealized portrait of Lucy, recognizable
even though 'embellished,' as her husband warned, 'with all the charms
the enraptured imagination is able to give them.' We see her first when
Wildgoose is introduced to her in her home: 'She was sitting (like the
divinity of the place) at the upper end of the room, at her needle, attended
by a boy, and a fine girl about five or six years old. Mrs Rivers received
Wildgoose, as her husband's friend, with a sweet smile; which, like the

sun-shine so much admired in the landscapes of Claude Lorraine, diffused an additional chearfulness over every other object.'9 That scene is impressed upon the reader's mind by means of a frontispiece to volume 2, based on a pen-and-ink sketch drawn by Graves himself (see plates 20 and 21). Clearly the author wished Lucy to preside over that volume as a kind of tutelary spirit of married bliss. From Lady Luxborough, Shenstone's lively friend who was seeing something of the Graveses, comes a glimpse of a lighter and warmer side to Lucy's personality. Lady Luxborough called her Graves's 'agreeable wife' and got from her the promise of a polyanthus root.10 Evidently Lucy not only had a green thumb but, in spite of her rusticity, knew how to cope with fashionable ladies.

Unlike his brothers and sister, Graves's friends accepted Lucy, at first probably out of deference to him but afterwards for herself. When Shenstone visited Whistler in Whitchurch early in 1751, he half expected to hear unfavourable comments on her behaviour with regard to 'forms and ceremonies,' on which Whistler and his family were sticklers. But he did not. Instead he had the satisfaction 'of hearing her person, her temper, and her understanding, much commended.'11 To what extent she shared Graves's social life outside the home and his inner circle of friends is unknown, but there is no reason for dismissing her as unacceptable in the society in which he moved.

Nevertheless, clouds darkened their relationship at times. The memory of their sin lingered and may have been alluded to even in a poem Graves wrote on Lucy's death:

> Yet smiles attest a soul serene;
>   Her mortal frailties are forgiv'n:
> Let Hope illume the tragic scene,
>   My Lucy's pardon's seal'd in heav'n.12

He seemed to lay the blame on her shoulders, but he was troubled in conscience on his own account too, though it is not always clear whether the cause was his sense of guilt or the unfortunate consequences his actions had had for his career. Though Lucy unquestionably held first place in his affections and was accepted by his friends, she could not satisfy his desire for more sophisticated society, especially that of lively and fashionable ladies. Many of his verses alluded to ladies of his acquaintance, and his volumes were dedicated to a great variety of genteel people, both men and women. Copies often turn up with handwritten presentation inscriptions, sometimes accompanied with a few lines of new verse scribbled on the endpapers. Lucy was evidently a little jealous, for Graves set out to placate her in a poem called 'Apology to Lucinda.'[13] The ladies who accepted his dedications and presentation copies, however, were so numerous that his relations with most of them must have been platonic. Lucy's jealousy of them was social rather than sexual.

Not all Graves's feelings for members of the other sex, however, were platonic. In 'An Apology for Unseasonable Rhymes,' written in 1767, he spoke of the difficulty he had in controlling his own 'stormy passions' and of being 'molested by Scandal's darts.'[14] Though he did not specify what Scandal was saying about him, it may have been harping still on the theme of his clandestine marriage and what went before it. But in his *Progress of Gallantry* (1774), an unusually frank poem about sex, there is a hint that he may also have been having an affair at the time with a titled lady. Dedicating the work to 'Lady ———,' whom he called Julia, he explained that he was attracted to her not just by her 'fine sense' or the 'splendor' of her rank and station –

> *No; 'tis your sex this homage claims:*
> *'Tis Beauty still my breast inflames.*[15]

The affair, if that is the right name for it, must have been over by 1776, for the dedication was withdrawn in the second edition, published in that year. Meanwhile, Graves may indeed have been transiently unfaithful to his Lucy. In the *Progress* he went on to describe the grip that his sexual desires continued to have on him:

> *Tho', stealing on with silent pace,*
> *The hand of Time has mark'd my face;*
> *Tho' wrinkles imitate a frown,*
> *And silver locks my temples crown;*
> *Old as I'm grown, and long despair*
> *Of smiles or favours from the Fair:*
> *His gentle sway Love yet maintains,*
> *Yet lingers in my stiffening veins.*[16]

During their married life Richard and Lucy produced two families, the first consisting of three sons, Richard (1747), whose baptism in London has already been noticed, Morgan (1749), born in Whitchurch, and Danvers (1750), born in Claverton. Then there was a gap of fifteen years, caused perhaps by strains in the marriage or by Lucy's ill state of health, followed by a second family, consisting of a daughter, Lucy (1765), and a son, Charles (1770).

CHART 2

Richard Graves's Family

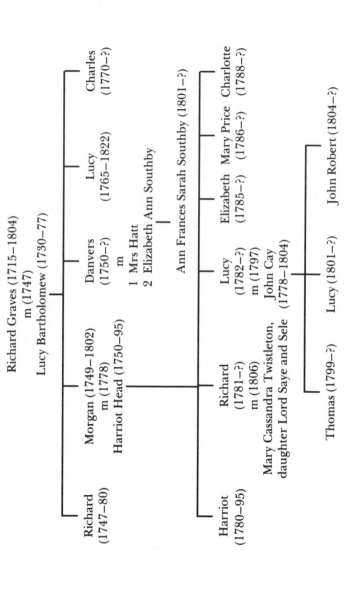

The history of Richard, the first born, is soon told. He matriculated in Oxford in 1767. Afterwards he took orders and served as curate to his father, first in Claverton and afterwards in Kilmarsden.[17] The rector paid thirty pounds a year to his son, who let it be understood that he would act in that capacity only until a better living became available. In 1774 accordingly he moved to Bishop's Lydiard, in the same county, where he had a better living than his father's. He died unmarried in 1780 at the age of 33.[18] His life was a bitter disappointment to his father. He plunged early into dissipation and left behind him mountainous debts that his father felt morally obliged to discharge. What form his dissipation took, whether women, horses, building, or any of the other expensive pleasures known to young men, is not specified, but its cost is ominously hinted at. Claims were still coming in seven years after his death. What made the situation the more galling was that young Richard never took his father's advice, and in fact there seems to have been little or no communication between father and son after the latter left home.

The second son, Morgan, was a different sort of man altogether.[19] He took after his great-grandfather, Richard of Lincoln's Inn, in being in a worldly sense an overwhelming success. He went to Oxford in the same year, 1767, as his older brother Richard and took his degrees in 1770 and 1774.[20] He owed his foothold on the ladder of church preferment to his father's old friend Sir Thomas Head of Langley in Berkshire, with whom he seems to have spent a lot of time in London after leaving Oxford, acting perhaps as secretary or domestic chaplain, or being at least a hanger-on. In April 1774 he became curate to Sir Thomas's brother Richard, vicar of Chieveley, and four years later he was presented by Sir Thomas to the vicarage of Compton, in Berkshire, only a mile or so from Aldworth, where his father and mother had first met some thirty years before. That was only the beginning of Morgan's rise to fortune. In the following summer he married Harriot James, daughter of the Reverend Richard Head, and shortly afterwards resigned the living at Compton in order to accept the rectory of Redgrave-cum-Botesdale in Suffolk, presented to him by the patron of that parish, Rowland Holt, Esquire, father of Lady Head. That was how things worked in the eighteenth century. The Holts were a wealthy family. Mr Holt's great-grandfather, Sir John, had been chief justice of the Court of King's Bench and had acquired the property at Redgrave, including a Tudor hall, from the Bacon family. Rowland, his great-grandson, was a member of Parliament for his county but devoted himself chiefly to improving his house and estate. With the help of Capability Brown, the most celebrated landscape architect of his time, and at a cost of some thirty thousand pounds he laid out a deer park of two hundred acres, studded with oaks and other trees and diversified with an ornamental lake of huge extent, and rebuilt the house in Palladian style, with a portico supported by four Ionic columns, commanding a view of the swans who lived on the lake.

Morgan's father, who visited Redgrave in October 1779, described the house and park and the spacious hospitality that reigned there in a poem probably written as a bread-and-butter letter. What struck him most favourably was the park:

> *Amidst those circling woods, in chastest style,*
> *How sweetly rises yon majestic pile!*
> *The silver lake, from its meand'ring tides,*
> *Reflects each object which adorns its sides.*
> *The gently-rising slopes, the opening glades,*
> *The varied scenes of mingled lights and shades,*
> *A landscape form, which Claude well-pleas'd might view,*
> *Tho' none but Nature's pencil ever drew,*
> *The traveller stops –, or, slowly passing by,*
> *Withdraws reluctant his enamour'd eye.*[21]

Hospitality was on a similar scale. In an old undated newspaper clipping there is an account of a ball given by Rowland Holt at Redgrave Hall. Forty guests arrived at three in the afternoon for a splendid dinner, after which they drank champagne and claret and danced until three in the morning, pausing only about eleven in the evening for a supper even more splendid than the dinner had been.

Morgan evidently throve in these gilded surroundings. In 1788 his patron presented him to a second living, Hinderclay, from which the income was five hundred pounds a year, in addition to his income, whatever it may have been, from Redgrave. Five hundred pounds alone was ten times the average clerical income in this period, and so Morgan's total income must have made him the envy of all clerical eyes. Evidently he hired others to do his work, for when his daughter was about to be married, the certificate of banns was signed by a curate.[22] It is pleasant to record that Morgan, unlike Richard, remained on good terms with his father and that there was coming and going between Redgrave and Claverton and young voices in the parsonage to cheer up the lonely old man. In 1797 Lucy, Morgan's daughter, thoughtfully brought her husband-to-be, John Cay, to Claverton so that they might be married there by her grandfather.[23] Of Morgan's five other children, his only son, Richard Charles Head, married Cassandra Twistleton, daughter of the thirteenth Baron Saye and Sele in 1806,[24] but in 1802 Morgan had died at the early age of 53.

With the third son, Danvers, the pendulum swung back again. He went to Oxford a year after his brother Richard and succeeded him at Kilmarsden for approximately a year before moving to Chieveley in Berkshire, where he was curate for nearly twenty years to the Reverend Richard Head, who had helped his brother in a similar fashion. Afterwards he moved to East Woodhay in the same country, where he was curate until at least 1802. According to Kilvert he died in France. Nothing more is known about him. Perhaps his father died knowing little more himself, for in 1804, in a poem written just before his death, he complained that he rarely saw his sons' faces.[25] Danvers, moreover, was as shameless a spendthrift as his older brother Richard. In his will, made in 1800, their father left nothing directly to Danvers but put money in the hands of his executors to enable them to discharge at least some of the debts and liberate his 'son Danvers Graves from the difficulties in which he had so imprudently or rather madly involved himself.' Strong language for a last will and testament!

The two members of the second family were in many ways closer to their father than were any of the older three children. Lucy, the only daughter, was in some ways the closest to him of them all. Twelve years old when her mother died, she suffered the fate of many daughters in her time and ours who forgo the prospect of a husband, children, and a home of their own in order to keep house for widowed fathers. Graves was in many ways in advance of his age in his understanding of the plight of unmarried women, adverting to it more than once in his writings, most specifically in an essay entitled 'The Consolation of Neglected Virgins,' in which he declared that in heaven, where there will be neither marrying nor giving in marriage, no individual of either sex will be the property of one or the other.[26] Unlike most of his contemporaries he seldom ridiculed old maids, treating them sympathetically in his novels and in *Plexippus*, the last of them, calling the ones he knew 'some of the most *useful*, and ... the most *agreeable* part of the human species.'[27]

Having been denied love, which her father declared in another essay to be the proper role for women,[28] Lucy fell back on being useful and agreeable to him. Graves, overreacting to his own experiences, was too protective of her. In a poem entitled 'Parental Affection,' written when she was fourteen, approximately the same age as his wife had been when he met her, he expressed his fears that his daughter might have to face problems similar to those that he had forced on his beloved and that she might not be as fortunate as his wife had been in achieving marriage and a happy home.[29] In spite of all his sympathy for unmarried women, his love for her, his fears for her well-being, and his sense of guilt combined to rob her of the fulfilment she had a right to expect. The comic plot of his opera, *The Coalition*, involves two proposed clandestine marriages not unlike his own, but they are circumvented, and one of the characters in the lyrical part of it gives voice to what were probably Graves's own feelings, when he sings:

> *a daughter of mine*
> *Should rather on chalk and on sealing-wax pine,*
> *Than marry before she's of age;*
> *I'd keep the fond slut*
> *In some cottage or hut,*
> *Pent up like a bird in a cage.*[30]

So Lucy stayed at home with her father and was rewarded with his parental love and gratitude. In the nineties, however, when she was approaching thirty, he sent her away, feeling that she ought to have some life of her own:

> *My daughter, so attentive, good and kind;*
> *Must not be always thus at home confin'd;*
> *Nor could I bear to see her youth engage*
> *Daily to nurse th'infirmities of age.*[31]

In *Reveries of Solitude* (1793) he complained of loneliness, and from that time to his death, so far as is known, he lived alone. Where Lucy went is unknown, but she apparently had friends or relations in both Bromley and London to whom she may have gone, for in 1822, when she died, she had been living in Bromley and was buried in St Martin's, Ludgate.[32] She died a spinster. In his will her father had provided for her generously, giving her at least as much money as he gave to each of her brothers, in addition to the advowson of the living at Claverton and a couple of small farms. She was also his residuary legatee. It was the least he could do.

The youngest son, Charles, was the apple of his father's eye, but his history, when it is not obscure, is melancholy. His father's efforts to shield him from infidelity while at Oxford have already been noticed. He took the degree of BA in 1790 and that of MA in 1793 and in the following year was instituted vicar of Kilmarsden, where two of his brothers had preceded him as curates. He stayed there until some time in 1804, a few months before his father's death,[33] but why he resigned and where he went are unknown and puzzling. For his sister Lucy, who inherited the advowson of Claverton from her father, was directed in his will to give the living to Charles unless, as the will went on ominously to say, 'he should meet with any obstacle to his getting possession' of it. Obstacle there apparently was, for Charles did not succeed his father. The nature of that obstacle, however, is unknown, though it was most likely raised by the 'villainous conspiracy' against the son of which his father complained in a letter to a friend in 1799.[34] In another letter, written two years later, Graves referred to 'an iniquitous Combination of *interested* and unprincipled Scoundrels' who were threatening his son. They probably included in their number the conspiracy of the earlier letter. Blackmailers, perhaps? Whatever they were, Charles disappears at this time altogether from the record. But in spite of anxieties Graves called Charles 'ye best of sons,' wanted him to have the rectory of Claverton, and left him his library. Charles was not a spendthrift like his brothers and was able to help Danvers out with a loan of two hundred pounds.

Graves's love for his wife survived the vicissitudes of family life and possible infidelities. In 1772 he was still sounding the same note as in earlier writings, referring to her in a prose essay as 'the dear partner of my joys and sorrows, who is chiefly responsible for what pleasure is experienced in a life full of vexations.'[35] Soon she was to inflict on him the greatest of his sorrows. In 1775 she suffered a dangerous illness,[36] and two years later, on 1 May, she died, at the early age of forty-six. When her husband noted her death and burial in his parish register, he added in the margin: 'Tristes Calendæ,' and he presently put up a handsome festooned urn in a niche in the south wall of the chancel of his church, with the following inscription:

LUCIÆ CONIUNGI CARISSIMÆ RICHARDUS GRAVES CONIUNX
INFELISSIMUS FECIT ET SIBI.

(Richard Graves, her inconsolable husband, has erected this urn in memory of Lucy, his dearest wife, and of himself.) It seemed to him in the agony of his grief that his own life was over too. He also wrote a poem, entitled 'On the Death of a Much-Lov'd Wife.' It expressed forcibly and at times movingly the distraught grief of a bereaved husband who longs to be reunited with his wife in another world and who still feels her unseen presence watching over him and their children. He worked the poem into the text of the novel that he was writing at the time, *Columella*, and two years later republished it in *Euphrosyne*, an anthology of poems, where it was embellished with an engraving of the festooned urn and the elaborately carved niche in which it sat (see plate 22). His grief is obviously sincere and his sense of loss devastating.

Graves was sixty-two when Lucy died and had another twenty-seven years to live. Love lingered for a long time yet. In his last poem, published in the year of his death, he wrote:

> *The lovely sex I still admire;*
> *But, ah! what hopes can they inspire?*[37]

At the age of eighty-nine his admiration had no doubt become at last platonic, but all his life he had been a strong advocate of sex, his feelings about it balancing uneasily with his puritanical conscience. As early as 1742 he had written a reply to a poem he had read in the *Derby Journal* called 'The Anti-platonic,' whose gist hardly needs to be summarized. In answer Graves wrote:

> *Could love secure a* lasting *bliss,*
> *Thy system were not much amiss.*[38]

Consequently, he went on, one must turn for lasting joy to virtue. He sounds as if he wanted to add the expletive 'alas.' In his last novel, *Plexippus*, he stated his simple hedonism even more explicitly: 'By a wise designation of Providence, the first and highest interest of mankind (next to their religious concerns) is their success in the mutual intercourse of the sexes. For, as the mere existence of the species is prior in the order of nature to their being rich or powerful, or otherwise distinguished, we see them daily sacrificing every other consideration to this most important one.'[39] Graves found it as hard to reconcile the claims made upon him by nature, matrimony, and conscience as most people do.

In spite of his beautiful surroundings and his fair share of matrimonial bliss, Graves's family was a mixed blessing to him. Though all his children were dearly loved and cared for in their infancy and the four sons were given Oxford educations, two of them disappointed him bitterly by their debts, their dissipation, and their rebelliousness. 'My children,' he wrote in 1772, 'whom I love beyond every thing are yet fresh sources of my solicitude, as the prospect of their future success in life seems very precarious; some of them appearing less attentive to procure a comfortable establishment in the world, than to grasp at every phantom of present pleasure; which must probably end in a habit of dissipation and a dislike of, and inaptitude for, any useful employment.'[40] What had gone wrong in what ought to have been a happy family? It is impossible to judge at this distance in time. But Graves's preoccupations may have stood in his way as husband and father, especially when he had twenty schoolboys living in the house with his family and competing for his attention. But the picture is not entirely black. Of Morgan, the second son, Graves must always have approved, and the two younger children shared many of his tastes and gladdened his heart.

CHAPTER ELEVEN

School

Writing to a friend in 1801 Graves recalled his having submitted 'daily to the Crambe repetita, of τύπτω, τύψω, τετύφε of above forty boys for near forty years.'[1] The Latin phrase he used, taken from Juvenal, is a proverbial one meaning monotonous fare (literally, warmed-over cabbage), and the Greek words are the three first principal parts of the verb 'I strike,' which the boys were learning by heart. Graves was referring to the daily grind he underwent as a schoolmaster during the greater part of his life in Claverton. Though the actual date is unknown, he must have set up his school shortly after his arrival there in 1750. He was short of funds (or thought that he was), and he was still young and vigorous, eager to have something to do more intellectually challenging than being shepherd to his little flock of parishioners. He must have given the school up in approximately 1790, when he was sixty-five. At first he took in just twenty boys, who slept in the parsonage house along with his family, a wing for their accommodation having been added to the building thanks to the generosity of his rich friend Ralph Allen. Eventually he had at least forty pupils, for whom he rented the top storey of the manor house next door.

The weight of the economic motive in Graves's mind for establishing a school is hard to estimate because the extent of his income from other sources is unknown. As capital he had the 'younger brother's fortune' that his older brother Morgan had given him when their father died. As for income there was, of course, a certain amount from his livings, but Claverton was tiny and the amount of its contribution to his income is unknown. Even when the ten pounds a year he earned at Kilmarsden is added to it, the total must have been small. Possibly Graves got a little extra from his sinecure as private chaplain to Lady Chatham, but it could not have been much. As for his publications, though they produced some money for him, the reward he sought in them was primarily psychological rather than financial. His letters to the Dodsley brothers, his usual publishers, contain many expressions of gratitude for presents of money and books, but there is little in them to suggest that the brothers felt themselves under any contractual obligation to him. What they sent him were free-will offerings.

Perhaps from all these sources Graves received enough to live on in the quiet way expected of a rural parson. But he had become accustomed to rich living in Tissington and at All Souls, and he probably had a share of the Graves family weakness of extravagance. Whatever his circumstances actually were, he set up a school and the school was a success and remained a success for nearly forty years.[2] Although in later years he occasionally complained of poverty, as when he regretted his inability to subscribe more than a couple of guineas to a literary project referred to him by a friend, protesting that until Lady Day he would not have enough cash on hand to meet 'domestic demands,'[3] at other times he seems to have been surprisingly well off. In 1790, for example, he was able to lend his nephew Walwyn, brother Morgan's oldest son, the large sum of £2,600,[4] and in 1794 he lost £1,000 in the failure of the Bath City Bank. (In order to lose £1,000 one must have £1,000.) And at various times he was able to make improvements to his church and parsonage house at his own expense.[5] When he made his will in 1800 he left legacies amounting to between £2,000 and £3,000, though he had to direct his daughter, to whom he had left the advowson of Claverton, to mortgage it in order to pay herself the legacy he had also left her. So he can hardly be described as either rich or poor. Generally speaking he was in comfortable circumstances, able to afford books and holiday trips to London. Probably he owed his position mainly to his school, and so the warmed-over cabbage of his pupils' recitations cannot have invaded his nostrils with too stale an odour.

His pupils were the sons of gentlemen and professional men, unlike those attending the King's School in Bath, who were the sons of local merchants. He treated his pupils as members of his family and had a gift for making friends of them. The size of his staff is another unknown. There were servant's, of course, to help with the work. In a comical poem written by him in 1766, after the school had moved into the great house, he referred to a Mrs B——, who was the cook, and a Mr B——, presumably her husband, who was an usher or under-master.[6] But the Graves family too must always have been much involved. Perhaps he enlisted the help of his sons with the teaching when they grew old enough and were not otherwise employed. But who darned the boys' stockings, looked after them when they were sick, and comforted them when they were lonely? Undoubtedly Graves himself and his wife. In the spring of 1758, for example, when he and his wife made a holiday jaunt into Berkshire and London, they took along with them one of their older pupils, a boy who had been with them for five years and who, as Graves explained in a letter to Robert Dodsley, was 'so destitute of friends amongst his own family capable of taking Care of him, that his Father had requested me to take him with me.'[7] The Graveses were obliged on his account to decline Dodsley's offer of hospitality. Even as late as 1763, when the school had grown to its maximum size, Graves had to call off a projected Whitsuntide holiday because the parents of two of his boys insisted that at least one of the Graveses stay home while they went away on a holiday.[8] At another time Graves was 'entirely engross'd' for a fortnight with another of his pupils, who had suffered an accident of some sort.[9]

But it was his sense of humour as much as his sympathy that helped Graves out in his relations with the boys. The humorous poem just mentioned originated in a typical situation. Dr Harrington, a Bath physician and friend whose three sons were among his pupils, had written them a letter in humorous verse. They took the ration of pocket-money he had enclosed to Mrs B——, who filled her oven with cakes and pies, and the letter to the headmaster, who read it and nearly 'burst his buttons with laughter.' He sat down and wrote another letter, also in humorous verse, that the three boys might send to their father in reply. The incident reveals the friendly atmosphere that prevailed in the school. Graves's letters are full of his concern for his boys, particularly at the end of term, when he sent them home for the holidays with 'proper instructions.'[10] He was at least as much interested in their personal development as he was in their learning, having only contempt for the usual product of the big public schools, who too often contracted an 'intrepid air and petulance, which too many young men discover, who have been hackneyed from their very infancy in some of our public seminaries.'[11] He understood boys well enough to know that such aggressiveness was usually a cover-up for insecurity and emotional starvation.

Graves's methods of instruction were most likely conventional, and his curriculum the course of reading in the Latin and Greek classics that constituted the intellectual heritage of the Western world. 'As for learning,' he made one of Dr Harrington's sons write:

> ... indeed we drive all before us;
> Read Virgil and Horace, and Martial and Florus.
> The two first are fine — but perhaps I am partial,
> For at present, methinks, I am fonder of Martial.[12]

It was characteristic of Graves to introduce his pupils to texts not often included in the courses of reading followed in the schools of his time and to make his boys enjoy them by his lively manner of presentation. In 1766, for example, on a suggestion from Bishop Warburton, whose son Ralph was another of Graves's pupils, he introduced Erasmus's *Dialogues*, 'a book,' as the bishop admitted, 'long out of fashion.'[13] How far afield Graves ranged it would be hard to say, but the tone of the preliminaries in several of his translations suggests that they originated in his teaching. If he had experimentally introduced the life of Commodus by the Greek historian Herodianus, of which he published an English translation under the title of *Heir Apparent* in 1789, he did so because of the useful lessons it taught of the 'baneful influence of *unlimited* power on the morals and conduct of those princes, who are possessed of it,'[14] and, although he did not say so, because he thought the boys would be entertained by the strange story of a Roman emperor who was also a prize-fighter. It would certainly have been an unusual school text, but Graves was never daunted by the unusual. He is likely to have had more faith in the rightness of his own tastes, however eccentric, than in educational theories, for which he had little use. In 1762, for example, he was reading a book on education by J.-J. Rousseau called *Emile* which had just been published, and reported on it to a friend: 'I am likewise in the middle of Rousseau's *Treatise* on Education, which makes some noise. There are some good observations on nursing and management of infants. But he is verbose, pedantick, and chimerical.'[15] A fair comment from an experienced, practical-minded teacher, not apt to be swept off his feet even by a book destined to make much noise in the world.

Unfortunately, no written records of Graves's school survive, but it is possible to identify a few of his pupils. Of the three Harrington boys, already mentioned, nothing further is known. Ralph Warburton, son of the bishop of Gloucester, whom Graves introduced to Erasmus, returned home from school in 1768, according to his father, 'taller, better, and wiser,'[16] but took sick and died at the early age of nineteen. He was buried in Claverton churchyard. Prince Hoare, son of the Bath artist William Hoare, is sometimes described as also having been one of Graves's pupils, but if he was it must have been for only a term or two, for he certainly owed his education mainly to the grammar school in Bath.[17] But he met Graves somehow and became a warm friend and admirer. He will be noticed at greater length in a later context. Henry Skrine, son of the lord of the manor of Warley who had presented Graves to the living of Claverton, was certainly one of his pupils in his early years, before going on to Winchester and Oxford. He earned some fame in later years as a writer, publishing among other works a book on the *Rivers of Note in Great*

Britain. Though Skrine spent relatively little of his time in later life at Warley, Graves kept in touch with members of his family, as numerous dedications and allusions in his works show.[18] Another boy who is said to have been one of Graves's pupils was Thomas Bowdler, who gave a new word to the language when he bowdlerized the text of Shakespeare's plays by cutting out all the naughty words and allusions.[19] If he was a pupil, however, he must not have caught Graves's love of the rough-and-tumble language of the people.

Undoubtedly the most famous of Graves's pupils was Thomas Robert Malthus, best known for his highly original *Essay on Population*. Son of the eccentric Daniel Malthus, according to his most recent biographer he spent nine years under Graves at Claverton, from the age of seven to that of sixteen, before going on briefly to a dissenting academy and then to Cambridge. A glimpse of his character as a boy, as well as of Graves's interest in his pupils' personalities, is given in two letters from Graves to Daniel Malthus. 'Don Roberto,' wrote Graves, calling the boy affectionately by his nickname, 'though most peaceably inclined, and seeming even to give up his just rights, rather than to dispute with any man, yet, paradox as it may seem, loves fighting for fighting's sake, and delights in bruising; he has but barely recovered his eye-sight, and yet I have much ado to keep him from trying again the chance of war; and yet he and his antagonist are the best friends in the world, learn together, assist each other, and I believe, love each other better than any two boys in the school.' Don Roberto won his tutor's heart by his sense of humour. 'He has finished Horace,' continued Graves, 'and has read five satires in Juvenal with apparent taste, and I never saw a boy of his age enter more instantaneously into the humour of the fifth satire, which describes so feelingly the affronts and mortifications which a parasite meets with at a great man's table.' Altogether the father must have found it a satisfactory report and must have been impressed with Graves's understanding of his pupil.[20]

CHAPTER TWELVE

Friends, Old and New

During the years immediately following his move to Claverton, the friends who meant most to Graves were still the two made in his youth, Whistler and Shenstone. Whistler was the closer of the two, for Graves had shared with him the secret of his marriage and accepted many kindnesses from him while keeping rather aloof from Shenstone and fending off his inquiries. Whistler was warm hearted, kindly, full of charm, and free from any desire to pass judgment. The sort of life he lived in Whitchurch with his mother and wealthy stepfather would not have been disagreeable to Graves, as it was to Shenstone, a life devoted, as Shenstone put it in a letter to Graves, to 'too much trivial elegance, too much punctillio ... and perhaps, as you express it, too much *speculation*.'[1] 'Speculation' did not here mean flights of abstract thought, which was in short supply at Whitchurch, but rather *gossip*, a sense of the word Graves probably picked up from *King Lear*.[2] Card-playing was their main occupation: 'I think they do nothing *else*,' complained Shenstone. Graves is not known to have been an ardent card-player, but he would not have felt out of place in the society of card-players as Shenstone did and would have enjoyed a visit there if he had been able to make one before Whistler died on 26 May 1754. Then he hurried over. Learning of his friend's death simultaneously through letters from both Whistler's brother John and Graves, Shenstone had been broken hearted and had had to make three or four attempts at a letter of condolence before he managed to write one that he could send. 'The Triumvirate, which was the greatest Happiness, & the greatest Pride of my Life,' he wrote to Graves, 'is broken! The Fabrick of our Friendship has lost a noble Column!'[3] He spoke for Graves too, whose own words on the occasion have been lost. Whistler had died prematurely at the age of forty, probably of gout, which had been plaguing him for some years. Nearly forty years later, in an essay 'On Intemperance,' Graves listed 'W——' among a number of his friends who had died of '*comparative* intemperance.'[4] By that time, however, he had become a bit of a health faddist and was rather proud of his own longevity.

If a coolness had developed between Graves and Shenstone, neither of them admitted to it and neither said anything that he had reason to regret afterwards. After 1750 their friendship was re-established, and visits back and forth occasionally took place. But the friendships of middle age are different from those of youth. Letters were less frequent, Graves having declared himself against 'a regular correspondence,'[5] and plans for visits sometimes failed to bear fruit. In May 1755, for example, Richard and Lucy did visit The Leasowes, though Shenstone confessed to Lady Luxborough that he would have put them off on account of other engagements except that he saw them so seldom.[6] The letters of this later period seem less full of personal feeling than the earlier ones, being devoted instead to common interests, especially literature. Shenstone's best creative period was over, but he was still writing occasionally, and he and Graves consulted each other about their work. They were also involved together in several literary projects, which will be described later, Graves's contributions to many of them being larger than appeared. For he insisted on almost total anonymity. Shenstone was undoubtedly sincere in wishing that Graves could bring himself to play a more public role as author, but probably he never considered the possibility that at least part of Graves's motive for not doing so was a desire to preserve his independence. Graves knew that his own talents, whatever they were, were different from Shenstone's, and he had no wish either to expose himself to the embarrassment of well-meant amendments from his friend or to be known as a disciple. During the fifties, for example, he wrote a substantial draft of *The Spiritual Quixote*, the work that most completely expressed his individuality, and apparently permitted Shenstone a quick look at his manuscript. But it is not clear that he accepted the advice that his friend volunteered. In fact, so far as is known he did not allow Shenstone the second and more leisurely reading he expected, and disappointed him by making no further references in his letters to his work in progress.[7] Graves was not quarrelling with Shenstone, whose pre-eminence as a man of letters Graves readily admitted, but he was protecting his own individuality.

Literature, however, was not occupying the whole of Shenstone's time. He was busy also making his farm at The Leasowes into a show-place that would attract devotees of taste from far and wide:

He built the ruinated priory [wrote Graves], adorned with the arms of his friends on gothic shields; he cut vistas to shew, from several points or view, the beautiful spire of Hales-owen; he erected urns, or placed up inscriptions, to his friends or to his favourite writers; he placed a cast of the Medicean Venus in his shrubbery, and one of the piping fawn in a small circle of firs, hazels, and other elegant shrubs, which were some of the most expensive ornaments of his place; for many of his seats and cascades were made by the manual labour of an old servant, under his own direction.[8]

In winter, when his *ferme ornée* was naked and shivered in the brisk Warwickshire winds, Shenstone busied himself indoors. But in summer crowds of visitors had to be shown all his marvels from the best points of view.

It was as a gardener that Shenstone made his first appearance in one of Graves's books, in volume 3 of *The Spiritual Quixote*. Wildgoose and Jerry visit The Leasowes, which, Graves writes, 'began to be frequented by people of distinction from all parts of England, on account of the natural beauties, which, by the mere force of genius and good taste, Mr. Shenstone had improved and exhibited to so much advantage.' Shenstone shows the two pilgrims 'his cascades, which are so deservedly admired, and the reservoirs that supplied them; the prospects of the country from various points of view; his grove, dedicated to Virgil; his urns, statues, and his admirable inscriptions.' Wildgoose is much impressed, but, being also troubled in conscience by such a display of what he considers paganism, he and Jerry under cover of darkness pull down one of Shenstone's naked statues and depart, leaving behind them a letter in which Wildgoose expresses his fear that Shenstone has set up idols in his heart. An engraving of the scene was chosen as a frontispiece, replacing the picture of wild nature in Derbyshire that Graves had intended, making Shenstone's garden preside over this volume of the novel (see plate 23). Though light-hearted, Graves was writing in sympathy with Shenstone, going out of his way to refer also to his friend's 'fine poetic talents and polite learning.'[9]

When a campaign was launched in 1762 to secure from the king a pension for Shenstone as a person of 'uncommon merit which has not met with an adequate reward from the random dispensations of Fortune,' Graves threw himself into it with a will. Robert Dodsley, the celebrated London publisher, seems to have acted as secretary to the committee, which also included some very socially distinguished persons. Acting presumably as a member of the committee, Graves wrote a letter on 24 December to an unidentified correspondent, scolding him for not having answered a communication from Mr Dodsley by return of post. He went on to explain why the government thought it necessary to take the step his correspondent had boggled at, of investigating Shenstone's actual financial position before making application to the king, and wound up this part of his letter by explaining his reasons for Shenstone's preferring a pension to a sinecure. His only criticism of the way the business was being conducted was that everything seemed to have to go through too many hands: 'To M^{rs} C—— by the hands of M^r D—— who is to communicate it to M^r W—— B & to M^r W—— a friend of Lord B——.'[10] Writing about the petition some years later, Graves said that he did not know that it had ever got as far as the king, but he did know that Shenstone believed that Lord Loughborough, then member of Parliament for Ayr, had spoken on Shenstone's behalf to Lord Bute, the prime minister.[11] No trace of any such petition now exists among Lord Bute's voluminous papers, but it would have come to nothing anyway because on 11 February 1763 Shenstone died. He was only forty-eight, and he made the second in Graves's odd list of friends who had been killed before their time by '*comparative* intemperance.' But earlier Graves had given the cause of death more plausibly as a 'fever of the putrid kind.'

Graves's feelings upon receiving news of the final dissolution of the triumvirate that had meant so much to him must have been melancholy, but no letters of that date have survived that might have recorded them. He wrote a poem on the occasion, however, later printed in *Euphrosyne*, a painful effusion in blank verse that was introduced by an epigraph from 'Lycidas' and that fully justifies all of Samuel Johnson's harsh strictures against pastoral elegies.[12] Perhaps his feelings were still too raw, or perhaps he was trying too hard, knowing what Shenstone would have expected from him. He expressed his feelings more conventionally but far more simply and movingly some years later in some verses carved on an urn dedicated to Shenstone's memory in Halesowen churchyard:

> *Reader! if Genius, Taste refin'd,*
> *A native Elegance of mind,*
> *If Virtue, Science, Manly Sense,*
> *If Wit, that never gave Offence,*
> *The clearest Head, the tenderest Heart,*
> *In thy esteem e'er claim'd a part;*
> *Ah! smite thy breast, and drop a tear;*
> *For know,* Thy *Shenstone's dust lies here.*[13]

Shenstone's death did not put an end to Graves's involvement in his affairs, for along with Robert Dodsley and John Hodgetts, Shenstone's cousin, he became one of the poet's executors, and although he could play only an inactive role because of his isolation in Claverton, he was caused endless trouble. The decisions of the executors were contested in the courts by Mary Cutler, Shenstone's housekeeper and, as some said, his mistress or even his wife, who spun out an ambiguity in the will into three suits in Chancery. She obviously felt that even an annuity of the amount she claimed under the will was an inadequate return for the services she had rendered the poet in his lifetime, whatever they had been.

The only part of Shenstone's estate with which Graves was himself actively concerned was the literary remains. Shenstone had left behind a quantity of unpublished manuscripts, including copy for a projected volume of collected poems over which he had been fussing for some time, at least since 1760, when Graves wrote some lines to be included among the commendatory verses.[14] These manuscripts had become the legal property of the executors, and Dodsley bought out John Hodgetts with a cash payment of three hundred pounds.[15] He and Graves then got together to peruse the lot and to revise and correct them for publication. Dodsley offered Graves a share in the profits from this venture in publication in return for his editorial work, but Graves thought it advisable on many accounts to refuse. Nevertheless, he was prepared to give Dodsley a good deal of help. 'Yet I hope you do not intend to deprive me,' he wrote, 'of the pleasure which I propos'd to myself of giving you all the Assistance in my power – to correct & prepare them for the press.'[16] Other literary people, such as William Melmoth and Dr Lowth, were to be consulted on the choice of poems, and Graves was to do most of the rest. He found that he could not go to London for the purpose as he had hoped, and directed that the manuscripts be sent to him at Claverton. In the following year the work appeared in two handsome octavo volumes, the first containing the poems and the second the prose works, along with a description and map of The Leasowes said to have been written by Dodsley and a sheaf of commendatory verses, including the one by Graves, to which he had uncharacteristically put his name. No credit was given to him, however, for his editorial work or to anyone else, except that the very brief preface was signed by Dodsley. The roles of editor, publisher, printer, and bookseller were not differentiated in the eighteenth century in the same way as they are today, and the way in which this work had been put together was not uncommon at that time. Graves did not feel that he had been treated ungenerously. The work he did on the collection was a labour of love, a tribute to his dead friend.[17]

In 1765 the third volume appeared, consisting of Shenstone's letters. Graves had not entirely approved of their publication,[18] knowing how easily remarks made in private to intimate friends may be misinterpreted when made public and probably also fearing lest information about his own private affairs, so long hushed up, should become common knowledge. What led him to change his mind was most likely his recollection of how Shenstone had felt when informed that his letters to Whistler had been destroyed by John Whistler: 'I am considerably mortified,' he wrote, 'by Mr. John W[histler]'s conduct in regard to my letters to his brother ... I look upon my letters as some of *my* chef-d'œuvres; and, could I be supposed to have the least pretentions to propriety of style or sentiment, I should imagine it must appear, principally, in my letters to his brother, and one or two more friends.'[19] Like many other eighteenth-century men of letters, Shenstone had undoubtedly anticipated the eventual publication of his correspondence and had written with one eye on posterity. But he was prepared to leave to the discretion of those into whose hands the letters fell the extent to which their more private bits might be made public.

Graves wrote the preface to the volume and almost certainly edited the letters themselves. The two manuscripts now in the Osborn Collection at Yale and the dashes and other marks of omission in the printed texts (many of which Graves filled in by hand in his own copy) give one a fair notion of how he went about his work.[20] He began by rejecting some letters altogether, such as the one Shenstone had written to him in June 1748,[21] probably because of extended references in it to the rumours that were circulating then about Graves's marriage and to his sister's love affair. Even in the letters that he included he not only often deleted proper names or reduced them to initial letters in the interest of discretion but sometimes also either deleted statements about personal matters or substituted evasive words. Occasionally he seems also to have made stylistic improvements. The printed text of Shenstone's letter to Graves on the occasion of Whistler's death, for example, differs considerably from the sent copy now at Yale, and the variants are almost all stylistic.[22] The existing evidence does not enable one to decide what actually happened: did Graves make the changes himself, or had he a revised draft in his hands as well as the sent copy? The letter had been written on a significant occasion, and such a letter by such a writer, once published, was likely to be quoted. So Shenstone may have drafted and redrafted it more than once. Or Graves may well have felt that he was rendering his friend a service by seeing to it that none of his chef d'œuvres appeared without the greatest possible propriety of style and sentiment.

Today Graves's editorial proceedings may seem odd if not dishonest, but they were entirely acceptable in the eighteenth century, when it was expected that the letters of a celebrity would be carefully vetted before being published so as to remove anything that might give offence or blemish the reputation of the writer. The letters of Pope and others clearly illustrate this point.

Ten years later, when William Mason published his *Memoirs of Thomas Gray*, Graves was distressed to find that Mason had let a number of harsh criticisms of Shenstone's poetry stand in the letters of Gray that he included in his book. Mason had not exercised the same editorial prerogative that Graves had when he edited Shenstone's. So in August 1775 Graves sprang to Shenstone's defence in an anonymous letter to the editor of the *Monthly Review*, naming ten or a dozen of Shenstone's poems that in his opinion had sufficient merit to shield him from Gray's *'ridicule and contempt'* and maintaining that Shenstone's 'natural genius' was not inferior to either Mason's or Gray's. Such faults as Shenstone's poetry suffered from, he maintained, were due either to premature publication or to the poet's lack of the urbanity that Gray's early contacts with the great world had given him. It was a warm tribute.[23]

This occasion may have been responsible for suggesting to Graves the subject of his second novel, *Columella*, published two years later. The title character had withdrawn from the great world and buried himself in the country in an effort to find happiness. Almost from the start he was identified in the public mind with Shenstone.[24] But though Graves had drawn upon his memories of Shenstone for his delineation of the character of Columella, yet Columella was not Shenstone nor Shenstone/ Columella. Graves could not possibly have intended Columella for a faithful portrait of the friend whom he had so much loved and admired and whom he was prepared to defend against what he considered unfair criticism. But he was also aware that Shenstone had had eccentricities if not weaknesses, that he had not made the fullest use of his considerable talents and had not derived as much happiness from his self-centred way of life at The Leasowes as he had expected. The novel was not a biography of Shenstone, much less a satire on him, but rather an apologue in which some parts of Shenstone's experience were used to illustrate a theme: the dangers implicit in a retired way of life.[25]

Columella was a success, at least at Bath. On its account a right reverend bishop took the author graciously by the hand (as Graves reported to James Dodsley, his publisher); the duke of Somerset expressed himself as much pleased with it; and Christopher Anstey, the poet, introduced him to Mrs Elizabeth Montagu, queen of the bluestockings, who invited Graves to dinner. She complimented him on his choice of subject and on his manner of executing it. In the course of their conversation she also remarked that Fénelon's 'Ode on Solitude,' written on a similar subject, was 'a beautiful thing' and ought to be translated into English. Graves took the hint, adding '2 or 3 more little things upon similar Subjects from Boileau and Fontenelle,'[26] and published his translations in a little pamphlet in 1784 under the title *Fleurettes*.[27] Shenstone was nowhere mentioned, but the collection was really a footnote to *Columella*.

Four years later Mrs Montagu spurred Graves into action again. Johnson's life of Shenstone, published in 1781 in volume 10 of his *Lives of the Poets*, contained some remarks about the Lyttelton family that irked her as well as a number of others about Shenstone that displeased Graves. So he undertook the assignment willingly, producing in 1788 his *Recollection of Some Particulars in the Life of the late William Shenstone, Esq.* Johnson's life had not been an attack on Shenstone, but Graves must have felt that the learned doctor had blown both hot and cold upon him and that his well-known prejudices against pastoral poetry, blank verse, and country life had warped his judgment. Graves chose a phrase from Horace for his motto – 'Vellem in Amicitia sic erraremus' – which he translated in these words:

> *In friendship I would wish to be*
> *Accus'd of partiality.*[28]

His book consists of a series of personal reminiscences and observations, clearly showing Graves's partiality but not marred by rancour or disrespect for Johnson, whom he had always admired. Graves took issue with him, however, on all the points on which Mrs Montagu and he felt that the great critic had erred, doing so with consistent good manners, an unusual quality in eighteenth-century literary controversy. His most severe remark was an objection to Johnson's comment that landscape gardening as practised by Shenstone demanded 'no great powers of mind':

But, in making this remark, he seems to have been contemplating some zig-zag shrubberies and wheel-barrow mounts in the tea-gardens near the metropolis, or at some inn on the road, rather than any of our pleasure grounds, which of late years have been laid out with so much skill, and in so sublime and beautiful a taste, round almost every nobleman's or gentleman's seat in Great Britain; the planning and disposing of which certainly discovers no common degree of genius, and seems to require as *'great powers of mind'* as those which we admire in the *descriptive* poems of Thomson, or in the noble landscapes of Salvator Rosa or the Poussins.[29]

His view of Shenstone's character and achievement was on the whole clear sighted. In fact, though the Shenstone he presented in this work was the real man rather than the fictional construct of *Columella*, he made his opinion clear that Shenstone, like Columella, failed to find happiness in his retirement: 'How little ... he consulted his real happiness, in adopting this inactivity in preference to a more busy plan of life, is but too evident from some of his letters to his most intimate friends; in one of which he expressly declares his conviction, "that the most *busy* man in the world is much happier than the most *idle* one."'[30]

Shenstone's death left Graves bereft of the friendships of his youth. In 1772 he wrote: 'The confidential friends and sprightly companions of my youth are, long since, either gone into the invisible world, or entirely separated from me in remote parts of the Kingdom.'[31] One of the friends who, though still alive, were separated from him was Sir William Blackstone, whose time was now divided between Oxford and London and who was busy beating his way to the top of the legal profession. Though in his later writings Graves often referred to him, dedicated one of his works to him, and once consulted him through a solicitor on a legal problem,[32] their friendship seems to have fallen into disrepair. His 'Anecdotes of Sir William Blackstone,' published in 1805, are vivid only for the Oxford years, though they contain at least one shrewd remark about his friend's character. Everything in Sir William, he wrote, was 'weighty and decisive': 'as a counsel, therefore, he had not that plausible superfluity of words, which gives some pleadings a show of eloquence; and never used those supplementary phrases, of "I humbly apprehend"; and "I beg leave to insist on it"; or "I can take upon me to prove; with all imaginable ease and facility, to the perfect satisfaction of your lordship, and the court," &c.'[33] In other words, he was a bit inflexible in temperament. Once the joyous years at Oxford had passed, the decisive Sir William must have had little time for the garrulous Richard Graves. But he cannot have entirely neglected the joys of life if Graves was right when he added him to his list of friends who died of '*comparative intemperance.*'

Nearby Bath provided Graves with opportunities for making new friends, even though for many of its sojourners, who came to drink the waters, it was only 'the great thoroughfare,' as he wittily put it, 'from this world to the next.'[34] The letters of his later years as well as his dedications and presentation inscriptions teem with the names of these new friends. He had always been gregarious, and he is known to have visited Bath nearly every day and to have attended the plays presented in the theatre there as often as he could, but he took little part in the fashionable life of the Pump Room beyond familiarizing himself with it enough to write the satirical chapters on it in *The Spiritual Quixote*.[35] His new casual acquaintances on the whole, however, gave him little comfort. 'And in these later acquaintance,' he wrote, 'whom mere vicinity, or other accidental circumstance, have thrown in my way, I find a cold reserve, or formal civility, ill calculated to supply the place of the warm and unsuspecting openness of my earlier friendships.'[36] Fortunately, among the new people he was able to form intimate friendships with a few kindred spirits whom he bound to himself with ties stronger than those of mere vicinity. The closest of these were among the more permanent residents, the physicians, the artists, the poets, the booksellers, the businessmen, and the clerics who attended to the wants of the visitors, as well as the gentry who inhabited the many great houses that dotted the hillsides. His poem called 'The Summer's Retreat' is a muster-roll of the great houses known to him in the neighbourhood.[37] To a few of these new friends we must be introduced more fully, but to catalogue them all would be tedious and unnecessary.

Graves must have met Ralph Allen, one of the most helpful of these new friends, soon after his arrival in Claverton, for Allen was not only a near neighbour but the best-known resident of Bath.[38] Having made a large fortune through his honest and efficient handling of a postal contract and through the operation of his stone quarries, from which most of the material used in the new building in the city was supplied, he became a philanthropist and patron of literature, befriending Pope, Fielding, Richardson, and Warburton, who often enjoyed his hospitality. *Tom Jones* is said to have been written in the vicinity while its author was a frequent guest at Allen's house. It is hard to get a clear impression of Allen's personality because of the blaze of panegyric that always surrounded him. Fielding based the character of Squire Allworthy in *Tom Jones* partly on him, called his a 'truly benevolent Mind,' and inserted a character sketch of him into the introductory chapter to book 8 among examples of 'the Marvellous.'[39] Graves's own tribute was to much the same effect:

> *But see the man of virtuous parents born,*
> *Whose useful life exalted acts adorn!*
> *With genius bless'd, whose ev'ry purpose tends*
> *T'improve his country or inrich his friends:*
> *Who pours his wealth on works of public use,*
> *In worthiest deeds still gloriously profuse,*
> *Whose pious care seeks merit in distress,*
> *His unknown hand whilst wond'ring wretches bless;*

Like some celestial planet's friendly rays,
To all around diffusive bliss conveys;
Who thus thro' life pursues one glorious plan
Is more than noble — is a godlike man![40]

Allen's great Palladian mansion-house of Prior Park, close to Claverton, situated so as not only to command a magnificent view of Bath and its surroundings but also to be seen from that city gleaming white among the trees on the top of the down, evoked rapturous praise from Fielding in both *Joseph Andrews* and *Tom Jones*. A cataract in the grounds, apparently gushing from a rock and appropriately presided over by a statue of Moses, was especially admired. The house was imposing to look at and, though inside cramped and dark, was splendidly furnished. It even had a private chapel where divine service was conducted regularly by the resident chaplain, the family entering their pew from the long gallery through a private door. Hospitality was also on a grand scale.

In 1758 Allen purchased the manor of Claverton with all the appurtenances and so became Graves's nearest neighbour as well as lord of the manor and patron of the living. Allen never lived in Claverton except when driven from Prior Park by painters and decorators, but he is said to have kept the house open and to have dined there once a week, in that way impressing the image of himself as lord of the manor, a genuinely aristocratic touch lacking in the nouveau riche splendours of Prior Park. His hospitality had already been extended to Graves, who mentioned meeting at Allen's table such people as William Warburton, later bishop of Gloucester, William Hoare the painter, father of Prince Hoare, Sir John Cope, the general who lost the battle of Preston Pans and distinguished himself by running away – an episode mentioned in *The Spiritual Quixote*[41] – Sarah Fielding, sister of the novelist, Richard Hurd, bishop and literary critic, William Mason, and many others 'distinguished by rank, learning, or eminence, in any profession, or public employment.'[42] Allen's generosity to Graves in building an addition to the parsonage-house to accommodate his school and securing for him the additional living of Kilmarsden and Lady Chatham's chaplaincy has already been mentioned. He also repaired the interior of the parish church, put up a stone altar, altar-piece, and font, built a gallery for the use of the singers – ironically first used on the occasion of his own funeral in July 1764 – and presented a bible, prayer-book, epistles, and gospels for the altar, all beautifully bound in morocco and nicely gilt. Unfortunately, no letters survive that might have shown how he and Graves felt about each other, but it is likely that Allen had neither the time nor the talent for writing letters except on business. Forty years after his death Graves put together a little collection of anecdotes about him that was published posthumously in *The Triflers*. Informal and at points inaccurate, it continues the tone of adulation conspicuous in his earlier poem, but it lacks the depth of personal feeling shown in his relations with Whistler and Shenstone.

Graves's friendship with the Dodsley brothers, Robert and James, London's most highly respected book publishers, is the most fully documented of all his friendships except for that with Shenstone, for seventy-seven of his letters to them have been preserved as well as two of their replies.[43] These letters were mainly on business, but business and friendship blended together so intimately in their relationship that it is hard to tell where the one ends and the other begins. At first Graves wrote to Robert, the older of the two brothers and the dominant one, who had once been a footman and had begun a career in literature by publishing a poem entitled 'Servitude.' He kept on with his writing even after becoming a busy and successful publisher and was able to be his own editor and reader as well as publisher and bookseller. But being loath to rely wholly on his own judgment, in the fifties he took on Shenstone more or less formally as his literary adviser. At the time a new and enlarged edition of the Dodsley's popular poetical anthology called *A Collection of Poems* was in preparation, and Shenstone submitted four poems by Graves along with a number from his other poetical friends. This occasioned Graves's first letter to Robert Dodsley, a deferential one, as from an unknown author to a well-established publisher: 'As I have the highest opinion of Mr Shenstone's judgment, I should have no reason to doubt that those little pieces of mine w^{ch} *he* has thought proper to transmit to you, deserv'd a place in your Collection – If I cou'd be certain that he was entirely unbiass'd by his regard for the Author.'[44] He was obviously a little in awe, but he had no objection to the publication of his four poems, one of which, a poem on ancient medals, Shenstone considered a 'small well polished gem.'[45] Graves even authorized Dodsley to attach his name to it, but when the book appeared in 1755, he was dismayed to find that Dodsley had carelessly extended that permission to all four of his contributions.[46]

The following summer Robert Dodsley appeared on Graves's doorstep in Claverton, having come at Shenstone's suggestion to consult him about *Cleone*, a tragedy he had just completed. Their time together was short. 'I a[ppeared] to you,' Graves wrote to him afterwards, 'in the same Dishabille of Conversation in which Mr Shen[stone] always indulges me.'[47] Nevertheless, he had time to look through the manuscript and, as Dodsley afterwards reported to Shenstone, pointed out 'several little Inaccuracies' that Dodsley hastened to correct. Dodsley also wanted an epilogue and mentioned his need to both Shenstone and Graves. Knowing Shenstone's habit of procrastination, Graves, who always wrote rapidly, sat down and dashed one off. In his covering letter to Dodsley he explained his notion of a good epilogue. *Cleone* being a highly emotional play, what was needed in the epilogue, he thought, was a 'Satyrical Contrast' that would defuse the tension and point a moral. So he wrote accordingly. The bibliographical history of this epilogue is too long and complex to be gone into here. No fewer than three versions of it exist in manuscript, each with interlinear and marginal corrections, and two in print.[48] Both Dodsley and Shenstone made contributions as the text was passed back and forth among the three friends, but about half of the words in the final version were Graves's, and the idea on which it was based was almost entirely his. Yet self-effacingly he described his epilogue as only a footman sent to the theatre early in order to keep a place in the boxes for his master, that is, the epilogue Shenstone had agreed to write. So entire credit was given to Shenstone. But in his own copy of Shenstone's *Works* Graves put under the title of the epilogue: 'I wrote this at his request.'[49]

Actual production of the tragedy was delayed for two years because Garrick rejected it at Drury Lane, allegedly describing it, not altogether unfairly, as a 'd——n'd, bloody, and improbable Tragedy.'[50] He was wrong about the 'd——n'd,' however, for when produced at Covent Garden, the rival theatre, it was a howling success. Graves did not see it there, but read it aloud to Lucy, his wife, who wept,[51] and when it was produced in Bath a few weeks later, he was on hand, afterwards reporting on the performance to Dodsley:

I fix'd myself ... in the Centre of the Pitt – In the Midst of young Milliners & Abigails – Whe[re I] had the pleasure of observing the Effect of your genius upon undisguis'd humanity – Neither indeed was there a young or handsome face in the Boxes but what [   ] being conceal'd with a handkerchief – shew'd that the [f]air Lady either was deeply affected – or was conscious that she ought to be so – I had the Satisfaction of silencing (with a single Hiss) one or two young fellows who either to shew their Stoical Conquest over their Passions – or their absolute Contempt of the rest of the Audience – were clamorously rallying Mrs Br——cas & two or three more very pretty women upon their amiable Sensibility.[52]

But was he thinking of *Cleone* several years later when he wrote in his Apology to *Euphrosyne*: 'I must confess with shame and confusion of face, that I have sometimes laughed to myself, even in the most bloody catastrophe of a modern tragedy'?[53] If he had wanted to laugh at *Cleone*, however, he stifled his laughter successfully, for friendship meant more to him than dramatic criticism.

Graves was elated by the success of the play and his epilogue, and wrote a panegyric on Robert Dodsley entitled 'On Tully's Head,' alluding to the sign that hung outside that publisher's London bookshop. Dodsley was embarrassed by Graves's extravagant adulation:

> *Yet He, I trow, in* CÆSAR's *Days,*
> *A nobler Fate had found:*
> DODSLEY himself *with gilded Bays*
> *Had been by* CÆSAR *crown'd.*[54]

Dodsley, however, continued to entertain the highest opinion of Graves's literary judgment, adopting his suggestion that a ghost be introduced into his ode to Melpomene,[55] accepting four more of his poems for a still newer and larger edition of *A Collection of Poems* to be published in 1758, and asking him to contribute to a three-volume collection of fables to be published by the famous type-founder and designer Baskerville in Birmingham and by Dodsley in London.[56] Graves was also consulted by Dodsley on a plate to be used in a splendid edition of Horace also to be published in collaboration with Baskerville, and was deeply enough involved in its preparation that in a letter to a friend he described the edition as '*our* Horace.'[57] In doing so he may have gone a little too far. However, Shenstone had evidently referred to him some queries from Dodsley on the edition; Graves replied that he thought it would appeal primarily to lovers of Horace and next to lovers of fine printing. But he objected to the plate that Baskerville had proposed using as a frontispiece, in which Horace had apparently been shown strumming on a harp. 'I am a little dubious,' he wrote to Dodsley, 'about the propriety of representing a real Poet with a[n] allegorical harp. It might lead a modern Gentleman into a mistaken notion that the Roman Poets sang their Ballads about the Streets to their Instruments.'[58] Evidently his advice was taken (see plate 25). And, of course, he helped Dodsley with the editing of Shenstone's *Works*. Meanwhile, their personal relations had become increasingly intimate. As early as 1759 Graves began to conclude his letters by signing himself 'y^r *affectionate* humble servant,' assuring him in one letter that 'no one has a greater personal regard' for him.[59] A present from Dodsley that Graves acknowledged in April 1764 may have been an honorarium sent to recompense him in part for his labours on Shenstone's *Works* in place of the share in the profits that Graves had declined, or it may have been sent out of mere friendship.[60]

When Robert Dodsley died in 1764, in the same year as Ralph Allen, James, his younger brother, was left in full charge of the business. At first there was little contact between him and Graves, but five years later a letter from Graves on business opened a correspondence that lasted almost until the former's death. Mainly it was concerned with business, for James Dodsley published Graves's books for a quarter of a century, but as in the correspondence with the older brother, personal matters more and more crept in. Eventually Graves again fell into the habit of signing off as James's *'affectionate'* humble servant and began to unburden himself of worries about his sons. On more than one occasion James sent him gifts. It is hard to gauge the extent of his generosity because his financial commitments in respect to Graves's books were so informal that a gift can seldom be distinguished from an honorarium, especially as his presents were sometimes bank drafts and sometimes parcels of books. But Graves seems to have considered them all free gifts and himself generously treated as an author at the same time, and once attempted to make the only return lying within his power: he sent Dodsley the manuscript of his third novel, *Eugenius*, to publish entirely for his own profit. But if that was his intention, he was frustrated, for a few months later Dodsley sent him another generous present.[61]

The Graveses, moreover, continued, as they had in Robert's day, to make Dodsley's house their headquarters on their London holidays. The business relationship, however, was terminated and their friendship put under strain by an incident that occurred in 1792. In the previous year Graves had written to Dodsley to announce that he had completed a translation of the *Meditations of Marcus Aurelius* and to ask if Dodsley wished to buy the copy.[62] Dodsley declined, explaining that 'it was not the sort of reading suited to the present age.' Though Graves knew that people in his age were 'not much given to *Meditation*,' he nevertheless found another publisher, and his translation came out in 1792. Dodsley, when he saw it, was 'a little piqued' to discover that for the first time Graves had put his name on a title-page, something he had never allowed Dodsley to do for him. Unfortunately, the letter that Graves wrote in explanation has been badly mutilated; all that is clear in it is that he felt himself in the right and tried to mollify the outraged publisher by sending him a turkey. But, as Graves himself wrote, the 'connexion between us as Author & his litt[er]ary Agent' had ceased; Dodsley published no more of his books.[63] Personal relations most likely were not completely cut off, though they must have cooled down, but no more letters have survived until one final one four years later in which Graves seems to have been trying to revive their business connection.[64] But his efforts were in vain, and in the following year James Dodsley died. It was a sad end to one of the most rewarding friendships of Graves's later life.

He does not appear to have had any close friends among the women he met for the first time in these years, though he loved to associate with them and take part in the elegant social events they patronized. One of the best known of the ladies who presided over literary society in Bath was Lady Miller, wife of an Irish baronet, who with her husband had built an elegant suburban villa at Bath Easton and after a sojourn in Italy began holding literary parties every second Thursday morning. The Millers moved in the upper circles of society. Graves recalled seeing more than fifty carriages one Thursday morning lining the road from Bath Easton to Lambridge and on another occasion counted four duchesses in attendance. Years afterwards he wrote a vivid account of these poetry readings:

when the company were assembled, those whom the Muses, or perhaps vanity, or the love of fame had influenced, produced their performances, and put them into an elegant antique marble vase brought from Rome, and placed on a pedestal in the bow window; when the company were seated, some young nymph put in her delicate arm, and took out a single poem, which the author, or some one who either had, or fancied he had an agreeable elocution, read to the assembly. When in this manner, the whole collection was gone through, the gentlemen retired into a contiguous apartment; where amidst a profusion of jellies, sweetmeats, ice-creams and the like, they decided on the merits of the several performances; from which they selected three, which were deemed the best; and of course entitled to prizes; which her ladyship distributed to the respective authors; a pompous bouquet of flowers to the first, a myrtle wreath to the second, and a sprig of myrtle to the third. These were then usually presented, by the successful candidate, to some lady who wore them in her hair or her bosom, the next morning, to the publick rooms.[65]

Though a glint of humour may be detected in that account, Graves took Lady Miller's salon seriously, writing many poems for it, which he eventually published in the various editions of his poetical miscellany called *Euphrosyne*, along with a poem or two in praise of the lady herself and, in the second volume, a prose preface devoted largely to a defence of her poetical society. For it had critics. Horace Walpole's derisive view of it, confided in a letter to Lady Ailesbury in 1775,[66] was probably not known to Graves, but the opinion of his old friend Dr Harrington of Bath probably was, who wrote in a satire published in 1782 that many of the people who attended her assemblies 'cannot in poetry distinguish

between a tulip and a bulrush.'[67] Graves himself noted the insipidity of high society in Bath,[68] which he had satirized in *The Spiritual Quixote*, but he praised Lady Miller for having raised its cultural tone. In his preface to the second volume of *Euphrosyne* he defended her again on the ground that her assemblies had given harmless pleasure and were in keeping with the spirit of a city dedicated to it. They were also much better conducted, in his opinion, than the Roman assembly derided by Juvenal in his third satire. Even the prevalence of the spirit of panegyric, only too evident to anyone who turns over the volumes entitled *Poetical Amusements at a Villa near Bath*, which Lady Miller edited at intervals between 1775 and 1781, he found acceptable. In panegyric, he said, strict veracity is not expected: the writer magnifies 'those good qualities, which he had *really* experienc'd in his friend or benefactor,' setting an example for others to follow. Significantly, he remarked that he himself was 'more inclined to panegyric than satire.' That had not always been so, for much of his most memorable early poetry was satiric or parodic. If it tended now to panegyric, that was a sign that his need for friendship had become paramount.

In addition to Lady Miller and, of course, Mrs Montagu, there was another literary lady among his acquaintance, Mrs Catharine Macaulay, whom he mentioned in at least two of his poems in *Euphrosyne*. She was the author of a history of England and was popular in Whig society in Bath, where she lived. On 2 April 1777, her birthday, a celebration took place in her honour, one of those elaborately festive occasions that were dear to the gentry of the eighteenth century but seem faintly ridiculous today. According to a printed account of it, the day began with the ringing of church bells and 'other public demonstrations of the general joy,' and in the evening a party was held at Alfred House, attended by 'a numerous and brilliant company.' Mrs Macaulay, elegantly dressed, was seated in state upon a dias, and when everyone had settled himself, six gentlemen advanced and, one after the other, declaimed odes. One of the odes, the account went on to say, was 'delivered with a grace and elocution that would have done honour to *Garrick*; and another, with an energy and action not unworthy of *Demosthenes*!' After two other gentlemen had made speeches and presentations, there were dancing and the inevitable refreshments: 'syllabubs, jellies, creams, ices, wines, cakes, and a variety of dry and fresh fruits, particularly grapes and pineapples.'

Graves had been waited on hat in hand some time before by the stage-manager of this show, the Reverend Dr Wilson, non-resident rector of St Stephen Walbrook in London, and asked to write some verses for the occasion. Though at first he demurred, in the end the wish to write was

too much for him and he 'wrote [a] few Heroic Lines,' almost certainly the first of the six odes.[69] Graves may well have been the Demosthenes, for he was always full of energy and action, and the first of the six odes, entitled 'Hortensia's Birthday,' though wretched stuff, sounds suspiciously like Graves's work, if only because of its opening salute to the University of Oxford. The latter part of the poem scales the heights of panegyric, attributing 'endless fame' to this quickly forgotten historian. There was only one cloud in it to screen the hearers from the full blaze of the poet's adulation, a reference to the frowns of 'envious Prudes,' saints, and bigots. The poet went no farther, but everyone present must have known that since the death of her first husband, Mrs Macaulay had been living with their host, the Reverend Dr Wilson. She was living with him, she said, for the sake of his library. And perhaps she was, for when she married shortly afterwards it was to a different man. Graves recalled this birthday party afterwards as a 'laughable' occasion, but his little innuendo was the only evidence of that feeling in his ode.

Occasionally a party of fashionable people enjoying an outing would arrive unexpectedly at Claverton and ask to see Graves's garden. Among the Bath-Easton poems included in *Euphrosyne* II is an amusing one called 'A Morning Visit,' modelled on Gray's 'A Long Story,' in which he described such a visit paid him by three 'goddesses,' one of whom was the celebrated beauty Lady Clarges:

> THREE *goddesses, divinely fair,*
> *To make a country parson stare,*
> *One pleasant morning, all agree*
> *To lay aside their quality;*
> *And, sending for an hackney chaise,*
> *With wondrous sprightliness and ease,*
> *Each nymph, apparell'd like a mortal,*
> *Came thund'ring at the parson's portal.*

'They laugh'd, they talk'd, they danc'd and flirt'd,' and made the blood in the aging parson's veins flow faster than it had done for years.

Graves had a talent for getting on with young people, and among the friends who cheered his later years was a group of young men, some of whom had been his pupils. One of these, Robert Malthus, the fighting Don Roberto of his school and author-to-be of the *Essay on Population*, had grown up in Claverton, for the Malthuses had lived in Claverton Hall as tenants and had only just terminated a tenancy there when they left their son behind to be one of Graves's pupils. In one of his poems Graves

celebrated their happy family life, adding a note in which he described them as 'a worthy family, who have happily united in their domestic œconomy, the elegant simplicity of the pastoral ages with the refinements of modern life.'[70] The Eckersalls also, the family into which Robert Malthus was to marry, were familiar visitors at Claverton and were living in the hall as tenants when Graves died. Robert was by that time a married man and in holy orders but, lacking a home of his own, was living there too for the time being with his pregnant wife. Called to the bedside of his old schoolmaster, he administered the last sacrament to him.[71] No personal letters or diaries survive that might tell us how often the old man and his famous pupil had seen each other and what they talked about when they did. But references to 'Malthus' occur several times in Graves's later poems and letters, which show that he had kept in touch with the family at least.

Prince Hoare was a different sort of young man from Robert Malthus, and a closer friend. Son of William Hoare, popular portrait artist, whom Graves had met at Prior Park, he was himself a painter, dramatist, essayist, and administrator – versatile and more brilliant than Malthus, if less profound and original in thought. His first play, a tragedy, was successfully performed in Bath in 1788, and two years later his farce-opera, *No Song, No Supper*, was produced at Drury Lane, the first of a series that kept the theatre in stitches for two decades. The libretto was a silly affair, of the sort parodied half a century later by W.S. Gilbert, full of heart-warming type characters, harrowing situations, and one obvious villain, who, of course, was ultimately defeated. But Prince Hoare had a more serious side as well. In 1799 he became foreign secretary to the Royal Academy, conducting its correspondence with other academies abroad, and he became a fellow of both the Society of Antiquaries and the Royal Society of Literature. Later still he began a periodical, called the *Artist*, aided by such contributors as Northcote, Hoppner, West, and Flaxman, a periodical somewhat in the manner of Addison but more professional in tone. Among other things Hoare campaigned for British art and for the establishment of a national gallery.

In 1801 Graves published a short poem in which he praised Hoare as a dramatist for his combination of satire and sentiment – 'Hoare ... / Laughs at our faults and *plays about* the heart'[72] – and in the same year he mentioned in a letter to a friend the obligation he was under to Hoare for 'his strenuous exertions in my late affliction.' The nature of his affliction was not specified in the letter, but it was almost certainly one of those mysterious lawsuits in which he was disastrously involved, for he went on to write that if Prince Hoare's friend, not identified, '[had] been as strenuous in our cause as he was I am convinced we should have carried our Cause.'[73] One of the same friend's correspondents, almost certainly William Meyler, wrote of Hoare that he was Graves's 'constant Correspondent, and most devoted friend.'[74] It is a pity that none of their letters has survived. But we do know that Hoare was in Claverton during the last few weeks of Graves's life and that he transmitted to the old man a suggestion from Richard Phillips, the London publisher who specialized in biographies and works of reference, that he write his autobiography. He got to work at once and filled 'several sheets of paper with matter at once pleasant, interesting, and connected.' The plan was to include numerous anecdotes concerning Graves's friends, in which task it is likely that he was to be assisted by Prince Hoare, who, in the *Artist*, was to show considerable talent as a biographer. But the work got no further. Within a week Graves was dead.

A third young man whose friendship meant much to Graves was John Skinner. Though born and brought up in Claverton, he was not one of Graves's pupils, but he must have made the rector's acquaintance by the time he became a student at Oxford, for while there he helped Graves by looking up in the Bodleian Library a few references relating to Graves's archaeological interests. After taking two degrees and finding out by experience at Lincoln's Inn that he had no aptitude for the law, Skinner returned to Claverton in 1797 to read for orders under Graves's direction, working, as he wrote in his diary, usually ten hours each day. He was ordained deacon later the same year and priest two years later. Predictably, Graves mingled archaeology with theology. Indeed, secular interests predominated in Skinner's later recollection of this time. He was fascinated by Graves's collection of Roman coins and on walks over the downs with him listened eagerly to what he had to say about the Belgic British earthworks on Claverton and Hampton Downs and the Roman vicinal road that connected Bath with Farleigh and Marlborough.[75] Skinner became obsessed with archaeology and spent a great deal of his later years travelling in the southwestern counties making notes and drawings of the antiquities he saw. He over-valued his work, which he recorded in a diary that eventually extended to ninety-eight volumes, all of which he presented to the British Museum, now the British Library. Few readers have troubled their repose on the shelves, but a one-volume selection of extracts from them published in 1930 sold well and led Virginia Woolf to include a sketch of Skinner in her *Common Reader* in 1932.

Our interest in Skinner's diaries stems from the fact that the first half of volume 3 is devoted to Richard Graves and Claverton.[76] It opens with a coloured portrait of Graves, probably a copy of the Gainsborough one, made by Skinner himself, and proceeds with a handwritten copy of Graves's biography from *Public Characters of 1799–1800*, corrected and brought up to date in a few particulars between 1801 and 1804. After that there is an extract from Collinson's *History of Somerset*, 1791, relating to Graves and Claverton, and then a list of rectors of the parish since the time of Queen Elizabeth, taken from the one made by Graves in the parish register. This section of the volume then winds up with descriptions of the parish church, the parsonage-house, and the great house, illustrated with coloured drawings made by Skinner (see plates 17, 18, and 19) and a portrait of Graves, also by Skinner. It is a remarkable tribute to Graves by Skinner, who gives no other person nearly so much space in his diary. Skinner left Claverton in 1800, moving to another Somersetshire parish, Camerton, where he got on badly with his parishioners and withdrew more and more into the ancient world. A tragic character, he took his own life in 1839 at the age of sixty-seven. Graves, if he had been still alive, might have saved him from that catastrophe, for when Skinner wrote about him in his diary, he remembered him 'even at this comparatively patriarchal age' as having 'the easy air, light-step, and brisk movement of a stripling.' Skinner needed the old man's light touch.[77]

This list of Graves's friends might be extended almost indefinitely, but particulars of their friendships to enliven such a list are lacking. Christopher Anstey, for example, author of the satire *A New Bath Guide*, was certainly a friend, but beyond a handful of casual occurrences of his name in Graves's writings and an anecdote mentioned earlier in this book, the history of their friendship is a blank. William Meyler is another example. Proprietor of a bookstore in the Orange Grove in Bath that Graves visited every day (see plate 26), he was probably the man described by S.J. Pratt in *Harvest Home* as a 'friend, who for the past thirty years has been in habits of the strictest intimacy [with Graves], and who perhaps knew more of him than any other person.'[78] Meyler had a hand in the preparation of the article on Graves in *Public Characters*, but their oral communication has left no record behind. Four or five letters survive from Graves to Thomas Percy, editor of the famous *Reliques of Ancient Poetry*, but their content is more literary than personal.[79] Percy's normal beat seldom took him near Claverton.

About Samuel Jackson Pratt, however, more may be said. In a letter dated 1796, Graves wrote of their 'long Acquaintance,' which must have begun as early as the mid-seventies, when Graves, Pratt, and Meyler were all members of Lady Miller's coterie.[80] At about the same time Pratt introduced into his strange, rambling novel entitled *Liberal Opinions* a character called Mr Greaves, who may owe some of his lineaments to Richard Graves, at least his good sense and probity. In 1781, according to the Reverend Richard Polwhele, Pratt knew Graves well enough to ask him to revise the manuscript of his forthcoming poem *Sympathy*. Graves did so, and told Polwhele that he had made upwards of a hundred corrections in the text.[81] The poem was a pastiche of all the most popular clichés: sentiment, lofty idealism, natural scenery, enamelled vignettes of rural society in the manner of Goldsmith. Polwhele confessed that he wished Pratt would write for a better motive than profit and fame; but if profit was what he was after, he got it, for the poem was a great success. Towards the end of the next decade Pratt undertook to compile a brief biography of Graves for *Public Characters of 1799–1800*, which he did with the help of William Meyler and at least one other friend and under Graves's watchful eye. It was the first time that Graves had come out into the open as an author, something he most likely would not have done except for a friend whom he trusted as much as he did Pratt. Pratt may have been a charlatan, but he evidently showed his best side to Graves, who responded to his warmth and kindliness.

For the most part Graves's friends were not the most talented people of his time, and he seems to have cultivated the acquaintance of few of the celebrities who visited Bath each season. He chose his friends for other, more personal, reasons. In an essay published in one of his latest books he explained why he valued them, and on this subject the last word shall be his:

the pleasure which we receive from the conversation of a circle of friends, does not arise from the fine things which are said, the shrewd observations which are made, the learning which is shewn, or the wit which is displayed, so much as from the benevolent disposition, and the exercise of the kind affections which accompany this friendly intercourse, and the ease and freedom with which every one delivers his sentiments, proposes his doubts, or unbosoms himself, of any remarks which he may have made, and which he wishes to communicate.[82]

He backed this statement up with a tag from Seneca: 'Amicorum conspectus ipse delectat' (The mere sight of one's friends is a pleasure).

CHAPTER THIRTEEN

Trifling

> On Isis' banks, where Chichley's turrets rise,
> (Long fam'd for arts, for sages learn'd and wise)
> This humble Bard first learn'd to tune his lyre:
> Tho' tame his muse, and void of native fire,
> She cheer'd his vacant hours; and Heav'n has still
> Form'd readers, suited to each grey-goose quill.[1]

At the university Graves, like many other Oxford men, wrote poetry, adopting the nonchalant attitude towards his efforts then fashionable in university circles. One of his earliest published poems, for instance, he said was written on horseback during a morning ride.[2] And when he published them he usually did so anonymously. It was not genteel to put oneself forward as a poet. But unlike most of the other academic poetasters Graves had Shenstone behind him, who took poetry quite seriously and who encouraged him and prodded him on. Shenstone said of the poem written on horseback that it contained 'several strokes that are picturesque and humourous,' and of another that it gave evidence of a talent for 'odd picturesque description.' He called it an 'important' poem and hung on to the manuscript for a year while coaxing Graves to let him publish it.[3] Gradually Graves must have yielded to such blandishments, for, as the chronological list in Appendix A shows, poems by him began appearing in magazines in the forties. The pressure on him to publish grew stronger when Shenstone became Dodsley's literary adviser and probably editor of the later volumes of that publisher's popular *A Collection of Poems*. Eight of Graves's poems appeared in it in 1755 and 1758, and in 1761 he contributed three prose pieces to the same publisher's *Select Fables*.[4]

In 1766, acting on a suggestion from William Frederick, predecessor of William Meyler in the proprietorship of the bookshop in Bath's Orange Grove, he published his first book.[5] Called *The Festoon*, it was an anthology of short poems or snippets from poems written by a variety of poets, supplemented by a large section of poems written by Graves himself, many of which had been published before in journals and miscellanies. He added a preface 'On the Nature of the Epigram.' All short poems, he wrote in his preface, like the ones he was introducing, are epigrams; all that is necessary to qualify them for that title is that each one exhibit a single view of its subject and that it be 'expressed in a concise and concluded in a forcible manner.' Though he did not like conceited language, he agreed that an epigram requires 'some striking thought, or poignancy of expression.' In short, it must have wit. All of Graves's original poems since he began writing in Oxford in 1740 were epigrams according to his own elastic definition of the term and fell into one or other of the six categories into which he divided the body of epigrammatical literature: panegyrical, satirical, amorous, moral, humorous, and monumental.

Festoon was successful in the bookstores, a second edition being required two years later, and as late as 1775 Graves informed James Dodsley that it was still selling 'like hot cakes.'[6] Altogether there may have been four authorized editions, for, although no copy of a third has turned up, one labelled 'fourth' was certainly published without date at some time after 1776. Moreover, two piracies were produced in Dublin under other titles in 1767 and 1784 respectively. It was an encouraging start.

Surprisingly, Graves published nothing more for eight years. Of course he was not a full-time writer and may have been preoccupied with other things. Or he may have been working hard on a number of manuscripts that he had put in his drawer and that were to come out in print in due time.[7] Of these the chief was *The Spiritual Quixote*,[8] which he had begun in the fifties and for some reason laid aside. How much work needed to be done on it by the seventies is hard to say, but a thorough revision of a long novel might have absorbed most of his spare time for months. Finally it was finished and sent off to James Dodsley, who published it in an edition of a thousand copies in 1773.[9] It must have sold well, for a second edition, dated 1774, came out in December 1773.[10] This time the print order was for 1,250 copies, and the three volumes were embellished with new copperplate engravings serving as frontispieces. A third edition came out in 1783, even though Graves had warned Dodsley earlier in the year that the sale had become 'rather languid.'[11] Dodsley's confidence, however, was justified, for a fourth was required in 1792. There were also unauthorized printings in Ireland and the United States as well as a German translation and a Dutch one. Copies of the English editions were even found on sale in German bookstores for the benefit of tourists.[12] Its author must have been elated. Though he never allowed his name to appear on the title-page, he was proud of his success and described himself on the title-pages of most of his later books as 'the Editor of *The Spiritual Quixote*.'[13]

The success in the bookstores of *The Spiritual Quixote* opened the floodgates and let out a spate of publications, nearly one new book a year down to a posthumous one in 1805. They are diverse in character, Graves following several parallel lines of interest simultaneously. In this flood there were three more novels: *Columella* in 1779, *Eugenius* in 1785, and *Plexippus* in 1790. None of them had the popular success enjoyed by *The Spiritual Quixote*, though along with it they are his best work and established his reputation. More will be said about them in the next chapter.

During these years Graves continued to write short poems, which differ little if at all in form from those of his earlier years, though they are less taut, less sparkling, and more occasional. At times the spirit of panegyric seems to have taken too much control. Unhappily Shenstone, the poetic mentor of his earlier years, had died in 1763, and Graves had joined the circle surrounding Lady Miller, which brought him into association with such minor poets as Edmund Rack, Mr Hinks, Richard Polwhele, John Hippisley, and William Meyler, who, along with Graves himself, were the six bards of Alfred House who had recited odes composed in honour of Mrs Macaulay. Inevitably the poems that Graves wrote under those auspices abound in clichés.

Our main interest in the translations that Graves also produced during these years is in what they tell us about his tastes and intellectual interests. *Galateo* (1774), the first of them, is a paraphrase of de la Casa's Italian text rather than a translation. It is even unclear whether he worked from the original Italian or from a Latin translation, but it is clear that he felt free to make minor changes in the organization of the book, to substitute English examples and words for Italian ones when it suited his purpose to do so, and to add occasional comments. He approached his task in much the same spirit as Pope had in his imitations of Horace. Clearly his concern was not to produce a scholarly translation so much as to communicate to the English reading public de la Casa's thoughts on what constitutes good social behaviour, a matter in Graves's mind closely related to virtue. It must have been virtue too that attracted him to Marcus Aurelius, of whose *Meditations* he published a translation in 1792. Equating old Roman stoicism with Christian resignation, Graves set out to get the emperor's meaning across even if he had to take liberties with the text: 'Litteral versions never give the full sense of the Original,' he wrote to James Dodsley, '& the language [that is, the emperor's Greek] is in general so bold and abrupt; that I hope that mine will be read with more pleasure.'[14] He aimed at achieving a smooth, elegant, and easily comprehensible version. He omitted numerous phrases and introduced paraphrases whenever he felt that a literal translation would be obscure or offend good taste. Nevertheless, he showed himself an able and careful scholar who knew his Greek and reproduced the substance of the *Meditations* with skill and good taste. Although there were many rival translations on the market, Graves's held its own and was reprinted several times.

The remaining three translations are relatively minor. Xenophon's *Hiero* evidently failed to inspire Graves, whose translation of it (1793) is often dull and flat, but he wrote with zest in translating the little-known life of Commodus by Herodian under the title of *Heir Apparent* (1789).[15] Meanwhile, in *Fleurettes* (1784) he produced his only translation from the French and his only one in verse. It is a small pamphlet containing his translation of two poems on the themes of solitude and country life, chosen presumably for their contrast: Fénelon's 'Ode on Solitude' and Boileau's 'Epistle to Mons. Lamoignon, VI,' with a few other shorter pieces thrown in for ballast. These too are paraphrases, but Graves transmitted the substance of the poems with fidelity as well as clarity and charm.

More and more in these later years Graves was turning to prose, publishing five volumes that are olios of prose and verse: *Lucubrations* (1786), *Reveries of Solitude* (1793), *Senilities* (1801), *The Invalid* (1804), and *The Triflers* (1805). The prose essays contained in these volumes generally carry the weight of the argument, while the verse provides decoration. The volumes are mixtures also in subject matter, serious essays on philosophy, politics, the rights of women, and health rubbing shoulders with amusing anecdotes and clowning. Graves seems to have wavered between developing a persona (Peter of Pontefract appears on one of his title-pages) and speaking with his own though nameless voice. He included several pieces of autobiography and had no hesitation over expressing personal opinions. In several essays he appears as a health-faddist urging on his readers his own regimen of fresh air, regular exercise, and a moderate diet. In his political essays he writes as a man of no party who advocates common sense in opposition to the speculative theories of Paine and Priestley. He argues that what his country needs is not constitutional reforms but moral regeneration. He praises the French for having become sensible of 'their late abject slavery,' but is not sure that they have 'virtue enough to be trusted with their freedom.'[16] Though he adheres to no party line in toto, he inclines towards the Pittite Whigs. Descending from the plane of high policy, he also wrote essays on the plight of unmarried women, on the treatment of servants, on the use of profane language, on the origin of gallantry, on private theatricals, and so on and so on. The volumes are all readable, and the opinions expressed in them, though sometimes eccentric, usually reveal a foundation in experience and good common sense.

To survey the whole of Graves's work one must add to the above-mentioned volumes a highly readable piece of biography – *Recollection ... of Shenstone* (1788) – a volume of sermons, a controversial essay on religious faith, the libretto of an opera, a didactic tale in the manner of Hannah More, pieces of social satire in *The Progress of Gallantry* (1774) and *The Rout* (1789), and a brief verse essay, *The Love of Order* (1773).

It is difficult to estimate the number of Graves's readers. Some of his books sold well, but others sold slowly. Even the existence of second editions of several of them cannot be relied upon as evidence of a brisk sale. Apparently *Eugenius* and the first volume of *Euphrosyne* sold well enough to justify new editions in a relatively short time. But other works, which had sold sluggishly, were given second editions by being used to fill out the copy for a new miscellany. Once at least, in an effort to stimulate sales, Dodsley stooped to tearing off the title-pages of the dust-covered copies of a second edition lying on his shelves and replacing them with new ones labelled 'third edition.'[17] But Graves never failed to find a publisher for any of his works. Perhaps Heaven, as he wrote in the poem quoted at the beginning of this chapter, was continuing to form readers suited to each of his grey-goose quills.

The reviewers, when they noticed Graves's works, were on the whole favourable. *The Spiritual Quixote*, for example, was reviewed at length in the *Critical Review* and the *Monthly Review* and briefly in the *Westminster Magazine*.[18] All three reviewers praised it highly, the *Monthly Review* declaring that there was 'something singular' in it and that it deserved 'to be distinguished from the common trash of modern novels.' Fourteen years later *Lucubrations* won praise, to its author's surprise, from a reviewer in Paris writing in *Le Censeur universel anglois*, a weekly devoted to English affairs: 'En effet, des idées saines, quelquefois neuves, toujours rendues sous une forme piquante, de la gaîté sans amertume, de l'esprit sans entortillage, de la variété dans les sujets, et de la consistence dans les principes; voilà ce que renferment les lucubrations.'[19] (Indeed, sensible opinions, sometimes new, always expressed in a striking way, gaiety without harshness, wit without conceits, variety in his subjects, and consistency in his principles, those qualities are what his lucubrations contain.)

Private readers also usually spoke favourably about Graves's works. Mrs Delany, for example, writing to her friend Mrs Port of Ilam in October 1773, when *The Spiritual Quixote* was still one of the new books, said: 'On your recommendation the Duchess sent for the Sp. Quixote, and we began the day before we came from Bulstrode, and were much diverted with it. There is excellent humour and satire in it.'[20] Generally speaking, common readers and reviewers alike enjoyed Graves's humour and exuberance, and although some of them found him long winded, as indeed he was, many were also alive to his counterbalancing gift for vivid and amusing language. What must have impressed them was what strikes readers today, his fertility. His pages teem with odd characters, absurd situations, curious colloquialisms, sudden changes of fortune, revealing ironies, allusions to out-of-the-way books, and other ingredients of boisterous comedy. The adjective *sprightly* became attached to him and turns up again and again in references to him in books, newspapers, and magazines, especially during his later years. Brevity may not have been the soul of his wit, but wit he had nevertheless.

As might have been expected from a man who distrusted the speculative reason as much as Graves did, he made few theoretical statements about his own literary principles. Something, however, may be learned from his practice. His prose essays are nostalgic in the sense that they are in the tradition of Addison and Steele, with overtones of the *Rambler* and the *Idler*. As a novelist too, especially in the first one, he hitched his wagon to Fielding's star. The influence of Richardson and Sterne is discernible too, and in *Columella*, of Johnson's *Rasselas*.

As a poet Graves belonged to the old-fashioned school of Pope and Gay and had little sympathy with the new poets like Collins and Gray who affected elaborate and often obscure Miltonic diction. Good diction was the great thing with Graves. Clarity of thought and simplicity of language were his ideals, a conviction he expressed in one of his earliest poems, one on riddles, which were apparently much in vogue at that time:

> *Abuse prophane of human speech!*
> *The greatest curse on this side hell!*
> *What heav'n design'd our thoughts to teach,*
> *These mortals use but to conceal.*[21]

In his translation of the *Galateo* (1774) he departed from the Italian text in order to give English examples of obsolete words that, he thought, ought not to be used in poetry, such as welkin, guerdon, lore, meed, eftsoons, except when a poet wishes to give solemnity to blank verse, or in other forms of verse when he is 'greatly distressed for a rhyme.'[22] In his preface to *Fleurettes* (1784) he returned to the subject, writing that he considered the age of Queen Anne to have been England's 'Augustan, or truly classical' age 'in regard to justness of composition, and purity of style.'[23] In *Lucubrations* (1786) he nailed his flag to the mast: 'A new æra or school of poetry seems to have commenced with Mr. Gray, as different from the simplicity of Addison, Pope, and Parnel, as Pindar's or Horace's Odes from Homer or Virgil; and, as the *sublime*, which is characteristic of Gray, often borders on *obscurity*, some passages in his poems might, perhaps, be interpreted according to the *inclination* of the reader.'[24]

Graves's concern for classical purity of style, especially with respect to diction, did not exclude an interest in the colloquial language of his own time and, when it was called for, the use of it in his novels without regard to the proprieties expected of him as a clergyman. Occasionally he was conscious of restraints. In the first edition of *The Spiritual Quixote*, for example, the language of a number of characters, especially Tugwell, is coloured by vulgarisms typical of their class and region, which would have been considered low by fashionable readers, and there are scriptural allusions and mild blasphemies that must have offended others besides Mrs Delany, who complained to her friend Mrs Port of his 'making use of such sacred names and parts of Scripture in so ludicrous a manner,'[25] even though she admitted that his subject justified them. But in his preface Graves defended those lapses on the ground that 'the truth of his principal character, not only justifies, but makes such allusions necessary.'[26] In the second and later editions the toning-down of those expressions may very likely have been done by Dodsley rather than Graves.[27] Though Graves deplored impiety and profanity, he knew that a certain amount of both was a constituent of the common speech of mankind and that its evil was often more apparent than real. He dealt with the subject several times in his prose essays[28] and added to his translation of *Galateo* a footnote in which he mildly differed with de la Casa when the Italian advised well-bred ladies always to avoid in their speech words that are indecent or impolite, even in sound. Graves, on the contrary, thought the lady of his acquaintance ridiculous who, when she wished to breed her canary hen, could not bring herself to utter the words 'cock bird.'[29] He preferred a more robust speech.

Graves either had or pretended to have no high opinion of his own literary works, referring both privately and in print to his poetry as 'middling' and to all of his productions as 'trifles,' even entitling his last book *The Triflers; consisting of trifling essays, trifling anecdotes, and a few poetical trifles*. In an Apology printed in the first volume of *Euphrosyne* he told his readers that many of his poems had been composed on the back of 'a jumbling horse' to save himself from boredom. He not only depreciated his own works in both verse and prose but also declared that all literature existed only to give harmless pleasure: 'the Poets ... seem to rest their cause upon a wrong plea, when they attempt to prove themselves of any great use to the world.' Poetry, he declared, was like the 'wild flowers with which Nature has enamelled our fields' and must be classified with the ornamental rather than the useful parts of creation. To that extent he differed, or appeared to differ, from the classical critics, who from Horace on down had said that all good literature provides useful lessons as well as pleasure. He gave his novels an air of artlessness that suggests a literary picnic rather than serious writing; they seem to be ramshackle structures thrown together to contain a thin main story and a loose collection of amusing anecdotes, sub-plots, and digressions, as if intended to divert the reader and make few demands on his attention.

But that appearance is deceptive. Some of Graves's poems were written and rewritten carefully, and a serious undertone is often heard in them. This undertone is heard even more persistently in the novels. The two mottos that he chose for the first volume of *The Spiritual Quixote* express his feelings about the reading public and hint at his serious purposes.[23] The first of them is from Young's *Night Thoughts*:

> *...Amusement reigns*
> *Man's great Demand*[30]

For the second he chose a sentence from Rousseau's *La Nouvelle Héloise* that he had apparently translated in his manuscript as:

Romances are almost the only Vehicles of Instruction that can be administered to a voluptuous People.

That is a reasonably faithful translation of the French –

Les romans sont peut-être la dernière instruction qu'il reste à donner à un peuple assez corrompu pour que toute autre lui sont inutile.[31]

By 'voluptuous' Graves meant no more than pleasure-loving or hedonist, not giving the word the pejorative weight that it usually carries in common usage today. (As a classical scholar he may have been influenced by the derivation of the word from the Latin *voluptas*, which can be given either a good or a bad sense.) Dodsley, however, not understanding such subtleties, altered 'voluptuous' to 'refined' in the first edition, much to the distress of Graves, who wrote to him explaining that he had used the word 'voluptuous' deliberately and that the change made nonsense of his point. He had intended to defend novels as the only means left to writers of conveying moral lessons to a pleasure-loving public.[32] In his prose Apology to the novel he wrote again to much the same effect: 'I am convinced that Don Quixote or Gil Blas, Clarissa or Sir Charles Grandison, will furnish more hints for correcting the follies and regulating the morals of young persons, and impress them more forcibly on their minds, than volumes of severe precepts seriously advanced and dogmatically inforced.'[33] The notion also turns up elsewhere in his works. In the preface to *Columella* he put it more precisely: 'The world is capricious and wants variety; they are tired of sermons and moral precepts, served up in the same tedious form. But maxims of life which are not new, or which are even so trite as to lose their effect, yet when tricked out in a more inviting dress, and set in a more amiable and striking light, may gain the attention of young people, who would not read even a Spectator or Guardian that was written fifty years ago.'[34] *Eugenius*, Graves's third novel, was written, as he explained in an unpublished letter, in order to defend a thesis,[35] and *Plexippus*, his last one, to take the place of a sermon, even though the author had many on hand, as he said, 'ready cut and *dried*' for the purpose.[36] Consequently, the critic who sets out to discover what Graves was about must penetrate the artless exteriors of those novels so as to reach their intellectual cores – to their theses, their maxims of life, their subjects of instruction. He must see them as they were intended to be seen, as novels of ideas containing social and moral content tailored to suit the capacities of the novel-reading public of his time. In the next chapter an attempt will be made to analyse the four novels according to this principle. As for the poems, Graves's didactic purpose is often either fully apparent, as in *The Love of Order* and *The Progress of Gallantry*, or else lacking altogether, as in his many poetic addresses to his friends. But when Graves is at his best, as in his parody of *The Seven Ages of Man*, the serious and the comic are beautifully fused together as in the novels.

CHAPTER FOURTEEN

The Novels

The four novels have received little attention from critics and historians of the novel, and that little has often been turned in unprofitable directions. Because *The Spiritual Quixote* contained satire on Methodism and because Methodism was a common object of ridicule, Graves has been typed as a satirist, even though satire was only one of several ingredients in any of his novels. An even more serious error has been to think of them as romans-à-clef. Keys to them have been published, and most of the critics who have written about Graves at all have had a shot at identifying one or more of his characters. But romans-à-clef are like crossword puzzles, the reader getting his reward from solving the puzzle, by identifying the characters and sniffing out the scandals alluded to. None of Graves's novels is at all like that, though he was fond of labelling characters and incidents in them as 'real facts,' without mentioning names or particulars. Like most novelists he drew heavily on his own experience. But too much concentration on this kind of source-hunting has turned attention away from the novels as works of literature and towards their biographical fringes instead.

The Spiritual Quixote, the first and best of them, won its popularity with its first readers by its satire on the Methodist preachers, who were becoming increasingly numerous in the 1770s, when the novel was published, and who had long been a popular butt of satire. Graves's satire is on the whole kindly. Feeling that the intentions of the Methodists were generally good even when their actions were unwise, he made them into comical figures rather than villains. But satire occupies only a part of this novel. Its theme is the experience of Geoffry Wildgoose, a young gentleman who, like Graves's brother Charles, has gone 'Methodistically mad.' Some old books of piety are the cause of his affliction, and he is brought back to his senses, and the Church of England, apparently, by a blow on the side of his head from a wine decanter. Or so it seems. The real causes are much deeper. The first and most obvious of these is the wise advice of his friends, which has been discussed at length in chapter 9. The rest is achieved by nature.

Graves was fond of nature, admiring the gardening done by his older brother at Mickleton and by Shenstone at The Leasowes, and imitating both in his parsonage garden at Claverton, within the narrow limits set by his income. But he did not take himself seriously as a gardener, offending Shenstone, who was proud of his *ferme ornée* at The Leasowes, by referring to his own place as his cabbage-garden *orné*.[1] His tastes were different, much as he admired those of his friend. When he makes Wildgoose and Tugwell visit The Leasowes and repay Shenstone's hospitality by throwing down in the night one of his naked statues, Graves seems to be writing in sympathy with his injured friend, but by some means, perhaps the level tone he adopted and the comical plate he used to illustrate the incident, he contrived subtly to make Shenstone's garden look a little ridiculous.

The truth is that Graves's preference was for wild nature, the nature he had read about in Fénelon's ode. It was wild nature that had taken him and his friend on a walking trip through Dovedale and into the Peak District just before he left Tissington and that drew out his most enthusiastic prose in *The Spiritual Quixote*. The countryside through which the itinerants travel – for this is very much a novel of the open road – beginning in the fleecy Cotswolds and the lush Vale of Evesham, moves Wildgoose himself to recite a few lines from *Paradise Lost*:

> *These are thy glorious works, Parent of good,*
> *Almighty! Thine this universal frame,*
> *Thus wondrous fair ...*[2]

This theme mounts to a climax in volume 3, in which Wildgoose and Tugwell undertake a missionary journey into the Peak District, a region well known to all devotees of nature, who were coming in increasing numbers throughout the eighteenth century to inspect such natural wonders as Mam Tor, Eldon Hole, and a land-locked lagoon called Peak's Hole, as well as rivers that flowed underground, thundering cascades, and other attractions.

The difference between Graves and Shenstone on the subject of nature was not trivial but symptomatic of a shift in imaginative sensibility that was taking place in mid-century. Shenstone agreed with Thomas Whately and

William Mason that gardening was a fine art. Indeed, his garden at The Leasowes with its artificial cascades, reservoirs, groves dedicated to Virgil, seats, statues, and inscriptions was a carefully composed stage set meant to be seen and enjoyed in the best lights by troops of visitors. Moreover, these gardeners expected a garden, like all other works of art, to teach useful moral lessons, though when they came down to particulars about those lessons, they often became a little silly: overly ambitious men, for example, may learn from a stream that water will not flow uphill, and lazy ones that it does not lie still.[3] For Graves, by contrast, the fine thing about nature was that it is natural, not the product of a scene-painter's art. Though it undoubtedly has a powerful moral effect on people, it does not teach little copy-book maxims. The true lover of nature, in this romantic view, approaches her works in solitude and with reverence, keeping silence unless, like Wildgoose, he breaks out in an involuntary hymn of thanksgiving. Ultimately he finds intense inward joy and peace. Nowhere does Graves elaborate any such semi-mystical philosophy of nature, but he adumbrates it by implication in many episodes in both *The Spiritual Quixote* and *Eugenius*.

Although Wildgoose receives pleasure from nature, he is also worried about that pleasure. When questioned he admits that 'the natural man cannot but be delighted with these terrestrial beauties' but goes on to express the old-fashioned view that mountains and other irregularities in the earth's surface are due to God's wrath at the fall of man. 'Considered in a religious light,' he continues, 'these stupendous rocks and mountains appear to be as the ruins of a noble palace, designed for man in a state of innocence; and, I own, it makes me serious, when I reflect on the fallen state of mankind; and that the whole creation suffers for our guilt, and groaneth for redemption.' Though the matter is not discussed far in the novel, one of his hearers, Lady Forester, does say in reply that 'the *natural man* is delighted with them, that is, every thing great, beautiful, or uncommon, is *naturally* agreeable to the imagination: and I can never think it unlawful to enjoy (under proper restrictions) what Providence has formed us for enjoying.'[4] Her reply, simple though it is, goes to the root of the matter. For the novel is an apologia for the natural man. From the start the countryside and all the happy vigorous outdoor life associated with it stand in bold ironic contrast to the asceticism of Wildgoose. External nature, indeed, symbolizes all those things in which the natural man takes pleasure, indoors as well as outdoors: sex, familial affection, the theatre, hunting, sports like those encountered at Dover's Games and Warwick Fair, tobacco, beer, and hosts of others, all of which are innocent when enjoyed, as Lady Forester says, 'under proper restrictions.' Graves was no libertine in his philosophy, but his novel is a manifesto declaring that it is wrong to reject the good things that God has created for man to enjoy.

It is not surprising that for Graves sex is one of those good things. Early in his adventures Wildgoose meets Julia Townsend and conceives a passion for her that grows steadily, in spite of separations enforced by his quixotic determination to leave everything and follow Jesus, until towards the end of the novel his passion becomes all consuming. Though Julia herself is something of a schismatic, their love for each other not only draws them together but brings them both into a new conformity with the traditional norms of behaviour. The impact of their love story on the reader is reinforced by 'Mr. River's Story,' which consequently has an integral place in the novel, however irrelevant it may seem at first. Regardless of what conventional moralists might predict, both Mr Rivers and Mr Graves achieved through passion happy and stable marriage relationships. From both 'Mr. Rivers's Story' and that of Geoffry Wildgoose and Julia Townsend it is clear that Graves ranked love high among the virtues and that for him love was neither platonic nor entirely spiritual but contained a large carnal ingredient. It is love, so defined, as much as the advice of his friends or external nature that shakes Wildgoose free from his delusions and induces him to return to the way of life normal for a young English gentleman.

The subjects that Graves chose at first for the three frontispieces that embellish the second and later editions highlight these three themes in the novel. In volume 1 there was to be a picture of Wildgoose preaching to a little knot of rustics in the village square; in volume 2, one of Mr Rivers's charming wife and children in their home; and in volume 3, a scene of wild natural beauty in Dovedale.[5] That plan was altered for unknown reasons, but the original intention was obviously to point to anti-Methodist feeling in the first, married bliss in the second, and wild nature in the third. Not all parts of this buoyant and high-spirited novel can be contained within the limits of that scheme, but even the apparently irrelevant episodes and characters attest to the author's vigour of mind and joyousness, and so are a real part of his message.

Columella, the second of Graves's novels, is like the first a novel of ideas, and in spite of structural weaknesses and a decline in *brio*, almost as good. A clue to its deeper purpose is provided on an early page in a passing allusion to Johnson's *Rasselas*.[6] Like *Rasselas*, *Columella* explores the various ways in which people seek happiness. The story of Columella himself, the principal character, is an extended exemplum, and clustered about it are several shorter stories having a thematic relationship with it.

The stories of Atticus and Hortensius, his college chums, for example, illustrate successful searches, Atticus having found happiness as well as usefulness where Graves would have liked to find it, in the mastership of an Oxford college, and Hortensius, like his friend Blackstone, in the practice of law in London. A Kentish squire and a canon of Bath Abbey also tell their stories, the first, one of wasted opportunity and the second, of successful ambition.[7] Several other stories are embedded in the texture of the novel, most of which illustrate aspects of the main theme. The intellectual core of the novel is a discussion of happiness that takes place among four of the characters, the substance as well as much of the language of which discussion Graves borrowed, in Shandean fashion, from one of his own sermons.[8] Though his doctrine has fewer moral and psychological insights than Johnson's, its main point is one that meant much to Graves himself and that Johnson would have agreed with, that happiness is not to be found in solitude and self-gratification but in integrating oneself into a community and contributing actively to its welfare.

Columella is best thought of not as a portrait of William Shenstone but as a fictional character who typically seeks happiness in retirement. In the eighteenth century that word had a broader meaning than it has today; then it meant 'a private way of life, as opposed to an active participation in a trade, a business, a profession, or politics.[9] In a society like that which existed in England in Graves's time, in which the social norm that many people aimed at was a life of leisure, the idea of retirement naturally had many attractions. It was even idealized by writers such as Richard Hurd, Richard Lucas, and James Thomson, whose works are mentioned in the novel and whose view of retirement approached the contemplative life described by Boethius.[10] But the novel has little to say about that and instead trains satirical guns on what in a private letter Graves called an '*Affected* love of Solitude & Retirement.'[11] In spite of having been given a good education and of possessing genuine talents, Columella has buried himself in the country, where he toys with landscape gardening and tries to convince himself that he is living an ideal life. Actually he is bored, frustrated, and lonely, bothered by his servants and harassed by his neighbours, incapable of the inner serenity necessary for the contemplative life. Even when he yields to the urging of his friends that he take more part in parish affairs, he does so unwillingly and badly and finds no relief for his mind. Eventually, being lonely, he falls victim to the amorous advances of his housekeeper, whom he marries and who offends his ears daily during the rest of his wretched life by her grammatical blunders. Obviously he has failed to find happiness.

In the minds of many eighteenth-century people retirement was also thought of as a means of improving one's social standing, since the possession of a country estate seemed to be a necessary part of the life of a gentleman. In one or two of the ancillary stories in this novel Graves alludes to the craze that raged among the newly rich middle classes of his time, which led many city people to give up their businesses as soon as they had made fortunes and go to live on estates purchased in the country, where they aped the manners of the gentry. Only a few generations back the Graveses themselves had done the same thing. Having no roots in rural society and not understanding its traditions any better than Columella did, most of these newly fledged country squires failed to play the true role of country gentry and instead were idle, dissipated, and bored. Graves was an admirer of the true country gentry; he recognized the numerous demands that society made on them and idealized the contribution they had made and were continuing to make in return. But he despised counterfeit ones.

Graves was interrupted during the composition of *Columella* by the death of his wife.[12] His had been a happy marriage, and he was deeply affected by his loss. How much of the novel had been finished before her death it is impossible to say, but the role in it of Parson Pomfret must have been enlarged, if not created, afterwards. For Pomfret, like Graves, loses his wife and composes an elegy on her death, which in fact is Graves's elegy.[13] Pomfret sends the novel off on a new tack, taking it away from amusing social satire and giving it a deeper and more universal moral significance. For Pomfret, before his loss, glibly preaches that 'every one has it in his power to be happy, if it is not his own fault,'[14] but afterwards flies to the other extreme, declaring that the world is a desert and wishing that he were dead. The episode is an imitation of the well-known one in *Rasselas* involving the 'wise and happy' philosopher who preaches the government of the passions until the sudden death of his daughter plunges him into despair. Time and the wise advice of his friends, coupled with the regular performance of his parochial duties, blunt the edge of Pomfret's grief, as they must also have done Graves's. Though the tragic irony of this incident may seem out of place beside the comic irony in Columella's story, the novel does not cease to be a comic one on that account. Pomfret is a comic character as Graves painted him, even if the tones he used are darker, and the lesson he teaches is that, though happiness is not within easy reach, a sense of humour does take some of the sting out of our misery. The novel is the richer for Graves's personal loss, though the theme as a result may be harder for the reader to get into focus.

Though *Eugenius*, the third novel, shows a further decline in power, it too is a novel of ideas and takes up again some of the themes of *Columella*. When sending the manuscript to Dodsley, Graves explained in a letter that he had had the work 'in Contemplation' for a year or two and that his purpose in writing it was to defend a thesis.[15] The thesis is that modern manners are superior to those of his own boyhood years. Eugenius, the central character of the novel and the narrator of almost all of it, is an idealist and optimist. In one of the opening chapters he declares that 'if we were to take a general view of the state of the world, in a religious or moral, in a civil or political light, I make no doubt but we should find it altered for the better almost within our own memory,' and he goes on for several paragraphs enumerating the ways in which this improvement has shown itself, in the development of such institutions as private and public charities, schools, hospitals, and asylums, concluding his speech with a prediction of world government and universal peace.[16]

The real hero of the novel, however, is not Eugenius but a Mr Hamilton, who is the living embodiment of Eugenius's views. He is either an updated version of Pope's Man of Ross or, more likely, Graves's counterpart to Richardson's Charles Grandison. A wealthy man, almost certainly of middle-class origins, he has done what many others of his class were doing; he has turned himself into a country gentleman, though not in the way condemned in *Columella*. Having bought a property in a remote and beautiful part of North Wales, he devotes himself to the welfare of his community, putting into practice economic principles that must have been novel in Graves's time. Though he gives generously to the poor when the need arises, as Christian charity requires, he believes that 'the best conducted charity is to *employ* the poor, and bring them to a habit of industry, which will be a constant fund for their support.'[7] Accordingly he establishes a woollen mill. As a result the people are happy, well dressed, and well behaved; roads are improved and new buildings constructed. The latter at first jar the aesthetic sensibilities of Eugenius, who is a devotee of unspoiled nature, but he accepts the explanation offered by Mr Hamilton, that considerations of taste must yield precedence to considerations of human need. The Golden Vale, as the locality is called, is a little utopia, more in keeping with the fictions of Thomas More and William Morris than the practices of the Industrial Revolution.

Even the most optimistic of sentimental novelists in the eighteenth century found it hard to get on without villains, and they often painted them in especially dark colours in order to set off the virtues of their good characters more strongly. Graves put two villains in *Eugenius*, but if all villains were as easily foiled as these two are, optimists would have nothing to worry about. Though there are no others in the body of this novel, in a prologue Graves produces a set of characters who are said to have been in possession of the Golden Vale before Mr Hamilton arrived there and who, though not exactly villains, are oddities reminiscent of Smollett illustrating the inferior manners of former times. They are dissolute, insensitive, and idle; they live only for their own amusement, and they corrupt the villagers by their extravagance and bad example. All but one of them have come to more or less bad ends before the main story begins. Their empty lives, more than any positive evil they do, set off vividly the virtues evident in Mr Hamilton and his family and friends, who are presented as typical of modern manners.

No explanation is explicitly offered for this improvement. One might have expected the author, a clergyman, to attribute it to a deepening of religious faith, but Christianity plays only a nominal role. A great deal of stress is laid instead on nature, as in *The Spiritual Quixote*. The Golden Vale is a beautiful spot in the mountains, and Mr Hamilton's house, called South Rocks, a picturesquely irregular building in keeping with the new romantic taste, commands a much-admired view of a little seaport and the sparkling sea beyond. In the woods near the house its owner has built a 'Druid Hall,' a kind of rustic summer house, in which important events in the story take place, including the final wedding feast. Both South Rocks and the Druid Hall are impressed visually on the reader's mind by means of frontispieces about which the author showed particular concern in his letters to Dodsley. A sensitivity to natural beauty when combined with good taste, according to Shenstone, has a moral function, and so it is not wrong for us to associate the good moral tone of the modern characters with their awareness of nature, which means nothing to the characters in the prologue. Mr Hamilton's home life is idyllic: virtuous thoughts and benevolent sentiments abound, and there is much music, dancing, needlework, and improving conversation. The society in which he moves embraces a lively group of young people of both sexes, and the story in the end calls for no fewer than five weddings. By contrast, the characters in the prologue are exclusively male and their social life a monotonous succession of bull sessions. Though Graves allows the contrast to speak for itself, the inference is clear that he felt that people of the present time had a healthier attitude towards sex than was prevalent in his youth and that the general improvement in manners was at least partly due to the larger role being given to women in social life.

Graves described *Plexippus*, the last of his four novels, as 'a more regular novel,'[18] perhaps because of the absence of a frame and of digressions, but more regular or not it is a failure not only because the characters are flat and uninteresting and the novel as a whole lacking in gusto but also because Graves did not treat his main theme seriously. It is explicitly stated at the outset: that a man of plebeian birth who has ability and a good character is more worthy of respect than 'the first nobleman in the kingdom, who has nothing but an *hereditary title* to boast of.'[19] (Graves may have had in mind Ralph Allen, whom he had hailed years before as the 'great plebeian.') But the issue is evaded when, in the final chapters, Plexippus, who has suffered through two volumes from being thought of as a man of lowly origins, not only inherits a fortune but turns out to have good family connections as well. Some irony may have been intended, but even so the thesis is weakened. A secondary theme has to do with marriage between Protestants and Catholics, which is dealt with after a fashion by preaching tolerance, scepticism towards the importance of doctrinal differences, and the duty of conforming with the laws of the land. All, of course, ends happily.

In none of these novels is Graves a writer of essays on timely topics however well disguised; he is a novelist and a comic one. The protracted discussions that occur in all of them of such serious matters as happiness, retirement, and the proper conduct of a priest are not pronouncements from the author himself but expressions of opinion from characters in the stories. In fact, Graves keeps himself out of sight as much as he can, putting his own name to none of the characters and inventing frames for all but one that allow him to retire to the sidelines as 'editor.' It is up to the reader to identify any spokesmen of the author's opinions.

When sending Dodsley the manuscript of *Eugenius*, Graves admitted in a covering letter that though he had been turning the subject of it over in his mind for a couple of years, he had not written the novel 'quite *seriously*,' and he described his thesis as a paradox.[20] According to Johnson, a *paradox* is 'a tenet contrary to received opinion; an assertion contrary to appearance; a position in appearance absurd.' In this novel Graves acted as a sort of intellectual clown, thrusting apparent absurdities in his readers' faces and turning their cherished prejudices upside-down for the purpose of making them think, still doing what Shenstone had recorded while they were both undergraduates in Oxford. In essence all four of Graves's novels were paradoxical. In *Eugenius* the argument that modern manners are superior to those of earlier times was iconoclastic in an age that usually looked for its norms to the past. *Plexippus* was equally paradoxical in the stratified society to which Graves belonged, however threadbare the subject may seem today. The paradox in *Columella* is that country life is not what it is held to be in the romantic imagination, a guarantee of peace and contentment. In *The Spiritual Quixote* readers must have been disturbed by Graves's suggestion that there was good in the much-reviled Methodist movement that the established church would do well to imitate. That these do not express the whole of Graves's mind is obvious to anyone who studies him and his work as a whole. His paradoxes were part of the dialectical game he was playing, in which he was testing the validity of received opinions and trying to make truth appear by indirection.

To justify his views Graves wrote a defence of laughter in which he defined man as 'a *Risible* Animal' because a rational one. Having made that promising start, he ought to have written more on the subject of humour and comedy, on which he must have often reflected, but instead he shyed away, treating the subject quizzically, winding up with a characteristic piece of irony: 'If (as some Divines have held) laughter be a symptom of reprobation; I will endeavour for the future to subdue this ungodly propensity.'[21] He had his tongue in his cheek, of course, but it amused him to glance in that way at one of Wesley's more eccentric opinions. He had alluded to it before, in *The Spiritual Quixote*, in an anecdote about a one-eyed Irish sailor who comes to Wildgoose as a penitent, confessing that his 'greatest affliction' is 'the being violently addicted to *laughing*, which,' he fears, 'is a token of Reprobation.' That sailor is a fraud and a villain, but Wesley, as his *Journal* shows, was firmly convinced that laughter came from Satan.[22] Nothing could illustrate better than that the gap that separated Graves from the Wesleys. The experience of his life convinced him that the comic outlook he had presented in poem after poem and novel after novel was a God-sent means of preserving peace of mind in a dark and frustrating world.

CHAPTER FIFTEEN

The Sprightly Mr Graves

In spite of advancing age and failing health Graves kept up his daily rides into Bath in winter as well as in summer. On one wintry occasion both he and his horse are said to have lost their way in a sudden snow squall and to have wandered about in the dark for hours before reaching home. But he suffered no injury either to his body or to his spirit.[1] On another occasion, at the age of eighty-three, he was thrown from his horse 'on the most unfrequented part of Claverton Down' and was unable to rise from the ground until he was providentially found and assisted by General Harcourt.[2] Such a mishap must have sapped his physical vigour, at least to some extent, but his mental energy remained unabated. When he was in his eighty-eighth year the Reverend Richard Warner sat beside him at a visitation feast and 'listened, with astonishment, to his uninterrupted flow of neat and epigrammatic impromptus; lively *jeux d'esprit*, and entertaining anecdotes.'[3] In the following year, that of Graves's death, Samuel Jackson Pratt responded to a letter received from the old man with these verses:

> *You talk of weakness and of age,*
> *And then, to* prove *it, fill your page*
> *With ev'ry mark of mental health,*
> *Vigour and intellectual wealth,*
> *And active, warm benevolence*
> *And all the energies of sense.*[4]

Though he kept up his spirits and often laughed at his infirmities, Graves complained at times of deafness and impaired vision. Once he was badly embarrassed when he failed to recognize Mrs Piozzi when she spoke to him on the street, and contritely wrote her a long letter of apology.[5]

Sometimes, however, he made a joke of his weaknesses. When he was led into the belfry of the church at Croscombe, for instance, during his induction there in 1802, he exclaimed: 'Where is the bell-rope, I *cannot see it?*' and, after he had pulled it: 'Does it ring; for I *cannot hear it?*'[6] He was shaking his bauble in the face of the grim reaper.

On 23 November 1804 he died, at the age of eighty-nine.[7] He seems to have been living alone at the time. Fortunately Prince Hoare was in the vicinity and was able to take a last farewell of his old friend. Another young man, Robert Malthus, recently married and in holy orders, was also living close by and gave the dying man the last rites of the church. Graves was buried in his own church a week later.

Looking back over his long life one is struck by his ceaseless activity and energy. He once described himself as a 'Bard, that was always in haste,' adding a bon mot of his friend Mrs B[ampfyl]d, 'that Mr. G—— would be a very agreeable man "*if he had but time*."'[8] He was in a hurry even when he dined with Ralph Allen at Prior Park, where he had the privilege of keeping on his boots in the dining-room, spurs and all, so that he might leave early and make a quick get-away. His get-away was so quick, in fact, that once as he left the table he trailed behind him to everyone's amusement his napkin entangled in his spurs.[9] He needed the quick get-away because he had many calls on his time and because temperamentally he could not sit still.

There was something a little frenetic in all this bustle. Underneath the surface, as his closest friends must have been aware, not all was serene. As early as 1786 there is evidence of a psychological crisis of some sort: he insisted upon using as a vignette on the title-page of *Lucubrations* the figure of an expiring lamp, and the autobiographical disclosures in his dedication of that volume have a despairing tone. Two years later he considered publishing a collected edition of his works as his final act as an author, and discussed possibilities with James Dodsley. The word leaked out to the press, the *Morning Chronicle* for 11 October 1788 printing this announcement: 'The sprightly author of Euphrosyne, the Spiritual Quixote, &c. means, we understand, to write no more, after he shall have put to press a complete collection of his works.' But no collection appeared; instead he went on writing and publishing. Eight years later, after publishing seven more books, he used as his epigraph for the eighth, *Reveries of Solitude*:

> *L'homme qui vivre dans la Solitude,*
> *(Pensant plus et agissant moins)*
> *Eprove à certain age, le besoin*
> *D'écrire.*[10]

(The man who lives in solitude [thinking more and doing less] experiences at a certain age the need to write.) His 'trifling' had grown compulsive.

Though Graves chose to present his works to the world as useless though amusing trifles, all of them, prose and verse alike, served a deep psychological purpose in his own life. Composing verses on horseback, he wrote in his Apology to *Euphrosyne*, not only relieved the tediousness of some particular journey but alleviated and amused 'the tedious journey of life.' It also enabled him 'to support the fatigue of a laborious profession, by diverting his thoughts, when unfitted by chagrin for more deep reflection.' Nor were those its only uses. Writing opened up to him a life of vicarious experience in which he was able to gratify in his imagination natural desires that he could not properly gratify in reality: 'He could never behold a fine prospect or a fine place [he wrote], much less a fine woman, or an animated countenance, without a sensible emotion; the most natural expression of which (to him at least) was in this way: which gratifying the imagination, has suppressed any illicit desires of invading his neighbor's property.'[11]

But not even writing could entirely remove the hurt. In March 1800 Graves made his will, voicing in it, as we have seen, some of the bitterness he felt over the misbehaviour of his son Danvers. His troubles weighed heavily on his mind, and they were numerous: the shipwreck of his academic career, his exile in Claverton, the hostility of members of his family, the misbehaviour of two of his sons and the persecution of another by unscrupulous villains, the sense of guilt he carried with him over his seduction of Lucy, her early death, and the loneliness that followed. So he kept busy. If he had not, he would have had nothing to do but listen to the silence around him.

In spite of his many troubles, however, in his old age the mellow elements in his personality gained precedence over the caustic. Richard Warner described him as 'ingenious, cheerful, and amiable.' The *Historic and Local New Bath Guide*, in its volume for 1805, used the adjectives 'amiable' and 'sprightly.' The *Bath Chronicle* in its issue for 29 November 1804, reporting his death a few days earlier, wrote of his 'benevolence and piety.' The memorial plaque put up in the church at Claverton described him as a 'good and exemplary man.' Such funerary rhetoric, of course, need not be taken very seriously, but in this case it was in keeping with the image of him that had become current. During his life in Claverton the more abrasive sides of his personality had gradually worn smooth. In 1783 he wrote in his preface to *Euphrosyne* II that he had 'always been more inclined to panegyric than satire.'[12] That 'always,' however, was not strictly true, for many of his earlier poems had a bite to them. But in later ones the wit was curbed. If he had wished to laugh, as he obviously had, at Mrs Macaulay's pomposity, he kept his laughter to himself. And he asked James Dodsley to remove the name of his neighbour Lady Vane from his list of illustrious modern whores in any possible new edition of his poem.[13] So the legend grew of this amiable and even beatific old man who lived on the fringes of things at Claverton and wrote sprightly books.

By the time of his death Graves had become a well-known figure. The Bath newspaper that had ignored his induction half a century earlier now made amends with a long and laudatory obituary notice dealing mainly with his personal qualities and only just mentioning his publications. Perhaps the editor still felt morally obliged to respect Graves's anonymity, though the secret had never been a closely guarded one and had been betrayed years before by Lady Miller in one of her anthologies.[14] Not many people living in his home territory who read books at all could have been ignorant of the identity of the author of *The Spiritual Quixote* and those other products of his imagination. Readers might have learned more from a footnote in the 1782 edition of *A Collection of Poems*, from John Nichols's fuller note in *The Biographical and Literary Anecdotes of William Boyer* (1782), or from *Public Characters of 1799–1800* (1799), which contained not only a lengthy biographical sketch but also a list of his writings.[15] After his death the august *Gentleman's Magazine*, which made a feature of its obituaries, published a short and inaccurate one in its November number that must have been thrown together by the office boy when the editor, John Nichols, who knew better, was not looking. However, the magazine tried again in its next number and succeeded much better. Full and fairly accurate information was consequently available to all who cared to look for it.

Externally the image that Graves presented to the world was a little odd and lent itself to caricature. His height was below average; according to his friend Dr Harrington he was a 'little man.'[16] Perhaps also the consistent avoidance by all the artists who painted his portrait of the full-face position hints that his face was lopsided. However that may be, one's impression of him on first meeting was apt to be unfavourable. If his sketch of Parson Pomfret in *Columella* is a piece of self-caricature, it reveals Graves as 'a poor, hectic, miserable-looking creature,' lacking in dignity. He wrote with his tongue in his cheek, no doubt, but not in complete disregard for the truth. Moreover, according to his own admission in *The Triflers*, he was a poor speaker,[17] and Dr Harrington explained that he stuttered and spoke thick. S.J. Pratt, however, in the poem and letter quoted a few pages earlier makes no mention of these speech defects. Probably one forgot them when in congenial surroundings Graves got into full spate and one was aware only of his wit and alertness.

Graves sat for his portrait several times during his life. In 1752, shortly after he moved to Claverton, he sent Shenstone a picture of himself by an unknown artist, which unfortunately has not been traced. In thanking Graves for it Shenstone declared it a good likeness, though he had two faults to find: the belly was too prominent, and the smile did not go with the gravity of the eyes. He proposed having the picture retouched when he could find a competent artist. But without waiting for that to be done, Shenstone hung it in his breakfast-room, where his friend could be with him, smiling or not, every day when he ate his morning meal. The portrait of a friend, he declared, meant more to him than a face he did not know, even if it had been painted by Raphael.[18] The disappearance of this picture is a loss indeed, for it would have been the earliest record of Graves's appearance. The artist, whoever he was, must have perceived the rare combination in him of the grave and the gay that eluded other and more famous painters.

The most famous of those others was Thomas Gainsborough, who did a crayon drawing of Graves that now belongs to the Pierpont Morgan Library in New York and that has been reproduced in black and white as a frontispiece to this volume.[19] No date appears on it, but though the face seems old for a man of forty-five, the most likely date for it is in the 1760s, when Gainsborough had his studio in Bath. Apparently he and Graves became acquainted, and in 1762 Graves wrote a poem in which he likened Gainsborough to Milton, declaring that he combined 'The Painter's genius, and the Poet's fire.'[20] In another and later poem he likened Gainsborough to Corregio: 'Nature's pupil, fraught with inborn genius.'[21] Gainsborough's drawing of Graves shows his head and shoulders only and, like all the other extant portraits, shows him side-face. The expression is serious enough to have satisfied Shenstone, and the tightly closed lips and beaky nose suggest the imminence of some barbed comment. The ironic part of Graves's character seems to have struck Gainsborough most strongly.

When Francis Kilvert, who had been curate of Claverton shortly after Graves's time, spoke to the Bath Literary Club in 1857 on the subject of Richard Graves, he had with him three portraits to show his audience. The first of them was the drawing by Gainsborough just mentioned, but the other two he identified only slightly. One, he said, was a 'profile,' done by a Mrs Sharples late of Clifton, and the other 'highly characteristic, but bordering upon caricature.'[22] One of these, though it is hard to say which, may have been the delightful and amusing full-length study reproduced here (see plate 27) from *Public Characters of 1799–1800*. It shows Graves, side-face as usual, dressed in outdoor clothes and striding along at a brisk pace, his walking stick clutched firmly by the middle and his gaze fixed on the far horizon. It is certainly a profile, is characteristic, and might be said to border on caricature. Unless this was one of them, Kilvert's two pictures are both unknown and cannot be traced on the basis of the meagre information given about them. Other portraits exist, some of which are probably copies. A coloured drawing made by John Skinner for his voluminous diary most likely in 1797 is obviously indebted to Gainsborough, but since Skinner was studying with Graves at the time, it may also have been drawn to some extent from the life. Skinner, however, was not so much an artist as a draftsman.[23]

In 1799 Graves was painted in the high style by James Northcote, RA, who exhibited his picture at the Royal Academy in the following year (see plate 28).[24] It shows Graves in clerical garb seated side-faced beside an open window through which his parsonage-house may be seen. The face is that of an old man, but the lips are as firm as they were thirty years before in Gainsborough's drawing. Graves was amused to discover how many of the people he met had seen his picture in London, though he attributed their interest in it more to his age than to his fame:

> *Tho' insignificant thro' life, I'm told,*
> *I famous grow, by merely growing old:*
> *Nor friends alone, but every man I meet,*
> *With gracious greetings stops me in the street;*
> *And seems to envy me my blest condition,*
> *To have my Picture in the exhibition.*
> *By Northcote painted! and so like, you'd swear,*
> *That I myself, in gown and scarf, were there.*[25]

Graves had a high regard for Northcote's gifts as an artist, considering him a strong rival to Reynolds.[26] Immediately after the exhibition this picture entered the collection of Graves's young friend Prince Hoare, who had most likely commissioned it.[27] The present whereabouts of the original are unknown, but good prints of it exist, one of which is reproduced here.

In its obituary the *Gentleman's Magazine*, after summarizing the story of Graves's life and listing his publications with moderate accuracy, attempted a little literary criticism. After declaring that Graves's works 'will always be read with pleasure, there being a sprightliness and epigrammatic turn in his writings which was peculiar to himself, and which he retained to the last,' it wound up by expressing the hope, unfortunately unfulfilled, that Graves's letters to Shenstone, Whistler, and Jago might be published. For the writer obviously it was Graves's personality as seen in his letters that attracted him also to the works; his bounce, his irony, his gift for unexpectedly apt phrases, his love of anecdotes, and his humour. But the prediction that Graves's works would always be read has not come true. *The Spiritual Quixote*, indeed, has been reprinted several times in the nineteenth and twentieth centuries. According to Elizabeth Gaskell, copies of it formed part of the stock in trade of every pedlar who made the rounds in Cumberland and Westmorland, along with copies of *Paradise Lost, Paradise Regained, The Pilgrim's Progress,* and *The Death of Abel.* She called them all 'grave, solid books' and may not have read Graves's novel. But certainly she had heard of it.[28] Three of his translations from the classics have also been reprinted and one of them is still in print. Of the rest, apart from a stray poem or two caught in his net by some compiler of an anthology, none has been reprinted since his death, and many are hard to come by even in great research libraries. It would be idle to maintain that this oblivion is entirely undeserved. Graves wrote too much and too rapidly, and he often set his sights too low. Moreover, he had no influence whatever on the development of English literature, which was about to change direction, for his tastes were old-fashioned and his models mainly in the past. *The Spiritual Quixote, Lucubrations,* and *Recollection ... of William Shenstone* merit a modern reader's attention, and an anthology of the best of his shorter pieces in verse and prose should attract many readers. Most of all, however, Graves deserves to be remembered for himself, as an interesting and complex personality who was at once very much a man of his time and one who suffered the miseries and perplexities and experienced the joys common to all mankind.

Abbreviations

Appendixes

Notes

Abbreviations

AW Anthony Whistler
BL British Library
GM *Gentleman's Magazine*
HP Hester Piozzi
JD James Dodsley
LL Lady Luxborough
MG Mary Graves
PRO Public Record Office, London
RD Robert Dodsley
RG Richard Graves
RJ Richard Jago
SJP Samuel Jackson Pratt
SQ *The Spiritual Quixote* (London: Oxford University Press 1967)
TP Thomas Percy
WS William Shenstone
ed Williams: *The Letters of William Shenstone* ed Marjorie Williams
         (Oxford: Basil Blackwell 1939)
Phillipps ms: Phillipps ms 13851 in the County Record Office, Taunton,
         Somerset

References to the *Gentleman's Magazine* are made in this form:
  GM 41.160 = page 160 in the volume for 1741.
All books cited were published in London unless another place of publication
  is indicated.

Richard Graves's Publications

All publications were anonymous except when the contrary is indicated. But the genuineness of most of them is assured by Graves's frequent references to them in his correspondence with the Dodsley brothers and others, and by his habit of identifying himself on title-pages by some such formula as 'the Editor of *The Spiritual Quixote*.' Notes on the authorship of works are included only when there is a special need for them.

Publications after 1805 are not included.

Generally speaking, the titles of individual compositions are listed only when they were published separately.

1740
'On a Favourite Little Cur' signed Æ. GM 40.460. Repr *Euphrosyne* I (1776)

1741
'To Chloe, on her Fondness for the Enigmatists' signed G. GM 41.160.
  Repr *Festoon* (1766) and *Recollection of Shenstone* 1788

1751
'The Heroines, or Modern Memoirs' *General Advertiser* 14 Mar. Repr *London Magazine* (1751), *Universal Magazine* (1751), Dodsley's *Collection* IV (1755), *Festoon* (1766), *Euphrosyne* I (1776)
'On Ancient Medals' or 'The Cabinet' *The Student* II. 230–2. Repr Dodsley's *Collection* IV (1755) and *Euphrosyne* I (1776)

1755
A Collection of Poems in Four Volumes by Several Hands (Dodsley) 4.330–6, contains Graves's 'The Cabinet,' 'Panacea,' 'The Heroines,' and 'The Parting,'

the author being identified as 'Mr Greaves.' There were many reprintings of this popular anthology.

1756

'On Tully's Head, in Pall-Mall.' *Birmingham Gazette* 20 Dec. Repr *Festoon* (1766)

1758

Epilogue to Robert Dodsley's *Cleone* (by Graves, Shenstone, and Dodsley). The play, including the epilogue, was reprinted 1758, 1759, and 1765. The epilogue by itself was reprinted in the *Annual Register* I (1758) and in the *Works* of William Shenstone (1764).

A Collection of Poems in Six Volumes by Several Hands (Dodsley) 5.62–9, contains Graves's 'To Lady Fane on her Grotto at Basilden,' 'The Invisible,' 'The Pepper-box and Salt-seller,' and 'Written near Bath,' the author being identified as 'Mr Graves.' There were many reprintings of this anthology.

1761

'The Patriot King, or George the Third' *Annual Register* 218. Repr *St James' Chronicle* 30 Jan–2 Feb 1762, *London Magazine* (1762), *Festoon* (1766), and *Euphrosyne* I (1776)

Select Fables ed Robert Dodsley. 3 vols, Birmingham. Graves contributed no 41 in vol. 1 and nos 16 and 17 in vol 3.

1762

'War Declared at Brentford, a Climax' *London Magazine* 44. Repr *Festoon* (1766) and *Euphrosyne* I (1776)

'On the Landskips, in Gainsborough's ... Portraits ...' *London Chronicle* June 24–6. Repr *Festoon* (1766) and *Euphrosyne* I (1776)

1764

'To William Shenstone, Esq., at the Leasowes, By Mr. Graves of Claverton' *Works* of William Shenstone, II, 374–5. Repr *Festoon* (1766) and *Euphrosyne* I (1776)

1765

Preface to vol 3 of *Works* of William Shenstone. Claimed by Graves in *Recollection* (1788) 133. Repr 1769

1766

The Festoon; a Collection of Epigrams, Ancient and Modern ... with an Essay on that Species of Composition London and Bath

The essay is by Graves and the final section of poems consists of original compositions also by him. The remainder of the volume consists of a large number of epigrams selected by him.

Repr 1767, 1776, and Dublin (under title *The Christmas Treat*) 1767, and Dublin (under title *The Bouquet*) 1784. Almost the entire contents were reprinted in *Euphrosyne* I (1776) and II (1780).

1773

The Spiritual Quixote 3 vols. Repr 1774, 1783, 1792. There was a German translation in 1773 and a Dutch one in 1798–9. There appears also to have been a Dublin edition in 1774. Graves himself was responsible for the date 1772 that appears in several works of reference, but no copy bearing that date has been found.

The Love of Order; a Poetical Essay Repr *Euphrosyne* I (1776)

1774

Galateo; or, a Treatise on Politeness, and Delicacy of Manners ... from the Italian of Monsig. Giovanni de la Casa

The Progress of Gallantry; a Poetical Essay Repr *Euphrosyne* I (1776)

1775

Poetical Amusements at a Villa near Bath

vol I (Bath 1775) 97–8: 'On omitting the assembly at Batheaston on Good-Friday' Rev. Mr. G——ves

vol II (London and Bath 1776) 106–10: 'On Beauty' By the Rev. Mr. Gr—v—s

vol III (London and Bath 1777) 10–12: 'Dreams' By Rev. Mr. Graves

vol IV (Bath and London 1781) 51–4: 'On the Transmigration of Souls' By the Rev. Mr. Graves of Claverton

A letter from a correspondent about William Shenstone. *Monthly Review* 53 (Aug) 191. See RG's letter to JD, 26 Dec 75, Phillipps ms, ff 121–2.

1776

Euphrosyne; or, Amusements on the Road of Life

vol I (1776). Repr 1780

vol II (1780; usually coupled with a copy of the second edition of *Euphrosyne* I): contains first printing of 'Echo and Narcissus.' Repr in *Coalition* (1794)

In 1783 three additional gatherings for *Euphrosyne* II were printed containing poems written for Batheaston. These were sold to customers who already possessed *Euphrosyne* II, and for new purchasers they were included in the work. New title-pages were also provided describing the work as the third edition.

1777

'Hortensia's Birthday' *Six Odes Presented to ... Mrs. Catharine Macaulay, on her Birthday* (Bath). Cf Emanuel Green *Bibliotheca Somersetensis* (Taunton 1902) I. 325–6.

1779

Columella; or, the Distressed Anchoret. A Colloquial Tale 2 vols

1784

'Werter to Charlotte,' a short poem added to the anonymous English translation of Goethe's *The Sorrows of Werter, a German Story*, published by Dodsley

Reprinted in editions of the translation published in 1785 and (by Osborne and Griffin) in 1794, as well as in the rival translation by J. Parsons published in 1786. The poem itself was reprinted in *Lucubrations* (1786).

The earlier editions of the anonymous translation published in 1779, 1780, 1782, and 1783 did not contain Graves's poem.

The translation of Goethe's work is by neither Graves nor Daniel Malthus, as often stated.

Fleurettes. The only known copies of this little volume of verse translations from the French are in the Alexander Turnbull Library in Wellington, New Zealand.

1785

Eugenius; or, Anecdotes of the Golden Vale 2 vols. Repr 1786 and Dublin 1786

1786

Lucubrations: consisting of Essays, Reveries, &c., in Prose and Verse by the late Peter of Pontefract

1787

A Letter from a Father to his Son at the University Oxford and London. Repr in Graves's *Sermons* 1799

1788

Recollection of Some Particulars in the Life of the late William Shenstone, Esq.

1789

The Heir Apparent; or, the Life of Commodus ... Translated from the Greek of Herodian
The Rout; or, a Sketch of Modern Life. Repr *Triflers* (1805)

1790

Plexippus; or, the Aspiring Plebian 2 vols. German translation, 1793. The only known copies of this novel are in the British Library in London and the Alexander Turnbull Library in Wellington, New Zealand.

1792

The Meditations of the Emperor Marcus Aurelius Antoninus. A new Translation from the Greek Original, with a Life, Notes, &c by R. Graves, Rector of Claverton. Bath and London

1793

Hiero; on the Condition of Royalty ... from the Greek of Xenophon Bath and London
'Sunday Schools – a Pastoral' in 'a morning paper.' Repr *Reveries of Solitude* 1793
    According to Graves this 'Jeu d'Esprit found its way lately into a morning paper, and was there said to have been written by Dr. Samuel Johnson, while at breakfast with a lady.' The paper has not been identified.
The Reveries of Solitude: consisting of Essays in Prose, a new Translation of the Muscipula, and original pieces in verse Bath and London

1794

The Coalition; or, the Opera Rehears'd, A Comedy Bath and London. Includes second printing of 'Echo and Narcissus'

1795

The Farmer's Son; a Moral Tale By the Rev. *P.P.* M.A. Bath and London. Repr *Triflers* (1805)

1799

Sermons By the Rev. Richard Graves, M.A. Bath and London

1801

Senilities; or, Solitary Amusements; in Prose and Verse Bath and London

1804

The Invalid: with the Obvious Means of Enjoying Health and Long Life
'To Mr. Pratt' GM 04.761. Repr *Triflers* (1805)

1805

The Triflers; consisting of Trifling Essays, Trifling Anecdotes, and a few Poetical Trifles By the late Rev. R. Graves. Bath and London. Prepared for the press by Graves and published shortly after his death by his daughter

A Note on Sources

LETTERS

Of the innumerable letters that Graves must have both sent and received, 161 have survived in either manuscript or print, or occasionally in both forms, not counting a few scraps of otherwise unknown letters quoted in books. Out of that number 97 were written by him and 64 were written to him by one or other of his friends. He was also sometimes mentioned in letters written by those friends to each other. All of these are valuable sources of information about what he was doing and feeling.

The earliest of his correspondences was that with William Shenstone, which began in 1741, after Shenstone left Oxford and before Graves did likewise, and concluded just before Shenstone's death in 1763. Sixty-one letters written by Shenstone to Graves survive and are available in two rival editions, edited respectively by Marjorie Williams and Duncan Mallam, both published in 1939.[1] (The Williams edition, the more satisfactory of the two, has been used here.) All of them were printed in the eighteenth century in either the third volume of Shenstone's *Works* (1765), for which they had been edited by Graves himself, or Thomas Hull's *Select Letters* (1778). Unfortunately only one of the letters that Graves wrote to Shenstone has survived, preserved by some accident in the Dodsley correspondence. When and by whom the remainder were destroyed is unknown, though the finger of probability points to Mary Cutler, Shenstone's housekeeper, who quarrelled with Graves, one of Shenstone's executors, after the poet's death. Some of the gist of Graves's letters, however, may be reconstructed from Shenstone's replies.

In 1754 Graves began a correspondence with the Dodsley brothers, the London publishers, that continued to 1786 and that overlapped the Shenstone correspondence for eight years. Of the 77 letters in this series the first 20 were written to

Robert, the older of the two brothers, who died in 1764, and the remaining 57 to James, the younger.[2] The sent copies of all but four of those letters survive in Phillipps ms 13851 in the Somerset Record Office in Taunton, three of the remainder being in the Bath Reference Library and the fourth in the Yale University Library. The provenance of the Phillipps ms is obscure, though before it passed into its present ownership it belonged to Miss Dorothy Skrine of Warley, near Claverton. At some time it was badly damaged, and to judge by gaps in the foliation, at least 14 of its letters were lost. Some of the surviving ones were also so badly damaged as to be virtually illegible, and almost all of them are illegible in places. (When quoting them I have indicated such spots by means of square brackets, any reading that appears between them being conjectural.) These letters, nevertheless, are invaluable for the insight they give into Graves's business relations with his publishers and into his personal affairs, for both brothers soon became his intimate friends. It is consequently most unfortunate that only two of the letters Graves received, both from Robert, have survived, in the Dodsley letterbook in the Birmingham Public Library. None of the Dodsley letters has ever been printed except incidentally and in part.

Those two are the only extensive correspondences that survive, but there are several short ones, many of them represented by only one letter. By some accident the Phillipps ms contains two such letters from Graves to other correspondents, the first of them to William Shenstone and the other to an unidentified friend. There are also other single letters in other repositories: to George Ballard, to the bishop of Bath and Wells, to Mrs Wigan of Birmingham, to Charles Burney, to William Bowen of Wells, to Sir Joshua Reynolds, to Mrs Piozzi, and to William Meyler of Bath. In addition to them, two important and somewhat longer series exist, the first, consisting of five letters, to Thomas Percy, written by Graves between 1792 and 1803, now in the Yale University Library, and the other, also consisting of five, to Samuel Jackson Pratt, written between 1799 and 1804, now is the Bath Reference Library. Finally, there is one letter by John Scott Hylton written to Graves in 1763, now in the library of the University of Texas.

Rich and varied as that collection may appear, its inadequacies soon become apparent. All the letters that must have been exchanged between Graves and his bosom friend Anthony Whistler have disappeared. Most likely Graves's letters to him were destroyed after Whistler's death by his brother, who also destroyed Shenstone's. But who destroyed Whistler's to Graves is a mystery. If Graves also carried on a correspondence with Richard Jago, as John Nichols thought,[3] it too has vanished. More serious still is the absence of family letters of any date. No letters either to or from Graves's father, his brothers, or his sister survive, and none to or from any of his own children. Fortunately, the gaps in the material caused by the loss of the Whistler and possible Jago papers may be partly filled from the letters of Shenstone and from Whistler's letters to Shenstone printed by

Hull. But the loss of the family correspondence is irreparable. As a result, much of Graves's family history is a blank.

LITERARY WORKS

In using any of the various episodes in the novels and other works that seem to have their origin in the author's own experience, one has to guard against the fallacy of assuming an exact correspondence between the fictional incident and the real one upon which it is based. Compilers of keys and some critics have fallen into that error. Thus for them Columella equals William Shenstone and Parson Pomfret equals Parson Graves. Several such equations have been examined in the preceding chapters and generally found invalid. Undoubtedly, in drawing the character of Columella, Graves used memories of his friend Shenstone, but Columella was a fictional character objectifying an idea suggested by one aspect of the real man's personality, not the whole man, and Parson Pomfret was not the whole of Parson Graves nor, indeed, even the image of Parson Graves that was current, but Graves's parody of himself, behind which he concealed his real self from the world.

The most important of these autobiographical episodes in the novels is the story of Mr Rivers that occupies most of book 6 of *The Spiritual Quixote*. That Graves told the story of his own courtship and marriage in it was understood by some of his friends almost from the start. Presumably William Shenstone, who had had a look at the unfinished manuscript of the novel, was referring to it when he wrote to Graves 26 October 1759 advising him not to make '*any* alteration in the narrative of your own story.'[4] When Thomas Percy, another friend, read the novel shortly after its publication in 1773, he noted in his diary that it was by 'M[r]. Graves of Claverton near Bath' and that the author had 'described the History of his own Marriage, under the name of Rivers & Charlotte Woodville.'[5] For both friends the source of that information must have been Graves himself. However, in editing Shenstone's letters for publication, Graves deleted all references to his courtship and marriage, though filling in the blanks in his own copy,[6] and in 1799, when he permitted the publication of a biographical sketch in *Public Characters of 1799–1800*, he saw to it that it was discreet and made no reference to Mr Rivers. Shortly after his death, however, the *Gentleman's Magazine* in its obituary notice made Mr Rivers's identity public knowledge for the first time, and Alexander Stephens, a great collector of literary scraps, repeated the information in a key to *The Spiritual Quixote* published in a magazine.[7]

'Mr. Rivers's Story' is charmingly told, but as biographical evidence it is woolly. It gives almost no dates and few particulars, and the nature of many of its incidents is left vague. Before accepting it I felt obliged to look for corroboration. The key fact in doubt was the date of Graves's marriage, which had been clandestine. Thanks to assistance rendered by Mr A.J. Phipps and the Genealogical Service of the Church of Jesus Christ of Latter Day Saints in Salt Lake City, Utah, I was able to put my hands on the actual registration of Graves's marriage among the Fleet Marriage Records in the Public Record Office in Chancery Lane, London. Quickly the rest of the picture then fell into place. Certainly 'Mr. Rivers's Story' parallels Mr Graves's, but Mr Rivers, who became a farmer, was not Mr Graves, who became a parson-schoolmaster-writer, and Mr Graves's story is considerably more sordid than the pretty idyll told by Mr Rivers. As biographical evidence it can be trusted only so far.

SECONDARY SOURCES

Such secondary sources as originated close enough to the time of the subject to contain primary material are also useful aids, though they have to be evaluated carefully. The chief of them is a sketch sixteen pages in length plus a full-page cut contained in a serial called *Public Characters*, which appeared in ten more or less annual volumes between 1798 and 1808. It was published by Richard Phillips at his bookshop at 71 St Paul's Churchyard, where he specialized in educational books and works of reference. The editors were anonymous, but one of them is known to have been the Alexander Stephens who has been mentioned already in another context.[8] His colleague or colleagues have not been identified, but one of them may have been Phillips himself, who had proven ability as a biographical writer. As for the contributors, the editors explained that each article was written by 'some friend of the party, whose intimate knowledge of the relative [sic] facts and circumstances qualify him to do ample justice to the character.'[9] The editors apologized for the lack of uniformity in style and manner resulting from their use of many different contributors, and apparently included basic matters of approach and method in their notion of style. The writer of each article, they asserted, was identified by an initial chosen at random, each contributor being given freedom to deal with his subject in the way that seemed most appropriate to him.

The author of the life of Graves was obviously a man of ability, but the life is patchy and oddly constructed. Only four written sources are cited in it, three of them published books (two by Graves himself) and the fourth a communication from 'a sensible correspondent who has the honour to be acquainted with Mr. Graves.' Though the writer posed as a man unacquainted with his subject, the greater part of his information must have come from Graves himself and the details about his appearance and characteristic behaviour from someone who knew him well. The life is also remarkable for the things it does not say. There is almost nothing in it about Graves's private life or his family, and the dry account of his marriage makes no allusion to the tale he based on it in *The Spiritual Quixote*.

Two of the unpublished letters by Graves to Samuel Jackson Pratt show beyond doubt that Pratt was the contributor of this life.[10] He was an old and trusted friend who wrote voluminously, often under the pseudonym of Courtney Melmouth. Graves's letters, written in September 1799, show that Pratt was then putting his sketch of Graves together – 'putting together' rather than 'writing,' because Pratt was drawing on several of Graves's other friends for materials; Graves, in fact, described him as the 'undertaker' rather than author of the article. It is hard to know how much of the actual writing is Pratt's. His, however, is the initial P with which it is signed. One of his collaborators is named in the letters, William Meyler, the Bath bookseller. He probably provided much of the intimate information. Another, though unnamed, may have been the 'sensible correspondent' previously mentioned. I have a suspicion, though no proof, that he was Thomas Percy, to whom Graves had recently sent information about his literary career in another unpublished letter, now at Yale. There may also have been other collaborators, such as Prince Hoare.

The letters to Pratt were written by Graves in a fit of anxiety lest anything be published that was '*improper* to be communicated to the public.' He had seen a draft of the article but had let it get out of his hands prematurely and was particularly anxious about an allusion to 'our Tory Club at Ashbourne,' discussed in chapter 6, which he thought indiscreet. The anecdote was accordingly cut. However, a statement made by him in one of these letters about his motives for writing his *Recollection of ... William Shenstone* was added almost verbatim.[11]

On the whole the life of Graves justifies the editors' assertions. The task had been entrusted to an intimate friend who had easy access to the facts and who in turn enlisted the aid of other intimate friends as well as that of the subject himself, who retained the right to censor the work before publication. Though the resulting biography avoided hurting anybody's feelings or violating the subject's privacy, it was vivid and reliable so far as it went.[12] Of course it did not go as far as one would have liked, but there is no reason to reject what it does say.

About other secondary sources little needs to be said. Francis Kilvert's *Richard Graves of Claverton* (Bath 1858) must be given some weight in spite of its errors because Kilvert had lived in Claverton and must have met some of Graves's friends and associates. W.H. Hutton's essay on Graves in his *Burford Papers* (1905) draws attention to some primary sources that otherwise might be missed. Little else of a biographical nature has been written about Graves, except for some brief articles by N.J.L. Lyons on his possible Methodist background and a useful monograph on his literary career by Charles Jarvis Hill.

Notes

CHAPTER ONE: FAMILY

1 Mickleton Parish Register. For much information on the family history I am indebted to Miss Mary Graves Hamilton of St Albans and Dr Charles Graves of Geneva, and to these two books in particular: F.A. Bates *Graves Memoirs of the Civil War* (London and Edinburgh 1927) chap 10; and [Treadway Russell Nash] *Collections for the History of Worcestershire* (1781–2); also the Parish Register of St Martin, Ludgate.

2 P 144

3 II, 83–9

4 Bates *Graves Memoirs*

5 R.B. Latimer *Cornhill Magazine* ns 47 (1919) 403–10

6 Bates *Graves Memoirs* genealogical table; J. Granger *Biographical History of England* (1779) III, 174

7 BL, King's mss, 84, ff 105–6. I owe this reference to the kindness of Professor Donald Greene.

8 *Remarks and Collections of Thomas Hearne* ed C.E. Doble, D.W. Rannie, et al, 11 vols (Oxford: Oxford Historical Society 1884–1918)

9 x, 182

10 'To Morgan Graves, Esq.' in *Festoon*

11 Bk II, chap 11.

12 P 99

13 P 275

14 *Recollection ... of William Shenstone* 49, and information from the Essex Record Office

15 Harrowby ms 905: 199: 68–82

16 Hearne VIII, 46

17 *The Invalid* 22–3
18 Quoted from Nash *Collections* I, 199
19 Hearne VIII, 329
20 'To Morgan Graves, Esq.'
21 Hearne X, 299
22 Harrowby ms 905: 199: 68
23 Hearne X, 299
24 Hearne X, 320; XI, 70, 217, 223
25 See chap 5.
26 Hearne X, 299
27 Information kindly furnished by W.W.S. Breem, Esq, librarian to the Honourable Society of the Inner Temple
28 *Correspondence of the Rev. Joseph Greene* ed Levi Fox (HM Stationery Office 1965) 76
29 P 332
30 Samuel Johnson *Poems* ed D. Nichol Smith and E.A. McAdam, Jr, 2nd edn (1974) 49–52
31 *Monthly Magazine* 55 (1823) 51; *Notes and Queries* 216 (1971) 63–7 and 218 (1973) 20–2; *London Magazine* 19 (1750) 523; *SQ* 249–57
32 *Notes and Queries* 217 (1972) 379–80
33 India Office Records, Letters from Bandar Abbas, 1745–65 (G / 29 / 2); cf *Columella* I, 196 ff.
34 Hearne X, 446
35 v: Nash *Collections*, and Bates *Graves Memoirs*
36 Hearne IX, 214

CHAPTER TWO: CHILDHOOD

1 Pp 13, 42, 469
2 RG to JD, 13 Oct 73, Bath Reference Library AL 2316
3 *Remarks and Collections of Thomas Hearne* ed C.E. Doble, D.W. Rannie, et al (Oxford Historical Society 1907) VIII, 11
4 Pp 390, 397–401
5 P 464
6 Quoted in Ernest Belcher *Rambles among the Cotswolds* (Evesham 1892) 7
7 *SQ* 21
8 *Monthly Magazine* 55 (1823) 51–2 (cf N.J.L. Lyons *Notes and Queries* 218 [1973] 20–2); William Hewett *History and Antiquities of the Hundred of Compton* (Reading 1844) 96
9 Cf H.J. Holden *Notes and Queries* 207 (1961) 18
10 P 52

11 For information about Dover's Games I am indebted to Mr Francis Burns, secretary to the Dover's Games Committee.

12 Pp 23–4

13 Michael Drayton *Works* ed J. William Hebel (Oxford 1931) IV, 298

14 P 377

15 *Recollection ... of William Shenstone* 115

16 Hearne X, 320

17 William Smith must have been born in 1678 if RG was correct in writing that he was ninety when he died (*Recollection* 116). He became curate of Mickleton in 1718–19 (not 1729, as posted in the parish church), signing the official transcripts of the parish registers, now in the County Record Office in Gloucester, from then to 1745–6 inclusive, describing himself each time as either curate or minister. In 1746 he became vicar of Toddington but probably continued to live in Mickleton, for he turned over his duties in his new parish to a curate, Henry Higford, who signed the Toddington transcripts regularly from then to 1767. Smith died the following year and was buried in the parish church, where his wife and two daughters also lie. A slab was set in the floor of the chancel in their memory by his son, which reads: '[In M]emory / of / the Revd Willm Smith / clerk, late Vicar of Toddington / [and] many years Curate of this Parish / [who] died Feby 22^d AD 1768; and of / Utrecia, his Wife / who died [November 7, A.]D. [1760.] Also of / Mary and Utrecia [their] two daughters. Mary died Jan. 23, A.D. 177[7]. Utrecia died [March] 5, 1743.' The bracketed letters, now illegible, have been supplied from Ralph Bigland *Historical Monuments and Genealogical Collections Relative to the County of Gloucester* (1791) I, 215

18 *Public Characters of 1799–1800* 377

19 For the history of Abingdon School see Douglas Macleane *History of Pembroke College* (Oxford Historical Society 1897) and James Townsend *History of Abingdon* (1920).

20 D / EP 7 / 144 A

21 P 114

22 From a private letter from Mr Nigel Hammond, master and archivist of Abingdon School

23 For the method of election see Anthony à Wood *History and Antiquities of the Colleges and Halls in the University of Oxford* (1668, repr Oxford 1786) I, 618. The three names are shown in the class list referred to above (n 20).

CHAPTER THREE: PEMBROKE

1 *Recollection of ... William Shenstone* (1788) 14–17

2 P 16. Cf Douglas Macleane *History of Pembroke College* (Oxford 1897) 374 n.

3 In a handwritten note added to page 48 of volume 2 of his copy of
Shenstone's *Works* (1764–9), RG recalled that a rumour ('clamor') went about
in the college that Shenstone, Whistler, and he had shut themselves up to
write character sketches of all the other members of the college (Hans Hecht
'Kleine Studien zu Graves, Shenstone und Percy' *Anglia* 58 [1934] 134).

4 P 4 and n

5 I, 12. Cf *Triflers* 22.

6 Cf John Wain *Samuel Johnson* (1974) 51–2.

7 Pp 46–8. Cf Hecht 'Kleine Studien' 134.

8 II, 109–12

9 Samuel Johnson *Prefaces, Biographical and Critical* x (1781) 'Shenstone' 4

10 *Recollection* 23

11 *Poems upon Various Occasions* (Oxford 1737)

12 *Recollection* 18n

13 The Osborn Collection at Yale has the sent copies of eleven of these letters,
ten of which were printed in Thomas Hull *Select Letters* (1778) I, 160–3, and
II, 22–60. All but one are undated.

14 *Recollection* 149

15 ws to aw [Nov 43], ed Williams, 75

16 *Recollection* 36 ff

17 *Recollection* 46

18 Cf N.J.L. Lyons *Notes and Queries* 217 (1972) 379–80.

19 ws to RG, Nov 42, ed Williams, 60

20 *SQ* 13–14 and n

21 'Careless! Oh, how you were mourned, and how worthy you were to be
mourned, by our muses!'

22 *GM* 52.192

23 *Sir Joshua's Nephew* ed Susan M. Radcliffe (1930) 17–18, quoted from an
unpublished paper by Dr J.D. Fleeman called 'Dr. Johnson and Oxford' that
he most kindly allowed me to read

24 Ibid

25 *SQ* 193

CHAPTER FOUR: ALL SOULS

1 Anthony à Wood *Antiquities of the Colleges and Halls in the University of Oxford*
(1786) I, 256–8; cf Charles Edward Mallet *History of the University of Oxford*
(1927).

2 *Memoirs of the Life of Edward Gibbon* ed G.B. Hill (1900) 57

3 I, 14–16

4 Ms Ballard 37, f 26

5 *Literary Anecdotes* II (1812) 266–70
6 The two finds are nos 235 and 67 respectively in R.G. Collingwood and R.F. Wright *The Roman Inscriptions in Britain* (1965).
7 At Magdalen a clerk is someone who helps out with the services in the chapel, today usually a member of the choir. Ballard is not known to have had a singing voice; perhaps he read the lessons. Cf J.H. Bloxam *A Register of the Presidents, Fellows, Demies ... and other members of ... Magdalen College* (Oxford 1857) II, 95–102.
8 Bodleian ms Autog b 1
9 Quoted in Lucy Sutherland *The University of Oxford in the Eighteenth Century, a Reconsideration* (Oxford 1973) 20
10 *Recollection of ... Shenstone* 27 n
11 P 94
12 Most of them were published, with editorial omissions, in Thomas Hull *Select Letters* (1778). The mss at Yale are the sent copies, later prepared to serve as printer's copy for Hull's book.
13 AW to WS, nd, Osborn Collection no 2, Hull *Select Letters* II, 22–4
14 AW to WS, nd, Osborn Collection no 11, Hull *Select Letters* II, 59–60
15 Pp 22–3
16 RG's 'A Few Trifling Anecdotes of the late Sir William Blackstone' *The Triflers* 53–9; biographical note by Isaac Reed in *A Collection of Poems* (1782) IV, 240–1; and information kindly supplied by Mr J.S.G. Simmons, librarian and archivist of All Souls
17 *The Triflers* 56
18 *A Collection of Poems* (1755, repr 1782) IV, 242

CHAPTER FIVE: THE GENTLEMAN AND THE CHRISTIAN

1 In this chapter I am indebted to the following sources: *The Journal of the Rev. Charles Wesley* ed Thomas Jackson, 2 vols (1849); *The Journal of the Rev. John Wesley, A.M.* ed Nehamiah Curnock, 8 vols [1904]; V.H.H. Green *The Young Mr. Wesley* (1961); Albert M. Lyles *Methodism Mocked* (1960); Maximin Piette *John Wesley in the Evolution of Protestantism* (1937); and the following papers by N.J.L. Lyons: *Richard Graves and the Methodist Background of THE SPIRITUAL QUIXOTE* MA thesis, University of Sheffield 1972; *The Spiritual Quixote*; A New Key to the Characters in Graves's Novel' *Notes and Queries* 216 (1971) 63–7; 'Another key to *The Spiritual Quixote*' ibid, 218 (1973) 20–3; and 'Satiric Techniques in *The Spiritual Quixote*' *Durham University Journal* 36 (1974) 266–77. Cf Graves's account of the beginnings of Methodism in Oxford in SQ 31.
2 Green *Young Mr. Wesley* 156

3 It can scarcely have been the Holy Club itself, which did not meet at Pembroke College, for Dr Dumaresq, the leader of the group RG joined, is never mentioned in any of the Methodist journals that I have seen. Though it imitated the Holy Club in one of its austerities, it occupied its time in reading Greek rather than in religious studies and the works of charity that had become the main concern of the Wesleys and their followers by 1732.

4 Charles Wesley's *Journal* I, 77

5 Ibid

6 *SQ* 325–7; cf *Journal* 20 May 1742

7 *Notes and Queries* 218 (1973) 21

8 Bk II, chaps 3–18

9 RG to HP, 1 Feb 99, Columbia University Library

10 P 380

11 *Life of Johnson* ed George Birkbeck Hill and L.F. Powell (Oxford 1934) II, 467

12 II, 215

13 Curnock, in a footnote in his edition of *John Wesley's Journal* (II, 151 n), misquotes this entry, making it say that Charles Wesley accused RG of driving Charles Caspar Graves insane.

14 Charles Wesley's *Journal* I, 70, 72, 73

15 Ibid, I, 76

16 John Wesley's *Journal* II, 152 n

17 *Life of Silas Told* (1786. repr 1959) 65 ff

18 John Wesley's *Journal* III, 40–2

19 John Wesley's *Journal* III, 253; cf 'Richard Viney's Memoranda' *Proceedings of the Wesley Historical Society* XIII (1922), XIV (1924), XV (1926) passim.

20 Charles Wesley's *Journal* I, 421–2

21 J.L. 'Original Memorials of Dr. Johnson's Religious Friends' *Christian Observer* 31 (1831) 1–13

22 F. Kilvert *Richard Graves of Claverton* (Bath 1858) 10

23 'A Letter from a Father to his Son' 2nd edn, in *Sermons* (1799) 210

24 *A Collection of Poems* (1758, repr 1782) v, 70

25 WS to RG, 24 Nov 59, ed Williams, 535

26 RG to unknown correspondent, 2 Dec 62, Phillipps ms, f 22

27 Though not published until 1773, this novel was almost certainly begun in the 1750s. How much was written then and how many changes and additions were made in the final revision before publication are unknown. So it is difficult to fit the attitude he shows in the book into the history of his feelings about Methodism.

CHAPTER SIX: TISSINGTON

1 Cf George Clark *History of the Royal College of Physicians* (Oxford 1964–72);

Thomas Lawrence *Franci Nichollsii M.D. ... Vita* (1780); George C. Peachey *A Memoir of William and John Hunter* (Plymouth 1924); Michael Donald Warren 'Medical Education during the 18th Century' *Postgraduate Medical Journal* 27 (1951) 304–11. Would-be surgeons fared differently; they were trained as apprentices to master surgeons working in hospitals.

2 P 379
3 Pp 23–5
4 MG to WS, 12 May 40, in Thomas Hull *Select Letters* (1778) I, 8–9
5 University and Diocesan Archives, Bodleian Library, Oxford
6 *Woodforde: Passages from ... the Diary of a Country Parson* ed James Beresford (1935) 13
7 P 411
8 WS to RG, 1 June 41, ed Williams, 25–6
9 29 May 1741, Tissington parish register
10 Diocesan Archives, Bodleian Library, Oxford
11 RG to SJP, 24 Sept 99, Bath Reference Library AL 2051. Graves, whose memory was now failing, addressed Pratt incorrectly as 'Samuel Johnson Pratt.'
12 *An Account of the Life of Dr. Samuel Johnson ... Written by Himself. To which are added, Original Letters to Dr. Samuel Johnson, by Miss Hill Boothby* (1805) 52, 113–15, 123. John Taylor of Ashbourne, a few miles from Tissington, Johnson's friend, was a Tory and may have had something to do with the Tory Club.
13 Bk x, chaps 7–31
14 James Boswell *Life of Johnson* ed John Wilson Croker (1831) IV, 524–5
15 Colonel Rappee was identified in one of the keys as 'Colonel Deane,' whoever he may have been, but obviously he also has resemblances to Sir John Cope (cf *SQ* 367 and n) as well as to Falstaff.
16 P 365
17 P 402
18 *GM* 53.170
19 *SQ* 366
20 Lichfield Diocesan Archives
21 Quoted from N.J.L. Lyons's Sheffield MA thesis, *Richard Graves and the Methodist Background to* THE SPIRITUAL QUIXOTE (1972) 185
22 *Public Characters of 1799–1800* (1799) 380
23 *SQ* 390–3
24 All Souls Archives
25 *Public Characters* 380–1. The archdeaconry of Berkshire is now a part of the diocese of Oxford.

CHAPTER SEVEN: UTRECIA

1 In *Festoon* and *Euphrosyne* I. In *Festoon* it was included in the section devoted to his own compositions and was described as the work of a schoolboy. The identification of the lady with Molly Aston is conjectural.
2 *Johnsonian Miscellanies* ed George Birkbeck Hill (Oxford 1897) I, 255
3 unà actæ memor pueritiæ
4 puellæ simplici, innocuæ, eleganti
5 *Recollection of ... William Shenstone* 115–16
6 C.J. Hill, in *Literary Career of Richard Graves* (Northampton, Mass 1934–5) 63, identified him with Graves, but N.J.L. Lyons, *Notes and Queries* 216 (1971) 63–7, pointed out the objection to that identification mentioned above.
7 Published in his *Poems upon Various Occasions* (Oxford 1737)
8 *Recollection* 44
9 ws to rg, June 42, ed Williams, 55
10 Hans Hecht 'Kleine Studien zu Graves, Shenstone und Percy' *Anglia* 58 (1934) 138
11 *Recollection* 116. Hill, in *Literary Career* 63, identified him with Graves. Neither identification is convincing.
12 Shenstone's eighteenth elegy, *Works* (1764) I, 65
13 My authority for this date is both the Mickleton parish register and the memorial slab to the Smith family, still to be seen in the church.
14 Christopher Whitfield *History of Chipping Campden* (Eton 1958) 181. He gives no basis for his statement.
15 Elegy IV, *Works* I, 21–2. In his own copy Graves identified Ophelia as Utrecia Smith and the person addressed as himself (Hecht 'Kleine Studien' 133).
16 *Works* II, 68–74
17 Pp 131–5
18 The 'Key to the *Spiritual Quixote*' in *Monthly Magazine* 55 (1823) 51–2 suggests the Cholmondley identification. Cf N.J.L. Lyons *Notes and Queries* 216 (1971) 63–7 and 218 (1973) 20–2. C.J. HILL, in *Literary Career* 63–4, supports the identification with Graves. The present writer in his notes to the Oxford edition of the novel (1967, p 483), held Hill's view, but does not do so now. For a judicious survey of all the relevant points see F.D.A. Burns *Notes and Queries* 218 (1973) 420–1.

CHAPTER EIGHT: LUCY

1 Diocesan Record Office, Salisbury
2 ws to rg, 6 Apr 46, ed Williams, 100–2
3 *Public Characters of 1799–1800* (1799) 381; Aldworth parish register

4 See Appendix B
5 WS to RG, June 48, Osborn Collection, Yale; cf ed Williams, 149–51.
6 *Monthly Review* 48 (1773) 384–8
7 P 188
8 P 190
9 WS to RG, about 1745, ed Williams, 94–6
10 BL, King's mss 80–97, f 107
11 I, 125–8
12 II, 80–91
13 WS to RG, 6 Apr 46, 11 May 46, and 1746 ('ineunte anno'), ed Williams, 100–2, 103, 104–6
14 WS to RG, 1746 ('ineunte anno'), ed Williams, 105
15 WS to RG, 21 Sept 47, ed Williams, 115
16 WS to RG, end June 48, ed Williams, 151
17 WS to RG, 'June y^e. 1748,' Osborn Collection, Yale; cf ed Williams, 150.
18 Cf N.J.L. Lyons *Notes and Queries* 216 (1971) 63–7 and 218 (1973) 20–2, as well as his Sheffield MA thesis, *Richard Graves and The Methodist Background to 'The Spiritual Quixote'* (1972).
19 Pp 381–2
20 *Some Account of London* 4th edn (1805) 194
21 *The Grub-street Journal* 27 Feb 1735
22 Cf John Ashton *The Fleet* (1888); John Sutherden Burn *The Fleet Registers* (1833); Alex. Charles Ewald 'The Fleet Marriages' *GM* 88. 466–78; and especially Laurence Stone *The Family, Sex, and Marriage in England, 1500–1800* (1977).
23 R.G. 7–546, p 2
24 R.G. 7–228, p 403
25 *Grub-street Journal* 10 June 1736
26 WS to RG, 21 Sept 47, ed Williams, 115–17
27 Oxford diocesan records
28 Parish register
29 *A Collection of Poems in Four Volumes* (1755) IV, 335–6
30 WS to LL, 18 Apr 48, ed Williams, 135
31 *Euphrosyne* I, 197
32 William Shenstone *Works* (1764–9) III, 162–3, Bodleian Library
33 WS to LL, 5 May 48, ed Williams, 140
34 20 Feb 1783
35 WS to LL, 5 May 48, ed Williams, 140
36 WS to RG, June 48, ed Williams, 149; Thomas Hull *Select Letters* (1778) II, 58
37 Parish register
38 AW to WS, 7 Oct 49, Hull *Select Letters* I, 102–6

39 LL to WS, 27 Feb 52, *Letters Written by Lady Luxborough to William Shenstone* 298
40 WS to RG, 21 Aug 48, ed Williams, 155–6
41 P 382
42 *Public Characters* 381
43 Francis Kilvert *Richard Graves of Claverton* (Bath 1858) 10
44 'A Cottage Garden' *Euphrosyne* I. 197
45 'Ennui' *Lucubrations* 120

CHAPTER NINE: THE CLERICAL CALLING

1 WS to RG, 21 Sept 47, ed Williams, 116; an obscure allusion
2 *Public Characters of 1799–1800* 382–3
3 *Bath Journal* 29 May 1749
4 Documents from the diocesan records in the County Record Office,
   Taunton: the presentation letter, the presentation register, and RG's bond
5 Claverton parish register
6 John Collinson *History and Antiquities of the County of Somerset* (Bath 1791) 145
7 His delay in moving to Claverton must have been due to prior commitments
   in Whitchurch. No doubt Claverton was served by a curate in the meanwhile.
8 'An Apology for Unseasonable Rhymes' *Festoon*, 2nd edn (1767) 158
9 *Lucubrations* viii. The anecdote as it appeared in print seems garbled, and so I
   have used only so much of it as I could be reasonably sure of.
10 WS to RG, 3 Oct 59, 26 Oct 59, ed Williams, 523, 527. Cf Shenstone's *Works*
   (1764–5) II, 368.
11 RG to unknown correspondent, 24 Dec 62, Phillipps ms ff 43–6
12 *The Triflers* 7
13 *SQ* 462
14 Repr *Euphrosyne* I, 22
15 I, 66–7
16 Pp 63–4
17 This sermon is undated, but it was put first in the volume and was described
   as a visitatorial one. In a letter to an unidentified correspondent, dated 1762,
   Graves mentioned having preached at a visitation twelve years before
   (Phillipps ms ff 43–6). The sermon he preached then was most likely this
   one.
18 Pp 12–13
19 *Public Characters* 386
20 *SQ* 432
21 *SQ* 350
22 Joseph Priestley *Letter to the Young Men, who are in a Course of Education for the
   Christian Ministry at the Universities of Oxford and Cambridge* (1787)

23 *Letter from a Father to his Son* (1787, repr in *Sermons* [1799]) 204, 216
24 II, 185
25 Pp 215–16
26 *The Love of Order* was published in 1773, but in a note at the beginning RG wrote that it had been 'sketched out many years since.'
27 *Lucubrations* 124–5
28 [E.J.D. Morrison] *The History of Claverton* (Bath 1962) 12
29 *Public Characters* 383, and RG to RD, 25 Apr 63, Phillipps mss, ff 47–9
30 Parish registers of Kilmarston, in Somerset Record Office, Taunton, D/D/Br
31 His letter of resignation in the diocesan archives at Taunton
32 Claverton parish register
33 Richard Warner *Literary Recollections* (1830) II, 19–21; RG to SJP, 21 Mar 1801 (apparently old style), Bath Reference Library

CHAPTER TEN: HOME

1 *A General Account of all the Rivers of Note in Great Britain* (1801) 236, 238
2 Richard Warner *An Historical and Descriptive Account of Bath, and its Environs* (Bath 1802) 144
3 *The Historic and Local New Bath Guide* (1805) 56; *The New Prose Bath Guide for the Year 1778* (Bath 1778) 58; *The New Bath Guide; or Useful Pocket Companion* (Bath 1776) 41–2; *The Bath and Bristol Guide* (Bath 1755, repr 1969) 27
4 John Collinson *History and Antiquities of the County of Somerset* (Bath 1791) I, 147
5 *Observations on Modern Gardening* (1770) 1
6 *The English Garden; A Poem* (Dublin 1786) bk I, ll 275–8
7 Cf *The Genius of the Place; The English Landscape Garden, 1620–1820* ed John Dixon Hunt and Peter Willis (1975), a useful anthology of essays on gardening in the period.
8 'Domestic Happiness' *Reveries of Solitude* 173–4
9 *SQ* 186, 188
10 LL to WS, 4 Dec 52, 1 Apr 53, *Letters Written by Lady Luxborough* 320,334
11 WS to RG, 16 Feb 51, ed Williams, 294
12 *Euphrosyne* II, 208
13 *Festoon*, 2nd edn, 183
14 *Ibid*, 158
15 Repr *Euphrosyne* I, 178
16 *Euphrosyne* I, 207
17 In the Somerset Record Office in Taunton there is a letter dated 20 June 1770 from RG to the bishop of Bath and Wells in which RG informs his lordship that he has appointed his son Richard curate of Claverton at

£30 per annum until he can secure a more valuable benefice elsewhere. With the letter is a note certifying that his son intended offering himself for ordination at the bishop's next visit. See also D/P/Kilm 2/1/3 in the same archive.

18 GM 80.298

19 I am indebted to the archivists at the Hampshire and Berkshire record offices for supplying information regarding the careers of Richard Head, Danvers Graves, and Morgan Graves at Chieveley and elsewhere. Francis Kilvert, *Richard Graves of Claverton* (Bath 1858) 10, supplied further information about the Graves family, derived from a Mr Bartholomew, grand-nephew to RG's wife. And I am particularly indebted to Mrs J.U. Todd for information from published as well as unpublished sources about Morgan Graves and the parish of Redgrave-cum-Botesdale. See also RG to JD, 1 Mar 73, Phillipps ms, ff 93–6.

20 Oxford University Archives

21 *Euphrosyne* II, 79

22 Claverton parish register

23 Ibid

24 Lord Saye and Sele committed suicide in 1788, owing, according to a family tradition reported in G.E.C., to an incurable headache. But that tradition is suspect, because RG told a similar story in *Columella* some years earlier. It was probably a stock legend that became attached to more than one name.

25 'Nepenthe' *The Invalid* 103

26 *Senilities* 1–30

27 II, 17. One exception is Miss Sacharissa Nonsuch, in *Columella*.

28 *Lucubrations* 42–51

29 *Euphrosyne* II, 198–9

30 'Echo and Narcissus' *Euphrosyne* II, 11; in 2nd edn (1794) the second line quoted was softened to read: 'Should rather neglected, in solitude pine.'

31 'Nepenthe' *The Invalid* 104

32 Register of burials 1813–48, under date 17 Mar, Guildhall, London

33 Diocesan records in Somerset Record Office, Taunton

34 RG to SJP, 24 Sept 99, 21 Mar 01, Bath Reference Library

35 *Lucubrations* 121

36 RG to JD, 23 Oct 75, Phillipps ms, f 117

37 GM 04.761

38 *Euphrosyne* I, 207

39 I, 193; cf motto on title-page of first edition (1774) of *The Progress of Gallantry:* 'The attachment between the Sexes is a natural principle; which forms, in a considerable degree, the happiness of human life.'

40 *Lucubrations* 121–2; see also 'Nepenthe,' *The Invalid* 103.

CHAPTER ELEVEN: SCHOOL

1 RG to SJP, 21 Mar 18 01, Bath Reference Library
2 There is no information on the size of the fees Graves charged his pupils, but in 1759 he may have indicated it when he remarked that he had lost over £50 by the death of an Irish baronet, if the baronet's son was to have been one of his pupils (RG to RD, 27 Mar 59, Phillipps ms, f 277).
3 RG to SJP, 21 Mar 18 01, Bath Reference Library; cf 'Nepenthe' *The Invalid* 104.
4 Harrowby ms 905: 199: 68–82
5 Claverton parish register
6 *Euphrosyne* II, 135–6
7 RG to RD, 25 Apr 58, Phillipps ms, ff 27–30
8 RG to RD, 25 Apr 63, Phillipps ms, ff 47–9
9 RG to RD, 27 Mar [59], Phillipps ms, ff 1–2
10 Eg, RG to RD, 21 May 63, Phillipps ms, ff 51–4
11 *Eugenius* II, 28
12 *Euphrosyne* II, 156
13 *Letters from a Late Eminent Prelate* 2nd edn (1809) 384
14 P 2
15 RG to unknown correspondent, 24 Dec 62, Phillipps ms, ff 43–6
16 *Letters from a Late Eminent Prelate* 428
17 Katharine E. Symons *The Grammar School of King Edward* VI, *Bath* (Bath 1934) 248
18 E.W.A. Walker *Skrine of Warleigh* (1936) 34–40
19 See Jasmine Profit in *Bath and West Evening Chronicle* 31 Jan 1986, 9.
20 Patricia James *Population Malthus* (1979) 15–17; also the memoir by William Otter prefixed to T.R. Malthus *Principles of Political Economy* 2nd edn (1836), espec xxix–xxxi. The extracts from RG's letters are quoted from this source.

CHAPTER TWELVE: FRIENDS, OLD AND NEW

1 WS to RG, 16 Feb 51, ed Williams, 293
2 Cf Johnson's *Dictionary* sv *speculation*, sense 2.
3 WS wrote to him at Whitchurch on 6 June; see ms in Osborn Collection at Yale. Williams printed it in her edition, 397–8, but misdated it the seventh and left out the address. Quoted here from ms. The reading in Williams is slightly different.
4 *Reveries of Solitude* 54; cf *The Invalid* introduction.
5 WS to RJ, 28 Mar 51, ed Williams, 303
6 WS to LL, 14 May 55, ed Williams, 449

7 WS to RG, 26 Oct 59, 24 Nov 59, 9 Feb 60, ed Williams, 528, 534, 549

8 *Recollection of ... William Shenstone* 69–70

9 *SQ* 329–30

10 RG to unknown correspondent, 24 Dec 62, Phillipps ms, ff 43–4

11 *Recollection* 165–6

12 I, 293–5

13 *Euphrosyne* I, 296

14 'See! the tall youth' *Works* of Shenstone (1764–5) II, 374–5; repr *Festoon* and *Euphrosyne* I

15 RG's answer to Mary Cutler's bill of complaint, PRO C 12/1892/22–8265

16 RG to RD, 25 Apr 63, Phillipps ms, ff 47–9

17 The following letters in the Phillipps ms deal with the editing of WS's *Works*: RG to RD, 25 Apr 63, Apr/May 63, 21 May 63, 20 June 63, 30 Mar 64, 9 Apr 64, ff 47–9, 281–4, 51–4, 55–8, 231–4, 59–62.

18 *Recollection* 133

19 WS to RG, 23 Oct 54, ed Williams, 413

20 Cf hans Hecht 'Kleine Studien zu Graves, Shenstone und Percy' *Anglia* 58 (1934) 131–9.

21 Cf ed Williams, 149–51; published in 1778 by Thomas Hull in *Select Letters*.

22 WS to RG, 7 June 54, ed Williams, 397–8

23 *Monthly Review* 53 (1775) 191. For evidence of authorship see RG to JD, 26 Dec 75, Phillipps ms, ff 121–2.

24 John Nichols *Biographical and Literary Anecdotes of William Boyer* (1782) 448n: 'Columella ... in which he is thought to glance at his friend Mr. Shenstone.' Cf C.J. Hill 'Shenstone and Richard Graves's *Columella*' PMLA 49 (1934) 566–76, and his *Literary Career of Richard Graves* Smith College Studies in Modern Languages 16 (1934–5) 76–84; and F.D.A. Burns *William Shenstone* diss, Sheffield 1970.

25 Cf Cassilde Tournebize 'Bonheur et excentricité dans le roman de Richard Graves, *Columella or the Distressed Anchoret*' in *L'Excentricité en Grand-Bretagne au 18e siècle* (Lille: Université de Lille 1976) 101–16.

26 RG to JD, 26 Aug [79], Phillipps ms, ff 271–4, and 20 Apr [84], ff 291–2. The proper title of Fénelon's poem is 'Ode à l'Abbé de Langeron.'

27 Only two copies of this work are known to have survived, both of which are in the Alexander Turnbull Library in Wellington, New Zealand. I am indebted to the kindness of its director for a xerox copy of one of them.

28 P 130

29 P 53

30 Pp 55–6

31 *Lucubrations* 120

32 See RG to RD, 6 Jan [64?], 30 Mar [64?], Phillipps ms, ff 293, 231–4.

33 *The Triflers* 53
34 *Columella* ii, 228
35 Vol i, bk v
36 *Lucubrations* 120
37 *Euphrosyne* i, 56–9
38 Claverton parish registers; Richard Graves 'Trifling Anecdotes of the late
   Ralph Allen, Esq.' in *Triflers* 61–80; Richard Graves *Festoon* 2nd edn, 171–2,
   213. Cf [Richard Warner] *An Historical and Descriptive Account of Bath and its
   Environs* (Bath 1802) 134–46; Benjamin Boyce *The Benevolent Man* (Cambridge, Mass 1967); and Howard Erskine-Hill *The Social Milieu of Alexander
   Pope* (New Haven and London 1975) 204–40.
39 *The History of Tom Jones, a Foundling* ed Martin C. Battestin and Fredson
   Bowers (1975) i, 4
40 'Mr. Allen, or the Great Plebian' *Festoon* 172
41 P 367
42 *Triflers* 66–8
43 They are mainly in Phillipps ms 13851 in the County Record Office in
   Taunton, Somerset. The rest are in the Dodsley letterbook in the Birmingham Public Library, in the Reference Library in Bath, and in Yale University
   Library. Cf Ralph Straus *Robert Dodsley, Poet, Publisher and Playwright* (1910);
   W.P. Courtney *Dodsley's Collection of Poetry* (1910).
44 RG to RD, 26 Oct 54, Phillipps ms, ff 1–2
45 WS to RG, 22 Feb 55, ed Williams, 427
46 For some unknown reason RG had altered the spelling of his name at this
   time to Greaves, and so in *A Collection* it appeared in that form. Cf WS to RG,
   21 Mar 55, ed Williams, 434.
47 RG to RD, 3 Sept [56], Phillipps ms, ff 285–8, mutilated). Other primary
   sources for the history of *Cleone* are RG to RD, 10 Sept 56, 7 Jan 57, 10
   Dec 58, Phillipps ms, ff 3–6, 11–14, 31–4; WS to RG, 27 July 56, 8 Apr 57,
   25 Nov 58, 6 Jan 59, ed Williams, 455, 467–8, 494–7, 501–3; and RD to WS,
   28 Aug [56], 5 Oct [56], 11 Jan 57, 4 Nov [58], 20 Jan 59, BL, Add ms 28959,
   ff 147, 113–16, 121, 231, 241, and passim). Cf Charles J. Hill *Philological
   Quarterly* 14 (1935) 181–4, and James Gray *Dalhousie Review* 54 (1974)
   207–27.
48 The three ms versions are RG's first draft in Phillipps ms, ff 285–8 (RG to RD,
   3 Sept [56]); RD to WS, 8 Oct 56, BL, Add ms 28959 ff 115–16); and back
   leaves of WS's copy of *Cleone* (1st edn, 1758), in the Bodleian (Dom e 574).
   The two printed ones are *Cleone, a Tragedy* 1758 (1st and 2nd edns); and
   Cleone, a Tragedy 1759 (3rd edn) and 1765 (4th edn) and *Annual Register* i
   (1758) 435–6.
49 Hecht 'Kleine Studien' 134

50 From Thomas Percy's note to ws's letter to RG, 25 Nov 58, in his copy of vol 3 of Shenstone's *Works*, now in the Bodleian

51 RG to RD, 20 Dec 58, Ph illipps ms, ff 31–4

52 RG to RD, 27 Mar [59], Phillipps ms, ff 277–80

53 I, vii

54 First published in the *Birmingham Gazette* 20 Dec 56; repr *Festoon*. Cf RD to RG, 30 Dec 56, Birmingham Public Library, and RG to RD, 7 Jan 57, (Phillipps ms, ff 11–14.

55 RG to RD, 22 Feb 57, Phillipps ms, ff 15–17, and RD to RG, 24 Oct 57, Birmingham Public Library

56 RG contributed three fables: 'The Mimic and the Countryman' in vol I and 'The Raven and the Magpie' and 'The Sunflower and the Tuberose' in vol III. See ws to RG, 3 Oct 59, 26 Oct 59, 24 Nov 59, 9 Feb 60, 7 July 60, 1 Mar 61, ed Williams, 523, 527, 534, 547, 556, 572); and RG to RD, 15 Oct 59, Phillipps ms, ff 35–8. Cf Hull *Select Letters* I, 264–70, 277–9.

57 RG to unknown correspondent, 24 Dec 62, Phillipps ms, ff 43–6)

58 RG to RD, 10 Jan 62, Phillipps ms, ff 39–40

59 RG to RD, 27 Mar 59, Phillipps ms, ff 277–80

60 RG to RD, 9 Apr 64, Phillipps ms, ff 59–62

61 RG to JD, 12 Apr [85], [25 Dec] 85, Phillipps ms, ff 251–4, 145–8

62 RG to JD, 16 Apr 91, Phillipps ms, ff 191–3); fragmentary letter, RG to TP, c1792, at Yale

63 RG to JD, nd [1792], Phillipps ms, ff 239–42

64 RG to JD, 25 Jan 96, Phillipps ms, ff 195–6

65 *Triflers* 12; cf preface to *Euphrosyne* II.

66 *Correspondence* ed W.S. Lewis et al, 39 (1974) 240–2

67 *Bath Anecdotes and Characters* by the Genius Loci (1782) 150

68 'On the Poetical Society at Bath E——n' *Euphrosyne* I, 47–9

69 *Six Odes presented to ... Mrs. Catharine Macaulay, on her Birth-Day* (Bath [1777]); RG to SJP, 18 Oct 02, Bath Reference Library; cf Emmanuel Green, *Bibliotheca Somersetensis* (1802), and G. Monkland *The Literature and Literati of Bath* (Bath and London 1854) 32–3.

70 'A Domestic Scene in Rural Life' *Euphrosyne* I, 38–40; cf 'On a Favourite Spring at Cl——n' *Euphrosyne* I, 36–7.

71 S.J. Pratt *Harvest Home* (1805) II, 491 (where the name is misspelled Matthias); *Bath Chronicle* 29 Nov 1824

72 'To Prince Hoare, Esq.' *Senilities* 174

73 RG to SJP, 21 Mar 18 01, Bath Reference Library

74 S.J. Pratt *Harvest Home* III, 488 ff

75 BL, Add ms 33.729, ff 4–5

76 BL, Add ms 33.635.

77 BL, Add mss 33.633–730, espec 33.635 and 729. Cf *Journal of a Somerset Rector, 1803–34* ed Howard and Peter Coombs (Bath 1930, repr 1971); and Virginia Woolf 'Two Parsons' *Common Reader* (1932).
78 III, 487–8
79 In the Osborn Collection at Yale
80 S.J. Pratt *Gleanings in England* (1803) III, xlvii–xlix
81 Richard Polwhele *Traditions and Recollections* (1826) I, 132–3.
82 'On Conversation' *Senilities* 74

CHAPTER THIRTEEN: TRIFLING

1 'An Altar to Vanity' *Euphrosyne* I, 171
2 GM 40.460
3 WS to RJ, after Sept 40, ed Williams, 11; WS to RG, Aug 42, Feb 43, ed Williams, 58, 63
4 No 41 in vol 1 and nos 16 and 17 in vol 3
5 RG to JD, 12 Oct 69, Phillipps ms, ff 71–4. The book was dated 1766 though actually published at the end of 1765.
6 RG to JD, 21 Oct 75, Phillipps ms, ff 117–20
7 Eg, *The Spiritual Quixote* (1773), *The Love of order* (1773), *The Progres of Gallantry* (1774), and perhaps others
8 There were several Quixotic literary works in England in the eighteenth century, and the name Quixote appeared in titles from Henry Fielding's play *Don Quixote in England* (1733) on down through the century. RG may have got the suggestion for his title from eitherCharlotte Lennox's *Female Quixote* (1752) or the anonymous *The Spiritual Quixote; or, the entertaining history of Don Ignatius Loyola* (1754). Cf Miriam Rossiter Small *Charlotte Ramsay Lennox* (New Haven 1935).
9 Charles Jarvis Hill has told the story of the publication of this novel at length in *The Literary Career of Richard Graves* (Northampton, Mass 1934–5) 16 ff. RG himself was responsible for the wrong date, 1772, often given for the first edition. RG to TP, c1792, 'List of my Trifling Publications,' Yale University Library. The statistics about the size of the first and second editions came from Bowyer's paper-stock ledger.
10 RG to JD, 18 Dec 73, Phillips ms, ff 107–10
11 RG to JD, 29 Jan 83, Yale University Library
12 RG to JD, 31 Jul 83, Bath Reference Library
13 He said editor rather than author because his novel was written through a persona.
14 RG to JD, 16 Apr 91, Phillipps ms, ff 191–3
15 For invaluable help with RG's translations from the Greek I am indebted to my brother, Dr H.L. Tracy.

16 *Reveries of Solitude* 23–4
17 When *Euphrosyne* was first published in 1776, it consisted of only one volume. It must have sold well, for in 1780 JD reprinted it along with a new second volume. The first volume was correctly labelled 'second edition,' and the second one was not labelled at all. In 1783 RG wished to add a sheaf of new poems, but there must have been too many unsold copies, for instead of printing a new edition, JD printed three additional gatherings, signed so as to fit them in at the end of the second volume, and sold them to customers who already owned the two-volume edition of 1780. For new customers the three new gatherings were included in their proper place. Copies of this edition have been seen with title pages to both volumes reading 'third edition.' In 1786, when RG produced still more material, JD wanted to issue a third volume (RG to JD, 17 Apr 86, Phillipps ms, ff 153–6). That was not done, but if it had been, it might have been the occasion for a 'fourth edition.'
18 *Critical Review* 35 (1773) 275–86; *Monthly Review* 48 (1773) 384–8; and *Westminster Magazine* 1 (1773) 211
19 Quoted from *L'Esprit des Journaux* (Feb 1787) 98
20 *Autobiography and Correspondence of Mary Delany* s2, 1 (1862) 561
21 GM 41.160
22 P 124 and n
23 P vii
24 P 218n
25 *Autobiography of Mary Delany* 561
26 *SQ* 4
27 Cf *SQ* xxi–xxii.
28 Eg, *Festoon* xix–xxi and *Senilities* 37–41
29 P 128n
30 P 11
31 J.-J. Rousseau *Œuvres* (Paris 1820) vi, 390
32 RG to JD, 22 Dec 72, Phillipps ms, ff 91–2. The reading finally adopted, 'refined and voluptuous,' was a compromise suggested by RG that must have satisfied neither party. RG, it must be noted, avoided the implications of Rousseau's 'corrumpu.'
33 P 3
34 II, 245
35 RG to JD, 12 Apr [85], Phillipps ms, ff 251–4
36 I, vi–vii

CHAPTER FOURTEEN: THE NOVELS

1 WS to RG, 28 Mar 53, and WS to LL, 2 Apr 53, ed Williams, 355, 358

2 P 43

3 William Mason *The English Garden: A Poem* (Dublin 1786) 83

4 P 396

5 RG to JD, 13 Oct 73, AL 287, Bath Reference Library. RG's sketches for these frontispieces are reproduced in this book as follows: for vol I, plate 3, for vol II, plate 21, and for vol III, plate 13.

6 I, 45

7 Whether or not the canon is happy is left uncertain, and his story looks as if it had been an afterthought.

8 None of the sermons in Graves's one published collection of them bears a date of composition, so I have merely guessed that the one on happiness was written before *Columella*. If it was not, then the borrowing was the other way. Cf C.J. Hill *Literary Career of Richard Graves* (Northampton 1934–5) 84–8.

9 Johnson's *Dictionary*

10 Richard Hurd 'On Retirement' in his *Moral and Political Dialogues* (1759); Richard Lucas *An Enquiry after Happiness* (1685+); James Thomson *The Seasons* (1728–30); cf William Cowper 'Retirement' (1765).

11 RG to JD, 21 Nov 78, Phillipps ms, ff 129–34

12 RG to JD, 21 Nov 78, Phillipps ms, ff 129–34

13 'On the Death of a Much Lov'd Wife': see above, p 97. Graves even forgot to alter the name of the dead wife from Lucia to Louisa when he incorporated the poem in the text of the novel.

14 II, 151

15 RG to JD, 12 Apr [85], Phillipps ms, ff 251–4. The word he used was not 'thesis' but 'paradox'; see below, p 142.

16 I, 17

17 I, 160

18 RG to JD, [1790], Phillipps ms, ff 201–2

19 I, iii

20 RG to JD, 12 Apr [85], Phillipps ms, ff 251–4. Cf above, p 144.

21 Apology to *Euphrosyne* I, vii–viii

22 P 259 and n. Cf *John Wesley's Journal* ed N. Curnock ([1904]), under dates 28 Feb 38, 9 May 40, and 21 May 40

CHAPTER FIFTEEN: THE SPRIGHTLY MR GRAVES

1 G. Monkland *The Literature and Literati of Bath* (Bath and London 1854) 19

2 RG to HP, 1 Feb 99, Columbia University Library; *Senilities* 144–5

3 *Literary Recollections* (1830) II, 18

4 Dated 31 Mar 1804, GM 04.761; repr Pratt's *Harvest Home* (1805) III, 490

5 RG to HP, 1 Feb 99, Columbia University Library

6 Richard Warner *Literary Recollections* (1830) II, 20–1; GM 02 (pt 1).580
7 Parish register
8 'The Needlework' *Euphrosyne* II, 251
9 Francis Kilvert *Richard Graves of Claverton* (Bath 1858) 8, quoting Mrs
  Stafford Smith, who was the widow of Bishop Warburton's chaplain, whose
  first wife had been Gertrude, niece of Ralph Allen and relict of the bishop
10 RG gave no source for this quotation, and its errors in French suggest that he
  was quoting hastily from an imperfect recollection.
11 Apology *Euphrosyne* I, ii–iii
12 II, xv
13 In 'The Heroines' *A Collection of Poems* IV (1755), 334–5; cf RG to JD, 1 Dec 74,
  Phillipps ms, f 115.
14 *Poetical Amusements* IV (1781)
15 See Appendix B.
16 *Bath Anecdotes and Characters* by the Genius Loci [Henry Harrington, MD]
  (1782) 147–8. Cf Kilvert *Richard Graves* 9.
17 I, 66
18 WS to RG, 3 Oct 52, ed Williams, 344
19 Pierpont Morgan Library, 1957. 12; cf E.K. Waterhouse *Preliminary Check-
  List of Portraits by Thomas Gainsborough* The Walpole Society 33 (Oxford 1953)
  50
20 *London Chronicle* (24–6 June 1762) 607; repr *Festoon* and *Euphrosyne* I
21 *Lucubrations* 140–2
22 Kilvert *Richard Graves* 9
23 BL, Add ms, 33635
24 Cat no 116
25 'My Picture' *Senilities* 233
26 See poem on p 180 in *Senilities*.
27 Information from Mr Malcolm Rogers, assistant keeper, National Portrait
  Gallery, London
28 'Half a Lifetime Ago' *My Lady Ludlow and Other Tales* (1906) 280

APPENDIX B

1 The Williams edition was published in Oxford and the Mallam in Minneapolis.
2 Actually, one of them was written not by RG himself but by his daughter
  acting on his behalf.
3 GM 04.1166
4 WS to RG, 26 Oct 59, ed Williams, 528
5 BL, Add ms 32.336, f 182. He repeated this information in marginalia in his
  own copy of Shenstone's letters, now in the Bodleian Library, Oxford, ms
  Percy 83, pp 162, 208, 354.

6 Cf Hans Hecht 'Kleine Studien zu Graves, Shenstone, und Percy' *Anglia* 58 (1934) 131–9.

7 GM 04.1165–6; *Monthly Magazine* 55 (1823) 51–2

8 *The Annual Biography and Obituary for the Year 1822* (1822) 412–22. *Monthly Magazine* (1 Oct 1821) 230. *Notes and Queries* 52, 12 (27 July 1861) 71. The statement made in DNB (sv Stephens) and copied into the *Catalogue* of the Library of Congress – that Stephens *wrote* most of the lives in *Public Characters*–is wrong.

9 No 1 (1798) viii

10 Dated 24 and 25 Sept 1799, Bath Reference Library

11 'My Intention was to vindicate him [Shenstone] from what Dr. Johnson says about the "unhappiness of his Genius" and from Gray's Ridicules, which Mason (who was jealous of him, as a gardener – so unnecessarily publish'd.' Cf *Public Characters for 1799–1800* 397: 'The Principal object of this little volume of Shenstonian anecdotes, which Mr. Graves published under the name of "Recollections" [sic], was, as we have observed, to vindicate him from the unjust censure of Johnson, and from Grey's [sic] ridicule, which Mason, who was jealous of him as a gardiner, so unsuccessfully published.' Pratt apparently misread the last word but one. Graves's handwriting had deteriorated and he complained of bad pens.

12 The only factual errors that I have found are in dates, about which Graves was always unreliable. The date of *The Spiritual Quixote* is given as 1772 instead of 1773. Graves had made the same mistake in a list of his works that he had sent to Thomas Percy c 1792 (see ms letter at Yale referred to above, chap 13, n 9). This error is understandable since it is almost certain that the novel was printed off in 1772, though no copy bearing that date has ever been reported. Also, the date at which Graves took orders is given as 1740, whereas he became deacon in 1741 and priest in 1743 (Oxford diocesan records).

Index